INSPIRE / PLAN / DISCOVER / EXPERIENCE

LONDON

LONDON

CONTENTS

DISCOVER 6

EXPERIENCE 66

NEED TO KNOW 332

Left: The skyscraping Shard in Southwark
Previous: The start of Regent Street, Piccadilly Circus
Front cover: Millennium Bridge, with St Paul's Cathedral
in the background

DISCOVER

An aerial view of London

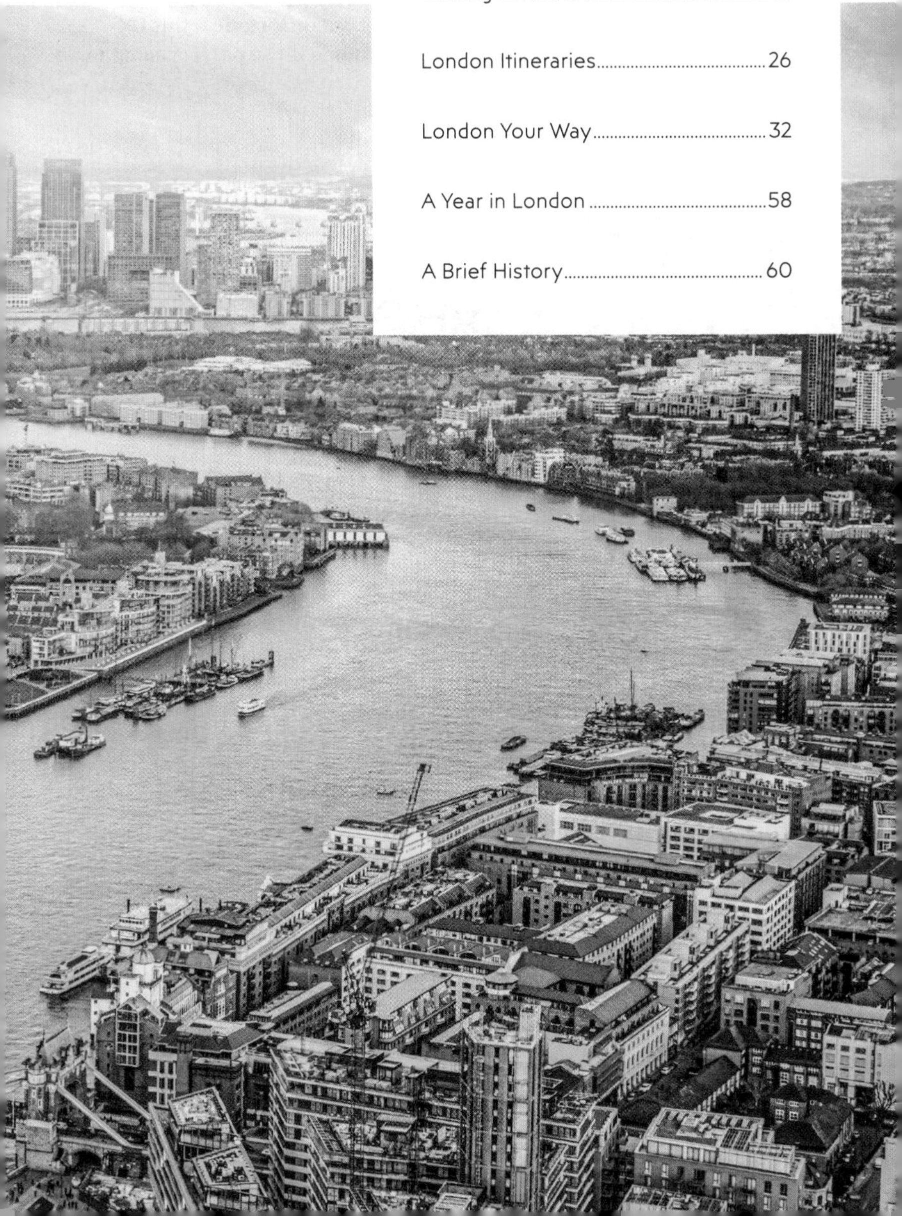

WELCOME TO
LONDON

For all its pomp and ceremony, London has always been a cosmopolitan capital. This diverse city has it all: amazing art and ground-breaking music, royal palaces and historic pubs, futuristic skyscrapers and picturesque parks. Whatever your dream trip to London includes, this DK Eyewitness travel guide is the perfect companion.

1 Relaxing on Hampstead Heath.

2 A typical London pub.

3 Admiring art at the National Gallery.

4 Royal Festival Hall on the South Bank.

It's easy to tread in the footsteps of kings and queens in London, steeped as it is in history, from the imposing Tower of London to graceful Buckingham Palace. The UK's capital is a cultural colossus, brimming with free museums and art galleries, from the National Gallery, with its Renaissance masterpieces, to the Tate Modern's cutting-edge performance works. London also boasts an excellent music and theatre scene. It's a paradise for foodies, where you can sample street food from around the world, and dine in an enticing array of Michelin-starred restaurants. Countless wonderful green spaces punctuate the city's heart, including eight royal parks, and swathes of bucolic bliss such as Hampstead Heath are never too far away; indeed, London became the world's first National Park City in 2019.

The city's charms extend beyond its centre. Head to places such as Brixton or Richmond to experience the diverse personalities of London's urban villages. Alternatively, escape the crowds at Kew Gardens or the Queen Elizabeth Olympic Park, ambling along the winding trails and landscaped flowerbeds.

With so many different things to discover and experience, London can seem overwhelming. We've broken the city down into easily navigable chapters, with detailed itineraries, expert local tips and colourful, comprehensive maps to help you plan the perfect visit. Whether you're staying for a weekend, a week or longer, this DK Eyewitness guide will ensure that you see the very best London has to offer. Enjoy the book, and enjoy London.

REASONS TO LOVE
LONDON

It's a world in a city. It's a buzzing metropolis. It has a story to tell on every corner. Ask any Londoner and you'll hear a different reason why they love their city. Here, we pick some of our favourites.

1 PRICELESS MUSEUMS AND GALLERIES

Take a turn through Ancient Egypt or meet a roaring dinosaur at one of London's unbeatable museums – and all without spending a penny.

2 WALKING THE THAMES PATH

With 45 km (28 miles) of riverside walkways between Richmond in the west and the Thames Barrier in the east, there is no better way to see the sights.

3 MARKETS

Will it be the tasty treats of Borough (p213) or the kaleidoscopic flowers of Columbia Road (p202)? Amble, browse and pick up goodies at any one of London's many markets.

POMP AND CEREMONY 4

The State Opening of Parliament, the Lord Mayor's Show and the extravagant Trooping the Colour showcase London's traditions at their finest (p59).

INCREDIBLE ARCHITECTURE 5

There are architectural treats all over the city. Discover staggering skyscrapers, Brutalist arts centres and even a majestic Hindu temple.

FESTIVALS 6

London offers a packed calendar of eye-catching festivals. Crowning them all is the exuberant Notting Hill Carnival (p268).

THE SOUTH BANK 7

Hugging a curve of the River Thames, the South Bank is filled with accessible-to-all institutions of theatre, film, art and music, and buzzing bars perfect for a sundowner.

PARKS AND GARDENS 8

In a city that hums with traffic and noise, it may be a surprise to find green spaces at every turn - so many in fact that London is officially the world's first National Park City.

9 THEATRELAND

From Shakespeare to Pinter, London has always enjoyed a wonderful theatrical tradition, particularly in the West End. Across the Thames, there's also the iconic Old Vic (p231).

10 GLOBAL RESTAURANT SCENE

Thanks to its multicultural population, London has an enviable array of culinary experiences to tantalize the tastebuds of any foodie.

HOUSES OF PARLIAMENT 11

The febrile centre of political power, the Gothic Palace of Westminster is a city icon *(p76)*. Explore the moody interior and discover centuries of turbulent and fascinating history.

A CITY OF PUBS 12

One of Britain's enduring institutions, the pub is the beating heart of London life. And the choice is staggering – from traditional affairs to hipster craft-beer bars.

EXPLORE
LONDON

This guide divides London into 17 colour-
coded sightseeing areas, as shown on
the map below. Find out more about each
area on the following pages. For sights
beyond the main city centre see p310.

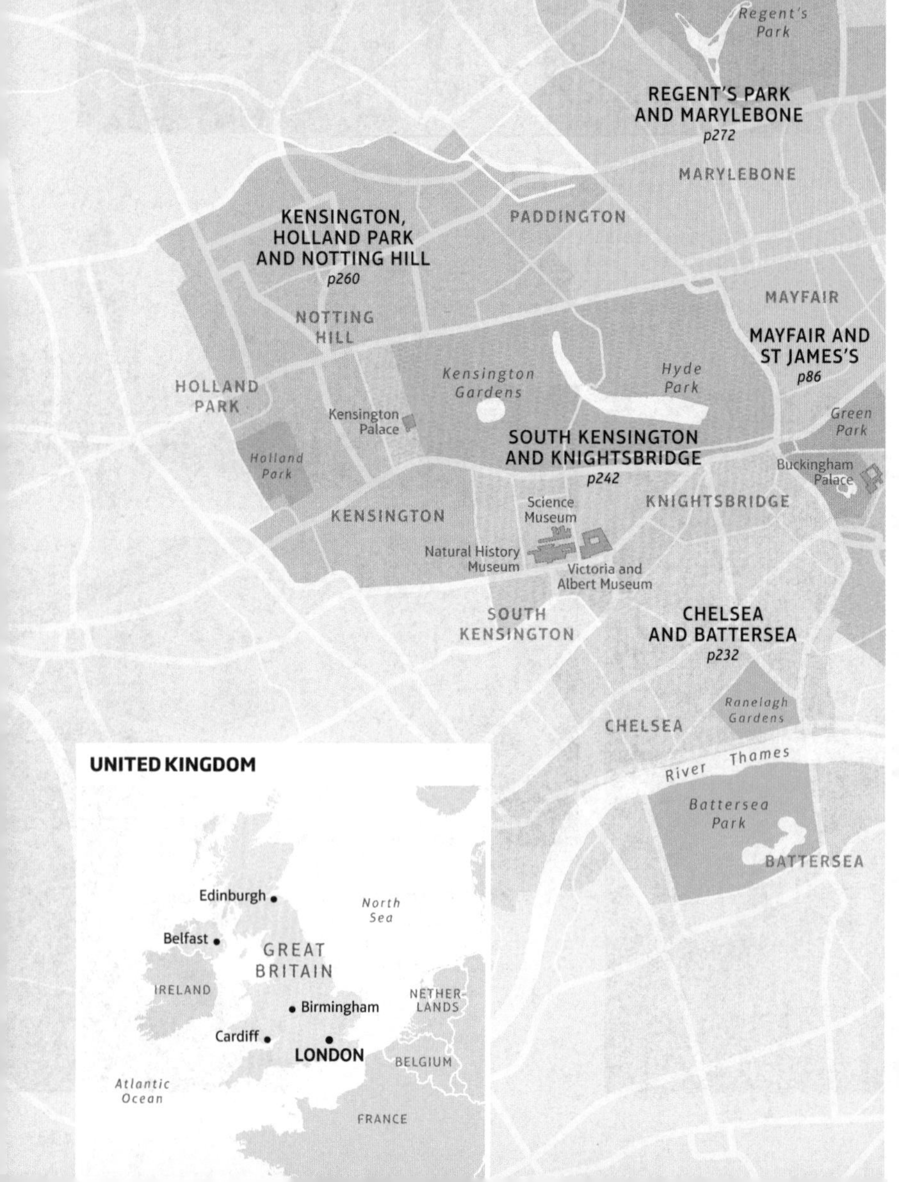

Regent's Park

**REGENT'S PARK
AND MARYLEBONE**
p272

MARYLEBONE

PADDINGTON

**KENSINGTON,
HOLLAND PARK
AND NOTTING HILL**
p260

MAYFAIR

NOTTING
HILL

**MAYFAIR AND
ST JAMES'S**
p86

HOLLAND
PARK

*Kensington
Gardens*

*Hyde
Park*

*Green
Park*

*Kensington
Palace*

**SOUTH KENSINGTON
AND KNIGHTSBRIDGE**
p242

*Buckingham
Palace*

*Holland
Park*

KNIGHTSBRIDGE

KENSINGTON

*Science
Museum*

*Natural History
Museum*

*Victoria and
Albert Museum*

**CHELSEA
AND BATTERSEA**
p232

SOUTH
KENSINGTON

*Ranelagh
Gardens*

CHELSEA

River Thames

*Battersea
Park*

BATTERSEA

UNITED KINGDOM

Edinburgh •

*North
Sea*

Belfast •

GREAT
BRITAIN

IRELAND

NETHER-
LANDS

• Birmingham

Cardiff •

LONDON •

BELGIUM

*Atlantic
Ocean*

FRANCE

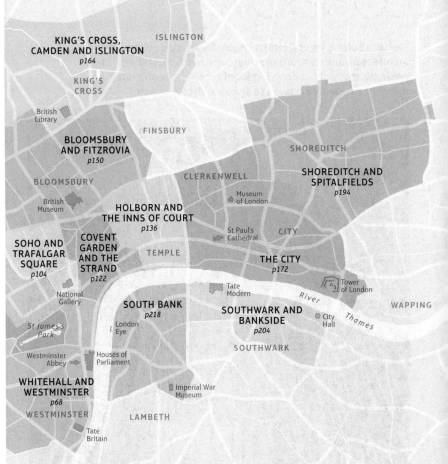

0 kilometres 1
0 miles 1

N

ISLINGTON

**KING'S CROSS,
CAMDEN AND ISLINGTON**
p164

KING'S
CROSS

British
Library

FINSBURY

**BLOOMSBURY
AND FITZROVIA**
p150

SHOREDITCH

BLOOMSBURY

CLERKENWELL

**SHOREDITCH AND
SPITALFIELDS**
p194

British
Museum

Museum
of London

**HOLBORN AND
THE INNS OF COURT**
p136

St Paul's
Cathedral

CITY

**SOHO AND
TRAFALGAR
SQUARE**
p104

**COVENT
GARDEN
AND THE
STRAND**
p122

TEMPLE

THE CITY
p172

Tower
of London

National
Gallery

Tate
Modern

River

WAPPING

Thames

SOUTH BANK
p218

**SOUTHWARK AND
BANKSIDE**
p204

City
Hall

St James's
Park

London
Eye

SOUTHWARK

Westminster
Abbey

Houses of
Parliament

**WHITEHALL AND
WESTMINSTER**
p68

Imperial War
Museum

WESTMINSTER

LAMBETH

Tate
Britain

FURTHER AFIELD

**HAMPSTEAD
AND HIGHGATE**
p286

**GREENWICH AND
CANARY WHARF**
p298

GETTING TO KNOW
LONDON

The UK's pulsing capital is best known for its iconic sights, regal architecture and cool, urban streets and neighbourhoods. Unsurprisingly, many of London's highlights are in its centre but there are visitor-friendly enclaves to discover all over the city.

PAGE 68

WHITEHALL
AND WESTMINSTER

The seat of government for a millennium, Westminster is synonymous with two of the most stunning buildings in London: the Houses of Parliament and Westminster Abbey. The area is packed with a curious mixture of civil servants and sightseers, many of them making their way up and down Whitehall, the grand street linking Parliament Square and Trafalgar Square. You'll find few locals here, with the area's traditional pubs mostly the haunts of government workers.

Best for
Sightseeing and iconic London landmarks

Home to
Westminster Abbey, Houses of Parliament, Tate Britain

Experience
A tour of the tombs of royalty at Westminster Abbey

PAGE 86

MAYFAIR AND ST JAMES'S

Home to some of London's wealthiest individuals (the word Mayfair screams "money"), neither of these elite areas are exclusively for the rich, with some good, affordable restaurants, cosy and welcoming pubs, and delightful gardens dotted around. South of ritzy, if traffic-clogged, Piccadilly, the streets of St James's are often surprisingly quiet, given this is the heart of London. There are historical buildings aplenty but, really, this is the place to shop for designer fashion and mingle with the moneyed.

Best for
Designer fashion and high-end men's tailoring

Home to
Buckingham Palace, Royal Academy of Arts

Experience
A shopping spree on Mayfair's Bond Street

PAGE 104

SOHO AND TRAFALGAR SQUARE

Trafalgar Square can lay strong claim to being the epicentre of touristic London, a well-placed launching pad for much of what the city has to offer. Nearby is the liveliest part of the West End, with clumsily commercialized Leicester Square, lantern-strewn Chinatown and cool, unconventional Soho, the main LGBT+ district of London. Many of Soho's streets are replete with excellent independent restaurants, bars and theatres, making it the perfect spot for an evening out.

Best for
Eating out and a buzzing, lively atmosphere

Home to
National Gallery, Chinatown

Experience
A night of theatre in the West End

→

COVENT GARDEN AND THE STRAND

The distinctive Covent Garden is always lively, attracting tourists and locals in equally large numbers to its dense mix of markets, independent shops and restaurants. There's usually a spirited family-friendly atmosphere as tourists gather on the piazza to watch applause-seeking street performers. Running along its southern border is the Strand, a busy road mostly worth visiting for grand Somerset House, with its large and elegant courtyard – often used for special events – cafés, restaurant and riverside views.

Best for
The buzz on Covent Garden Piazza

Home to
Covent Garden Piazza and Central Market, Somerset House

Experience
The brightly painted warehouses of Neal's Yard

HOLBORN AND THE INNS OF COURT

This is one of the calmest areas of central London. The traditional home of the legal profession, its relative absence of shops and restaurants means there are almost as many lawyers as visitors. The Inns of Court themselves are subdued havens of tranquillity, a maze of alleyways and gardens overlooked by lawyers' chambers. Add to this the excellent small museums and the lovely Lincoln's Inn Fields, and you have a great place to escape the bustle and crowds.

Best for
Hidden and quiet corners in the heart of London

Home to
Inns of Court, Sir John Soane's Museum

Experience
A picnic in the green squares of the Inns of Court

PAGE 150

BLOOMSBURY AND FITZROVIA

Though not exactly avant-garde, these relatively genteel districts have a pleasingly bohemian, laid-back air. Parts of Fitzrovia are densely packed with an enjoyable mix of restaurants, akin to Soho but turned down a few notches. Bloomsbury is the student quarter, home to several university institutions, a variety of independent bookshops and large garden squares. Its most famous sight by far is the British Museum, but elsewhere Bloomsbury is characterized by a pleasing sense of studious calm.

Best for
A laid-back, cultured atmosphere and a strong literary heritage

Home to
British Museum

Experience
Some of the world's greatest treasures at the British Museum

PAGE 164

KING'S CROSS, CAMDEN AND ISLINGTON

Imaginatively converted from a downbeat industrial landscape into a collection of culinary, commercial and artsy hotspots, King's Cross has undergone staggering transformation in recent years. Not entirely finished, it's still gaining reputation – the same of which cannot be said of neighbouring Camden, where the alternative market and raucous venues keep the place thriving day and night. Adding yet more to the mix is well-heeled Islington, a more bourgeois district full of gastropubs.

Best for
Canal walks and a wide range of shopping and dining options

Home to
Camden Market, St Pancras Station, British Library

Experience
Off-beat fashion and food at Camden Market

→

PAGE 172

THE CITY

The towering skyscrapers of the City loom over London's traditional financial district, where corporates in suits scurry around during the week, making it a bustling place at lunchtimes but an eerily deserted one during the weekend. It is also the historical heart of the city, with traces of the Roman occupation in places. The City's sights are dispersed over a relatively wide area, but there are plenty of them, including London's highest concentration of medieval and early modern churches, crowned by the most famous church of all, St Paul's Cathedral.

Best for
Getting up close to London's staggering history

Home to
St Paul's Cathedral, Tower of London, Barbican Centre

Experience
The gore and glory of the centuries-old Tower of London

PAGE 194

SHOREDITCH AND SPITALFIELDS

These districts have attracted and spawned a once cutting-edge, much caricatured and now simply trendy local population. Though gentrification has firmly set in, there is still an alluring energy here, particularly in lively Shoreditch. It's not entirely hipster-centric though, with Brick Lane home to a large Bangladeshi community, and markets like Old Spitalfields and Columbia Road continuing traditions that stretch way back before the latest incarnation of the neighbourhood.

Best for
Feasting on street food and people-watching

Home to
Columbia Road Flower Market, Brick Lane

Experience
Some of London's most vibrant and eclectic markets

PAGE 204

SOUTHWARK AND BANKSIDE

Over the river from the City, Bankside, in the borough of Southwark, contains some of the most popular tourist attractions on the Thames. Tate Modern and Shakespeare's Globe, along with waterside restaurants, pubs and Borough Market, ensure that there's a constant buzz along this stretch of the Thames Path. The recently developed area emanating out from London Bridge station has plenty of new places to eat, a few of them in Western Europe's tallest building, the Shard.

Best for
Urban river walks and riverside sightseeing

Home to
Tate Modern, Shakespeare's Globe

Experience
Striking and strange modern art at the Tate Modern

PAGE 218

SOUTH BANK

At night this is the liveliest part of the river, but it is cultural institutions rather than nightclubs that draw in the after-dark crowds. The Southbank Centre's concert halls and gallery, alongside the National Theatre and the BFI Southbank, form a striking line-up of architecture along the river. Any gaps are filled mostly with mediocre chain restaurants, though bookstalls, a skate park and a food market provide a more homespun angle. The South Bank is always busy in the daytime too, the views from the promenade – and from atop the London Eye – having cemented it as one of London's must-visit areas.

Best for
A sundowner and an evening's entertainment

Home to
Southbank Centre, Imperial War Museum, London Eye

Experience
A stroll along the Thames Path

$\rightarrow$

PAGE 232

CHELSEA AND BATTERSEA

Sitting on opposite sides of the Thames are wealthy Chelsea and energetic Battersea. Flashy sedans and 4WD vehicles, often derided as Chelsea tractors, ply Chelsea's main shopping street, King's Road, where upmarket fashion boutiques sit next door to more humdrum high-street stores. Away from King's Road the area is largely residential, though there are some decent pubs, worthwhile museums and gardens. The glorious park, trendy shops and varied restaurants of Battersea are a welcome retreat from the touristy sights of central London.

Best for
Upmarket shopping and riverside parks and gardens

Home to
Saatchi Gallery, Battersea Park

Experience
A spot of shopping along the King's Road

SOUTH KENSINGTON AND KNIGHTSBRIDGE

PAGE 242

London's museum quarter, South Kensington is home to three of the largest and best museums in the city, exhibiting stunning natural history, science and decorative arts collections. In keeping with the spirit of learning that pervades here, the wide streets house several important royal colleges and societies. In contrast, Knightsbridge, just up the road, oozes ostentatious wealth and is the location of one of the city's most iconic department stores, Harrods.

Best for
World-class free museums

Home to
Victoria and Albert Museum, Natural History Museum, Science Museum

Experience
The weird and wonderful skeletons and species inside the Natural History Museum

KENSINGTON, HOLLAND PARK AND NOTTING HILL

From well-to-do High Street Kensington, the neighbourhoods to the north drift uphill through expensive townhouses, some original little museums and Holland Park. Partially wooded and beautifully landscaped, the park reflects its upmarket location with its pricey restaurant and outdoor operas. To its north is Notting Hill, more touristy than High Street Kensington, in part because of the eponymous film, but also because of its market on Portobello Road.

Best for
Markets, parks and beautiful neighbourhoods

Home to
Design Museum

Experience
Browsing for bargains on Portobello Road

REGENT'S PARK AND MARYLEBONE

With one of London's more high-brow high streets, a thriving restaurant scene, leafy squares and elegant brick façades, Marylebone attracts the well-heeled. There is a distinct change in tone on the main road between here and Regent's Park to the north, where the massive queues for Madame Tussauds are accompanied by non-stop traffic. This all melts pleasantly away in the attractive park itself, with its canalside location providing universal appeal.

Best for
Georgian architecture, open-air theatre

Home to
London Zoo

Experience
The splendid shelves of the marvellous Daunt Books

$\rightarrow$

HAMPSTEAD AND HIGHGATE

PAGE 286

Separated by the rolling fields and woodlands of Hampstead Heath and the atmospheric Highgate Cemetery, two of the biggest draws for visitors, Hampstead and Highgate have maintained much of their quaintness and villagey charm, despite London's rapid urban expansion. The jumbled streets graced with boutique shops and upscale restaurants that make up the old villages are great for a stroll in a part of the city where the pace is noticeably slower.

Best for
London villages and vast swathes of heathland

Home to
Hampstead Heath, Highgate Cemetery

Experience
A dip in the chilly Hampstead bathing ponds

GREENWICH AND CANARY WHARF

PAGE 298

Separated by the river, but joined by a foot tunnel underneath it, Greenwich and Canary Wharf are as different from one another as it gets. Built around the old docks in the 1980s, the business district of Canary Wharf lacks soul but is full of hidden history and dockside walking routes, the sum of which makes it unlike anywhere else in the city. In contrast, Greenwich has history seeping from its pores, populated as it is by a swathe of prominent royal and historical buildings and museums, an ancient park and a handsome town centre.

Best for
Maritime London

Home to
National Maritime Museum, Cutty Sark, Greenwich Park, Royal Observatory

Experience
The home of Greenwich Mean Time in Greenwich Park

BEYOND THE CENTRE

Though it has a distinct city centre, the sprawling capital of London reaches far beyond the urban banks of the Thames. Make the effort to venture out to the suburbs and you'll find the locals: urban families and young professionals, multinational and multicultural, all fiercely protective of their backyard, and with good reason. There are some big-name attractions out here – royal palaces, stately homes and lush gardens to name a few – but a trip beyond the centre is really a great opportunity to get to know the locals behind this multifaceted city.

Best for
Local life and getting off the beaten path

Home to
Hampton Court, Kew Gardens, Warner Bros. Studio Tour: The Making of Harry Potter

Experience
The sights, sounds and smells of energetic Brixton

←

1 Looking towards the iconic Tower Bridge.

2 Tate Modern, housed in a former power station.

3 St Paul's Cathedral.

4 The London Eye.

With so much to see and do in London it can be difficult knowing where to start. Here we suggest a few itineraries to help you get the most out of your visit.

1 DAY

Morning

By following the river you can fit an awful lot into one day without having to travel too far or rely on public transport. Begin at Butler's Wharf; located close to Tower Bridge (p188) and lined with decent river-facing restaurants, it's a great spot for breakfast. From there, walk across the world-famous bridge to the Tower of London (p180) and immerse yourself for a few hours in a thousand years of royal history and scandal. Ready for lunch? Follow the river to London Bridge and cross back over to the south side where you can pick up tasty street food or a gourmet picnic from Borough Market (p213).

Afternoon

Wander through the streets of Southwark past the *Golden Hinde* and along Clink Street. Soon you'll reach Shakespeare's Globe (p210) and the Tate Modern (p208). Stop at the Millennium Bridge to enjoy a picture-perfect view of St Paul's Cathedral

(p176) before heading into the gigantic old power station to admire – or puzzle over – modern art. Check out the views from the top floor of the Blavatnik Building before having a coffee in the gallery's cafe (the view from here isn't bad either). Revitalized, continue along the Thames Path, around a bend in the river, to the South Bank (p218). Pause to watch skateboarders and browse the popular second-hand book stall under Waterloo Bridge before joining the queues for the London Eye (p228), which is open until at least 6pm on most days of the year.

Evening

It's a half-hour walk back along the river to Southwark (p204). Have a spot of dinner at one of the many restaurants in the area – there are some terrific ones on the streets around Borough Market – before ending the day with a pint at London's only remaining galleried pub, the 17th-century George Inn (p213).

←

1 Canalboats cruising along Regent's Canal.

2 The Cenotaph.

3 Renting bikes in Hyde Park.

4 A street performer in Covent Garden.

2 DAYS

Day 1

Morning Enjoy a full English breakfast in Art Deco style at the St Pancras Brasserie, right inside St Pancras station (p169). It's a short stroll to the innovatively resurrected King's Cross neighbourhood (p168), where you can wander the city's newest independent hub, grab a coffee from one of the cafés in Granary Square or Coal Drops Yard and relax in Camley Street Natural Park. From here, follow the winding Regent's Canal path to infamous Camden Market (p170) for quirky, offbeat shopping and a casual lunch.

Afternoon From Camden Town Tube station take the Northern Line down to Embankment – from there it's just a 600-m (655-yd) walk along the north bank of the river to the Houses of Parliament (p76), one of the great wonders of London, and only another 300-m (330-yd) to the architecturally awe-inspiring Westminster Abbey (p72).

Evening Make your way up Whitehall, past 10 Downing Street (p81) and the Cenotaph (p81), towards Trafalgar Square (p114). Once at the square stroll up through Chinatown (p112) to the edge of Soho, the West End's most vibrant and eclectic restaurant district. Get a taste of one of London's current culinary crazes by dining on the delectable Peruvian tapas at Ceviche Soho (p115), before popping across the road to Ronnie Scott's, the city's most famous jazz club – there are dozens of great bars near here too.

Day 2

Morning Have a traditional English breakfast at the atmospheric Café in the Crypt (p115), below St Martin-in-the-Fields church just off Trafalgar Square. Afterwards, cross the road to the National Gallery (p108) and explore one of the world's greatest art collections. Pick up something delicious for lunch from one of the many cafés in nearby Soho.

Afternoon From here, head back south to cross lively Piccadilly Circus (p114) and thread through the regal streets of St James's to the beautifully landscaped St James's Park (p95). Wander past the pelicans on the lake and over the blue bridge, a great spot for photos of Buckingham Palace (p90). If they're open, visit the grandiose State Rooms in the palace itself; otherwise admire the precious art collection at the Queen's Gallery or the ornate carriages at the Royal Mews. Pick up bikes (p339) at the other end of Constitution Hill from the palace and see out the daylight hours cycling around the expansive Hyde Park (p257).

Evening Park the bikes at a docking station near Knightsbridge Tube and hop on the Piccadilly Line to the lively Covent Garden (p126). Enjoy the street performers in the atmospheric piazza and then settle into dinner at one of the many fine restaurants in the heart of Theatreland. See out the evening with a drink – and great views – on the riverside terrace of Somerset House (p128).

7 DAYS

Day 1

Morning Start at the Shard – there's no better vantage point from which to survey the city (p214). Down at street level, stroll along the cobbled alleys of Southwark and pick up lunch at Borough Market (p213).

Afternoon Head west along the Thames Path, popping into the cavernous Tate Modern (p208) to see what's new in the world of modern art.

Evening Finish at the Southbank Centre (p222) for a spin on the London Eye (p228) and, afterwards, dinner and drinks.

Day 2

Morning Choose from three of the city's top museums: the Natural History Museum (p250), the Science Museum (p252) or the Victoria and Albert (p246). Any one could occupy you for a day, but as they're free, split your time across two or perhaps all three.

Afternoon Have a picnic in nearby Hyde Park (p257) before trying your hand at a bit of boating on the Serpentine lake.

Evening If you've pre-booked tickets, enjoy a performance at the refined Royal Albert Hall (p254), or go out for dinner in smart Kensington (p267).

Day 3

Morning Head east to the City and explore the history of the capital at the Museum of London (p185).

Afternoon Have lunch at Leadenhall Market (p190). Next, take the Docklands Light Railway to Greenwich to discover centuries of maritime history (p302).

Evening Walk to the top of Greenwich Park (p303) to enjoy the sunset.

Day 4

Morning Take the Tube north to enjoy the alternative vibe at Camden Market (p170). Browse the stalls until lunchtime – there's plenty here to feast on.

Afternoon Head to the characterful villages of Hampstead and Highgate. Walk between the two via the heath (p290) and Highgate Cemetery (p292).

1 Leadenhall Market.
2 The Southbank Centre in the sunshine.
3 Camden Market and its food stalls.
4 Deer graze at lush Richmond Park.
5 Columbia Road Flower Market.

Evening Have a relaxed dinner at one of Hampstead's excellent pubs, such as the Holly Bush (p295).

Day 5

Morning Travel south to Dulwich Picture Gallery (p325) in upper-crust Dulwich Village, taking in the gorgeous park (p325) over the road.

Afternoon Catch a train at West Dulwich station for livelier Brixton. Do the full circuit of the Brixton Village and Market Row arcades (p328), a foodie's haven, before settling down for a late lunch.

Evening Stick about in Brixton for a spot of live music at one of its venues, catch a film at the Ritzy cinema or simply chill out in Pop Brixton, a complex of shipping containers packed with street food start-ups and bars.

Day 6

Morning Catch the train from London Waterloo to Kew Bridge; from here it's a short walk to the gardens of Kew (p318).

Afternoon Follow the river path at a relaxed pace to the attractive riverside town of Richmond (p329). Have lunch on the go or, better still, take a picnic to the expansive Richmond Park.

Evening Keep close to the Thames and enjoy a riverside dinner as the evening draws in.

Day 7

Morning Sunday morning is the only time Columbia Road Flower Market (p202) operates and it's well worth a visit, whether or not you want to buy flowers. Here you'll catch sight of the sellers or "barrow boys" flaunting their impressive displays of flowers and foliage.

Afternoon Check out what's on at the Barbican (p184) or Rich Mix (p202), both of which have an ever-changing roster of film screenings, exhibitions and talks.

Evening Spend the evening in super-cool Shoreditch. There are plenty of trendy places to eat, drink and relax in, not least on Brick Lane (p199), the curry capital of Europe.

DIVERSE DISTRICTS

Brick Lane
AKA the "curry capital of Europe" and home to a large Bangladeshi community *(p199)*.

Ealing
The unofficial Polish capital of Britain – over 6 percent of people here speak Polish.

Stockwell
Nicknamed "Little Portugal", there are over 30,000 Portuguese in the local area.

Stamford Hill
London's largest community of ultra-Orthodox Jews live in this area.

Southall
Home to the biggest Punjabi population outside of India.

Did You Know?

One in three people who live in London were born in another part of the world.

LONDON IS
A WORLD CITY

Sit on the Tube and listen. You'll hear conversations in Polish, Chinese, Yoruba and 300 other languages besides. These are the voices of London, one of the most wonderfully multicultural cities in the world. Wherever you go, you'll find slices of life from every continent begging to be explored.

Places of Worship

Lighting up neighbourhoods from east to west are spectacular places of worship, many of them open to the public and each one a crash-course in understanding the cultural traditions they serve. From the largest Hindu temple in Europe *(p322)* to the towering mosque in Regent's Park *(p280)*, these architectural anomalies spice up the urban landscape wherever they stand.

→

BAPS Shri Swaminarayan Mandir, an incredible Hindu temple in Neasden

Festivals

Aside from the popular Chinese New Year (p112) and Notting Hill Carnival (p268), there are plenty of festivals that showcase London's locals. St Patrick's Day in March is celebrated with all-out revelry, as is Australia Day in January, less raucous in numbers only. Plaza Latina in August unites the Latin American communities for parades and merriment, and the fireworks of Diwali in the autumn sparkle over the city's skies. Whenever you visit, there's sure to be something to celebrate.

←

Entertainers contribute to the party atmosphere at the Notting Hill Carnival

↑ Vibrant Chinatown, the original home of London's Chinese population

Welcome to the Neighbourhood

West Indian barbershops to the south, Turkish grocers to the north – London's diversity is palpable whichever way you turn. Head to the East End to find the traditional heart of immigrant London, where so many have settled and dispersed into the cultural soup that is London.

A snapshot of the café culture in Brixton Market ↑

Ceremonies and Traditions

A number of centuries-old royal ceremonies and traditions continue today, despite the sometimes baffling outfits and proceedings. Most famous is the Changing the Guard, which takes place at Buckingham Palace and Horse Guards Parade on Whitehall. Once a year, in June, the far more elaborate military parade Trooping the Colour is staged to celebrate the Queen's birthday. Tickets must be booked online (www.household division.org.uk).

→

Queen Elizabeth II waving to the crowd during the military parade Trooping the Colour

LONDON FOR
ROYALTY

London has been the royal capital of the UK for almost a thousand years and most of the royal family, including the Queen, live in the city. Over the centuries, successive monarchs have done much to shape the character of the city, from the landscaping of royal parks to the landmarks they left behind.

The Legacy of Victoria and Albert

We have much to thank Queen Victoria and her husband Prince Albert for. The Christmas tree, housing projects for the poor and the superb museums in South Kensington are just some of the things accredited to the forward-thinking pair. Give them a nod at the Queen Victoria Memorial outside Buckingham Palace and the Albert Memorial in Hyde Park.

←

The stunning Natural History Museum, a legacy of Prince Albert

Tower of London

At times a royal palace, at others a prison and place of execution for fallen monarchs or rejected courtiers, the story of the Tower of London *(p180)* is to some extent the story of the English monarchy itself. Built by William the Conqueror in the late 11th century, this was where Anne Boleyn awaited her fate after falling out of Henry VIII's favour and was later beheaded. Curiously, for 600 years it was also home to the royal menagerie, a collection of exotic wild animals, including lions and an elephant, gifted to the monarchy. It is now one of London's most popular attractions.

↑ Trooping the Colour, a parade to celebrate the Queen's birthday

💬 INSIDER TIP
Sneak Preview

You can catch members of the Household Cavalry leaving the barracks on the south side of Hyde Park at 10:28am on weekdays and 9:28am on Sundays on their way to the Changing the Guard at Horse Guards Parade.

↑ The forbidding fortress of the Tower of London

Royal Palaces

Go behind the scenes of royal households to discover how the upper echelons of power have lived over the centuries. Hampton Court *(p314)* is arguably the most impressive with its long and rich history, while Kew Palace, surrounded by its beautiful gardens *(p318)*, is relatively modest by royal standards. Pop by the famous Buckingham Palace *(p90)*, the official London residence of the monarch since 1837, to say hello to the Queen - if the Royal Standard flag is flying, she's at home.

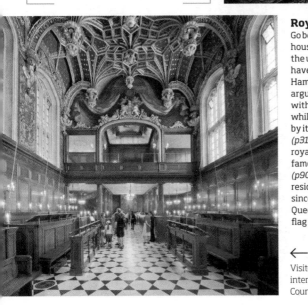

Visitors exploring the interior of Hampton Court Palace

Royal Parks

During a day of sightseeing take a detour to the former stomping grounds of kings and queens. Boat on the lake in expansive Hyde Park (p257), wander handsomely landscaped Kensington Gardens (p256) or take in the view of famed Buckingham Palace from St James's Park (p95). Venture a little further out and spend the day exploring the rural landscapes of Richmond Park (p328). A hike up the hill in Greenwich Park (p303) provides sweeping views across the river, the perfect end to any day.

→

Relaxing by the lakeside in the vast Hyde Park

LONDON FOR
GREEN SPACES

With its eight million trees and 3,000 parks, London is one of the greenest capitals in Europe – in fact in 2019 it became the world's first National Park City. Take a break from the city hubbub and venture to any one of these green spaces.

An English City Garden

The English have long had an unabashed love affair with their gardens. The green-fingered should make their way to the gorgeous gardens that surround manor houses like Chiswick House (p331) and Syon House (p329). If it's respite you're after, any of the public garden squares in the city will do, particularly those in Bloomsbury (p158). The breathtaking Kew Gardens (p318) crowns them all and is a must for any budding gardener.

←

The exquisite Kew Gardens, a veritable haven for the green-fingered

47

Percentage of green space in Greater London, most of which is open to the public.

Back to Nature

There are more than 40 nature reserves and pockets of woodland across London, some of them not so far away from the centre. Go bird-watching at Walthamstow Wetlands, hunt for creepy-crawlies at Camley Street Natural Park *(p169)* or walk through ancient woodland in sylvan Highgate Wood.

$\longrightarrow$

Sifting for creepy- crawlies at the Camley Street Natural Park

A Walk on the Wild Side

Linking a lot of the city's green spaces together, along rivers, canals, old train tracks and park paths, is the Capital Ring, a painstakingly plotted 126-km (78-mile) circular walking route. It's well signposted throughout the route (or download the routes to your phone for free on the Go Jauntly app).

$\longrightarrow$

A couple of couples on the Capital Ring trail

Football in London

The capital city of the country that invented the game has more professional football clubs and large football stadiums than any other on the planet. Premier League games are usually booked up well in advance, mostly with corporate guests and season-ticket holders. Your best hope of watching some top-level action is to try to book in a cup match, particularly a League Cup game, when tickets are not only more widely available but a bit cheaper too.

→

Ecstatic Arsenal players and fans celebrating a goal

LONDON FOR
SPORTS FANS

Britain is a nation of sports fans and its capital is no exception. London, the only city to have hosted the Olympic Games three times, puts on a dazzling range of sporting events and tournaments, from football to boxing and everything in-between.

An Olympic Legacy

Head to the Queen Elizabeth Olympic Park *(p312)*, which played host to the 2012 Olympics and Paralympics. There are frequent events here ranging from international track cycling competitions to all-star basketball championships, plus a range of first-class facilities, fit for any budding Olympian.

→

The Queen Elizabeth Olympic Park, with the ArcelorMittal Orbit

Sports Museums and Stadium Tours

London's sporting heritage is unparalleled, with legendary areas dotted all over. Given their long histories they all have stories to tell, and a tour is the best way to hear them. Walk through the players' tunnel at Wembley, go behind the scenes at the home of rugby in Twickenham or explore the grass courts of Wimbledon. The oldest sporting museum in the world, the MCC Museum at Lord's cricket ground, is a must-visit for fans.

←

England's national stadium, Wembley

The Sporting Calendar

The Six Nations Rugby tournament kickstarts the year, with some games held at Twickenham. The hotly contested Boat Race brings in spring, followed swiftly by the London Marathon and people's favourite the FA Cup Final. Expect strawberries and sunburn in summer, as crowds watch Wimbledon and cricket internationals. After the frenzy of the transfer window, the Premier League kicks off in mid-August. Rugby Union Internationals and a series of NFL games round off the year.

→

Pounding the pavements for the London Marathon *(above)* and enjoying a game of tennis at Wimbledon *(inset)*

↑ The gorgeous Albert Bridge, illuminated at night

LONDON
ON THE RIVER

Like many cities, London grew up around its river. The Romans used it as a line of defence, the Victorians established it as the world's largest port and today it's one of the most famous waterways. Take to the water to see London landmarks from a different angle.

Follow the Thames Path

Twisting and turning along the river through London and out into the countryside is the Thames Path. Starting far to the west of the city in the Cotswold Hills, this National Trail's London section stretches from the floodplains of Richmond *(p329)* to the Thames Barrier *(p307)*, hardly ever losing sight of the river. The best stretch for sightseeing is between Westminster Bridge and Tower Bridge, but there are some pretty sections, dotted with pubs and full of greenery, between Kew Bridge and Hammersmith Bridge in the west.

→ A section of the Thames Path, running past City Hall

Spanning the River

For centuries, right up until 1750, London Bridge was the only bridge across the Thames in London. Now there are more than 30 – and tunnels too. Instantly recognizable is Tower Bridge *(p188)*, with its twin towers and famous bascule bridge. A favourite for many Londoners is the attractive 19th-century Albert Bridge, near Battersea Park *(p238)*, spectacular at night when it is illuminated by thousands of lights. The somewhat eerie Greenwich Foot Tunnel *(p305)* links the Isle of Dogs, the home of Canary Wharf, and Greenwich – it's an unusual way to get from one bank to the other. Snap great shots or take in the view of the riverscape from the pedestrian Golden Jubilee Bridges, flanking Hungerford Bridge *(p224)*.

← A legend of London, the turreted Tower Bridge

EAT

Skylon

This cool, refined restaurant on the first floor of the Royal Festival Hall, offers a fine river view and classic British dining.

🗺 J6 🏠 Southbank Centre 🌐 skylon-restaurant.co.uk

£ £ £

Sea Containers

Tuck into a seafood platter or half a lobster on the marvellous riverside terrace.

🗺 K5 🏠 20 Upper Ground SE1 🌐 seacontainers london.com

£ £ £

A Thames Clipper coasting the river ↑

From the Water

Board a Thames Clipper rather than a sightseeing boat to cruise the river and see the sights for a fraction of the price. There are four main routes, all of them covering the busiest section of the river between the London Eye and London Bridge. There are boats roughly every 15 minutes at peak times.

LONDON
ON TAP

Londoners, like most Brits, come together in pubs. They eat and drink in them, they chat and dance in them, and they watch comedy and sport in them. And whether you're on the river, in a park or on a busy street, no matter the neighbourhood, there will be a pub just round the corner.

Brewing a Beer

While London's craft brewers come up with ever more inventive beer styles, be sure to try traditional draught "real" ale, hand-pumped from casks and served at cellar temperature. Still, London's taste for hoppy IPAs shows no sign of dissipating, and there are more than a hundred microbreweries and brewpubs across the city. Tackle the Bermondsey Beer Mile on a Saturday to try some of the best.

$\longrightarrow$

Some of the London-brewed ales on offer at a local pub

A Traditional Public House

The title of "oldest pub in London" is claimed by quite a number of pubs. Though very few pub interiors are more than 200 years old, there have been pubs and inns in the city for over a millennium and there are certainly a select few establishments whose current building dates to the 16th century. Look out for timber-framed interiors and compartments separated by frosted glass screens – the classic tells of a Victorian-era pub.

← The Victorian Churchill Arms, in Kensington

DRINK

Hoop and Grapes
This 17th-century pub is one of the oldest still standing in London.

📍04 🏠47 Aldgate High St 🌐nicholsonspubs.co.uk

Ye Olde Mitre
Elizabeth I danced around the cherry tree still standing at this 16th-century pub.

📍K4 🏠Ely Place 🌐yeoldemitreholborn.co.uk

↑ A pint of traditional draught ale, which goes down well with pub grub

Pub Lunch

Since the 1990s, there has been a gastropub explosion in London. Though many pubs have stuck to traditional pub grub, some can compete with top restaurants for quality. Among those most renowned for their food are the Anchor & Hope in Waterloo, the Harwood Arms in Fulham and the Marksman in Hackney.

↑ Serving up an impressive Sunday roast dinner at a London gastropub

Independent Cinemas

Intimate arthouse venues, Golden Age auditoriums, brick-lined railway arch establishments and trendy industrial-style spaces are just some of the places you can watch big screen films around the city. The historic Regent Street Cinema, the Electric Cinema on Portobello Road, with its diner and leather armchairs, and the Art Deco Phoenix in East Finchley, which opened in 1912, are among the most memorable. Look out, too, for a branch of the excellent cinema chains Picturehouse, Curzon and Everyman.

> **INSIDER TIP**
> **Summer Cinema Tickets**
>
> Tickets for summer screenings go on sale months in advance and often sell out. The best site to check for multiple venues is thelunacinema.com. Screenings are rarely cancelled so don't expect refunds if it rains, and bring an umbrella.

The plush setting of ↑
the Electric Cinema
on Portobello Road

LONDON FOR
FILM BUFFS

From the grimy, sinister streets of Victorian London to the romantic home of middle-class bumblers and eccentrics, the capital has been the backdrop to countless movies over the decades. Here, we round up the best of London's film scene.

Big Screen Scenes

Finding the streets of London familiar? It's no surprise, given the city's role in film. Hugh Grant wooed Julia Roberts in *Notting Hill* and Cillian Murphy faced a post-apocalyptic Westminster in *28 Days Later*. James Bond fans will recognize landmarks at every turn, particularly after Bond's high-speed chase down the Thames. And let's not forget a certain boy wizard, who boarded the train to Hogwarts at King's Cross Station – look out for the staged Platform 9¾ *(p169)*.

←

Film fans on their way to
Hogwarts at Platform 9¾

British Film Institute

The British Film Institute (BFI) aims to promote and preserve film-making in the UK. Its headquarters at the BFI Southbank building (p225) are equipped with a four-screen cinema, a film shop and a publicly accessible film archive. The BFI organizes the London Film Festival, which runs for 12 days every October at cinemas around the city.

←

The shop at the BFI Southbank

Summer Cinema

Every summer, dates are set for outdoor cinema seasons. Among the big names is the central courtyard at Somerset House. Rooftops are a favourite, with screenings at the Bussey Building in Peckham and the Queen of Hoxton pub in Shoreditch, among others. Look out for the Luna Cinema, which has a jam-packed summer schedule at over a dozen parks and gardens as well as royal palaces.

→

Settling down to watch an open-air film screening at Somerset House

Classical, Opera and Ballet

The classical music calendar in London is dominated every year by the Proms, eight weeks of summer concerts climaxing at the Royal Albert Hall (p254). There is plenty going on the rest of the year – check out programmes at the Royal Festival Hall (p225), the Barbican (p184) and Wigmore Hall (p281). For opera and ballet, head to the sumptuous London Coliseum (p133) and the Royal Opera House (p129).

→ The enthusiastically attended Last Night of the Proms

INSIDER TIP
Getting Tickets

Head to the TKTS booth on Leicester Square for on-the-day last-minute and discounted tickets for some first-rate West End productions.

LONDON FOR
LIVE SHOWS

"When a man is tired of London, he is tired of life," Samuel Johnson famously declared and that is as true in the 21st century as it was in the late 1700s. With an overwhelming choice of live entertainment, from a thriving comedy circuit to world-class theatre, visitors to London really are spoilt for choice.

Take Me to Church

There is much more to church music than stuffy choirs and organ recitals. Free lunchtime events are common and St Martin-in-the-Fields (p114) has weekday concerts. It also stages regular jazz concerts at its Café in the Crypt. St John's on Smith Square (p83) in Westminster has ticketed concerts almost every afternoon or evening. Frequently named the city's best live music venue, the Union Chapel in Islington is a special place to hear world and contemporary music.

→ A performance at the atmospheric Union Chapel

Did You Know?

Licensed Tube station buskers must pass auditions judged by music industry professionals.

Pub Performances

Some of the future greats of British music started their careers gigging on the London pub circuit, and legendary venues like the Windmill in Brixton and the Dublin Castle in Camden still host regular live performances. London's pubs also play a major role on the comedy circuit: check out the Camden Head pub in Angel and Banana Cabaret at the Bedford in Balham.

←

A band playing at the Dublin Castle in Camden

A City of Theatre

The West End is the city's answer to Broadway, and commercial theatre, much of it of a very high standard, is in rude health. Independent theatre is thriving too. The National Theatre (p229) and the Barbican (p184) provide audience-pulling platforms for first-time directors and experimental productions, injecting an extra dose of creativity into London's theatre scene.

→

The renowned Les Misérables in the West End

A Fashion Mecca

When it comes to style, London is a city where just about anything goes. Iconic designers to look out for include Vivienne Westwood and the late couturier Alexander McQueen, a graduate of Central Saint Martins, the London art and design school renowned for churning out superstar designers. Check out the experimental and the edgy at London Fashion Week, which takes place in February and September.

←

A Vivienne Westwood show presenting her unique collection

LONDON IN
FASHION

London is Europe's undisputed heavyweight champion of shopping. Perhaps best known for its luxurious department stores, the city's thriving markets also provide much to delight in. In these festivals of independent retail, the walk through is at least as much fun as the eventual purchase.

Hit the High Street

Oxford Street is a bustling 2 km- (1 mile-) long parade of over 300 shops and stores. Find here the staples of the British wardrobe, with flagship stores for perennial favourites John Lewis, Marks & Spencer and Topshop. On adjoining Regent Street are famous national and international names, such as Hackett, Barbour and Ted Baker.

→

The ever-popular Oxford Street

Embrace Your Independents

On every corner there are chances to find something unique, whether high-end goods or vintage bargains. For the best suits in the city, head for the unbeatable tradition of Savile Row and Jermyn Street. Independent boutiques abound in Notting Hill and Hampstead, while for vintage and alternative fashion you can't do much better than Brick Lane and Camden.

←

Browsing the wares at a vintage shop in trendy Notting Hill

↑ Cutting-edge tailoring at a London boutique

TOP 5 LONDON MARKETS

Camden Lock Market
A canalside market, best for alternative fashion.

Portobello Road
A long road lined with antiques-loaded stalls.

Old Spitalfields Market
A covered market with themed days, like vinyl.

Columbia Road Market
Cut flowers, plants and seedlings at great prices on Sunday mornings.

Petticoat Lane Market
Historic street market, with great leather goods.

↑ The interior of luxury department store Liberty

World-Class Department Stores

You can shop till you drop in London's top department stores – and certainly your jaw will drop when you see some of the prices. The sheer extravagance of Harrods is absolutely worth braving the crowds for, as is the historic Liberty, housed in a Tudor revival building. Selfridges, second only to Harrods in size, has built a reputation not just for the staggering breadth and quality of its stock, but for its artistic and innovative window displays.

LONDON
ON THE ROOF

London is in the midst of a tall-building boom, and as fast as the towers shoot up, so the trend for socializing up high thrives. Popping up on London's rooftops are open-air cinemas, adventure playgrounds for adults and buzzing bars – and all with superlative views of the cityscape.

Sky-High Jinks

Take to the rooftops for an evening of summer entertainment. Roof East in Stratford is a riotous activity playground with crazy golf, batting cages and bowling lanes surrounded by the obligatory street-food pop-ups. Rooftop Film Club shows classic movies from a height, supplying their audience with wireless headphones and rows of deckchairs to settle back in. Choose from one of three venues and book your ticket in advance.

$\rightarrow$

A screening of *Saturday Night Fever* at Peckham's Rooftop Film Club

Rooftop Gardens

Some of the most delightful rooftops are those with gardens, a number of which are open to the public. Book (free of charge) to see the terraced palms and ferns of the Sky Garden (p189), or walk through the landscaped flowerbed of the Crossrail Place Roof Garden in Canary Wharf. The greenery of the Queen Elizabeth Hall Roof Garden may be modest, but its riverside location more than makes up for it.

←

The Sky Garden's panoramic views and (inset) the Crossrail Place Roof Garden

EAT

SUSHISAMBA London
An inventive menu, served 38 floors up.

📍N4 🏠110 Bishopsgate, EC2 🌐sushisamba.com

£££

Oxo Tower Restaurant
Thameside location offering adventurous global dishes.

📍K5 🏠Barge House St, SE1 🌐harveynichols.com

£££

Madison
In-your-face views of St Paul's from the terrace.

📍L5 🏠One New Change, EC4 🌐madison london.net

£££

Take in the View

The Shard (p214), western Europe's tallest building, provides miles of eye-busting views from its 72nd-floor viewing platform. The price of a ticket is high, too, but you can opt for one of the bars on a slightly lower floor, where the view is the cost of a cocktail. Even closer to earth are some of the city's more long-lived buildings; the viewing galleries of St Paul's and Westminster cathedrals present captivating vistas along with a satisfying sense of history.

↑ The lights and landmarks of London, as seen from the Shard

Diana Memorial Playground in Kensington Gardens ↑

LONDON FOR
FAMILIES

You won't struggle to find places geared up for kids in this city, with its innovative museums, abundance of expansive parks and family-friendly restaurants. Although some attractions are a little pricey, there's a huge range of free and low-cost activities to be found.

Rainy-Day Activities
Given the unpredictable British climate, it's lucky that some of the most entertaining experiences for kids are indoors. The standout is the Science Museum *(p252)*, a veritable world of wonder that pairs well with a trip to the Natural History Museum *(p250)*. A far less wholesome experience is to be had at the London Dungeon *(p230)*, where gory moments in the city's history are brought to life. The similarly macabre Clink Prison Museum *(p214)* will delight fiendish teenagers.

←

Coming face-to-face with the specimens at the Natural History Museum

Let Off Steam

The hundreds of parks in London – both large and small – provide, at the very least, a space for kids to run around. Take your pick of St James's Park *(p95)*, Holland Park *(p266)*, Regent's Park *(p276)* and Kensington Gardens *(p256)*, all of which have playgrounds. As well as climbing frames, a swing set and slide, Hyde Park also has a lido and a boating lake *(p257)*. Don't miss Coram's Fields *(p161)* in Bloomsbury, a park designed solely for children and young people, with adventure play areas, a city farm and a paddling pool.

> INSIDER TIP
> **Kids Go Free**
>
> Under-11s can travel for free on public transport when they're accompanied by an adult and can gain admission to most attractions for a reduced price. At many sights, entry is free for under-5s.

Urban Safari

Inexpensive or free, London's city farms are great places for families on a budget. One of the biggest is Mudchute Park and Farm, near Canary Wharf *(www.mudchute.org)*, home to over 100 animals. For more exotic creatures, head to the children's zoo at Battersea Park *(p238)*, which counts monkeys, snakes and emus among its residents, while for the biggest beasts make a beeline for London Zoo *(p277)*.

$\rightarrow$

Feeding the donkeys at Mudchute Park and Farm

Acting Up

From traditional puppet shows to cutting-edge plays, there are plenty of theatres for children. The marionette shows at the Puppet Theatre Barge in Little Venice *(p268)* and Richmond offer a unique, floating setting, while the Unicorn Theatre in London Bridge puts on several kids' shows a year *(www.unicorntheatre.com)*.

$\leftarrow$

A performance at the Puppet Theatre Barge

Dickensian London

Inspired by the city and its people, Charles Dickens is inextricably linked to London. Read *The Pickwick Papers* and *Oliver Twist* to get you in the mood, then tour the streets he made famous with Charles Dickens Walks and Tours *(www.dickenslondon tours.co.uk)*. To get to know the man himself, visit his house, now the Charles Dickens Museum *(p159)*.

←

Victorian interior of the Charles Dickens Museum

LONDON FOR
BOOKWORMS

If you're a lover of books you'll be a lover of London. Writers and readers alike have much to celebrate in the city, with the world's largest library and Europe's largest bookshop, a thriving independent bookshop scene and a literary heritage stretching back centuries.

Recommended Reads

Dickens classics aside, there are plenty of London-set novels to devour. Patrick Hamilton's *Hangover Square* is set in the Earl's Court area in 1939. There's a strong sense of place in Zadie Smith's *White Teeth* and Sam Selvon's *The Lonely Londoners*, both examinations of the immigrant experience. John Lanchester's *Capital* explores the dynamics on a London street around the 2008 financial crisis.

→

Browsing at the Foyles store, Charing Cross Road

Take a Tour

A Bloomsbury tour is a must for bibliophiles. Walk in the footsteps of the Bloomsbury Group (p158) in and around Russell Square and Gordon Square. Look out for towering Senate House (p162), the inspiration behind George Orwell's Ministry of Truth in his prescient 1984, then make a beeline for the British Library, home to riches from the literary world (p168).

→

Researchers at the British Library, and the imposing Senate House (inset)

SHOP

Foyles

This renowned store, one of London's biggest, is a haven for book-lovers and dates back to 1903, when brothers William and Gilbert began the venture by selling the textbooks they didn't need. The five-story flagship store on Charing Cross Road includes a jazz music concession, an excellent foreign-language books section and over 6 km (4 miles) of shelving.

📍R1 🏠107 Charing Cross Rd 🌐foyles.co.uk

LONDON FOR
FOODIES

You can sample food from hundreds of countries in every imaginable setting and on any budget in London. Shining with Michelin-starred restaurants, the city is also in the midst of a sparks-flying street food explosion. Here, we explore some of its must-eats.

Festival Seasoning

For more food stalls than you can wave a bread stick at, time your visit to coincide with one of the city's summer food festivals. In June, bag a ticket for Taste of London, a fine-dining jamboree in Regent's Park *(london. tastefestivals.com)*. In July, Feria de Londres at the Southbank Centre celebrates Spanish cuisine and culture. Looser and livelier are the StrEATlife festivals held between May and August at Alexandra Palace *(p322)*. The vibe is more like a music festival here, with DJs and bands providing the soundtrack for grazing while gazing out over London.

→

Trying out nibbles at the Taste of London festival

Eat the Street

There are plenty of restaurants jumping on the street food bandwagon, but genuine on-the-hoof eats - sold from market stalls, shipping containers, trucks and more - are popping up wherever there are crowds of people. The best-known option - although on the pricey side - is Borough Market (p213). The Southbank Centre Food Market (p224) is also slap-bang in the middle of the tourist circuit and sells breads and cheeses, as well as a mix of British and international dishes. For a more authentic street experience, head to Leather Lane Market (p147), Berwick Street Market (p118), Camden Market (p170) or Maltby Street Market (www.maltby.st).

←

Street stall at Borough Market selling freshly baked breads

TOP 5 **LONDON FOOD HUBS**

Brixton Village and Market Row
Old market arcades now heaving with cafés and restaurants (p328).

Flat Iron Square
Food counters in a set of railways arches (p214).

The Prince
A polished street food hub with alfresco dining (theprincelondon.com).

W12 Studios
Street food in the old BBC TV Centre (w12 studioslondon.com).

Bang Bang Oriental
A specialist Asian cuisine food hall (bang bangoriental.com).

↑ Le Gavroche, and (inset) a dish from the Connaught Restaurant

Fine Dining

With over 60 Michelin-starred restaurants, the fine dining scene is booming. Most of the extravagant eateries are found in the West End, the City, Kensington and Knightsbridge. They tend to be formal affairs, but there are hipper exceptions, such as industrial-chic tapas joint Barrafina (p115) and Cantonese favourite Hakkasan (hakkasan.com). Most of these places build their reputation on their chefs, like Michel Roux Jr of Le Gavroche (le-gavroche.co.uk) and Gordon Ramsay, whose eponymous restaurant is one of only three in the city with three Michelin stars (gordonramsayrestaurants.com).

A YEAR IN
LONDON

Whatever the season, and whatever the weather, Britain's capital welcomes an array of festivals, with floral displays in the spring, musical offerings in the summer, cosy cinema days in the autumn and Christmas celebrations in the winter.

Spring

London brushes off the cold weather and kick starts the spring season with a flurry of sporting events, including the historic Boat Race between Oxford and Cambridge university and the London Marathon. Spring also sees the city's parks blossoming with flowers as well as the sophisticated horticultural displays of the RHS Flower Show, held during May.

1. Crowds gathering on Hammersmith bridge to watch the Boat Race

Summer

Londoners make the most of the warm weather (sprinkled with a few summer showers), socializing in the sun on rooftop bars, lounging in parks throughout the weekend and cooling off in the city's lidos. Festivals sweep through the streets, with Pride celebrating the LGBT+ community in July and Notting Hill

RELIGIOUS CELEBRATIONS

London celebrates a variety of religious festivals. Jewish communities gather to celebrate Hanukkah in November and December, and a giant menorah is lit up in Trafalgar Square. In October/November, Diwali is also celebrated with lively street parties and light shows.

Carnival revelling in the rhythms of Afro-Caribbean music in August. Food markets also attract crowds seeking local and international grub.

2. An extravagantly dressed participant at London's Pride parade

Autumn

September still welcomes a few outdoor events but as the weather cools, Londoners spend their weekends in galleries and pubs, or on brisk walks in the park. Festivities head indoors: the BFI Film Festival takes over the city's screens and Open House Weekend allows the public into iconic buildings for free. Come November, Remembrance Sunday sees the city gather to commemorate the country's war veterans.

3. Exploring the Victoria and Albert Museum, the ideal spot on a cold autumn day

Winter

By December, London's central squares and streets are bright with fairy lights and Christmas trees – plus several pop up ice rinks. Families flock to Hyde Park for the magical Winter Wonderland and cosy up indoors at traditional pantomimes. As the city enters the New Year, a spectacular display of fireworks ignites the skies *(inset)* followed by lanterns and parades in Chinatown for Chinese New Year.

4. Skating at the Natural History Museum's popular winter ice rink at dusk

TOP 4 ROYAL EVENTS

Queen's Birthday Salute
Gun salutes at Hyde Park and the Tower of London herald the Queen's birthday in April.

Trooping the Colour
In mid-June a show of military pageantry celebrates the Queen's Birthday Parade.

Buckingham Palace State Rooms Open
From July to September, Buckingham Palace's opulent state rooms are open to the public.

State Opening of Parliament
Shortly after the general election, the Queen travels by coach to Westminster to address the new Parliament.

3

4

A BRIEF
HISTORY

Founded by the Romans, London changed hands many times in its first thousand years. Devastated by fire, plague and war during the subsequent millennium, the city rebuilt itself every time to become a centre of world trade and the largest metropolis on the planet.

Roman London

The first permanent settlement on land within what is now London was established after the first Roman invasion of Britain in 55 BC, though it was not cemented until almost a century later, following another, greater invasion in AD 43. The Romans bridged the river and built their administrative headquarters, Londinium, on the north bank, the present site of the City of London. The Roman occupation lasted some 350 years, but following its withdrawal in the early 5th century during the decline of the Roman Empire, the city lay more or less abandoned.

1 A map of London from 1570.

2 Work begins on Westminster Abbey.

3 The Battle of 1066.

4 Thousands were killed by the Black Death of 1348.

Timeline of events

55 BC
Julius Caesar invades Britain.

AD 43
Londinium founded.

AD 61
Londinium is sacked by the Iceni, British Celts led by their queen Boudicca.

200
Romans build a wall around the city.

410
Romans withdraw from Britain.

Saxons and Vikings

Saxon and Viking invaders fought over the city over the following centuries, during which time its importance fell below that of others like Winchester and Canterbury. It wasn't until 1016 that it recovered its status as the capital under King Canute. Edward the Confessor, one of the last Anglo-Saxon kings of England, moved the base for royal government to the City of Westminster, a distinction that remains to this day. Edward also founded Westminster Abbey where, following the subsequent Norman invasion, William the Conqueror was crowned in 1066.

Norman and Medieval London

William allowed the City of London a degree of independence, reliant as he and his successors were on the City's backing, with all its wealth, for the maintenance of power. City tradesmen set up their own institutions and guilds and the first City of London mayor was appointed in 1189. By the early 14th century London enjoyed a period of relative prosperity, though much of the population, thought to be around 80,000 by this time, lived in poverty. This number was cut in half by the arrival of the bubonic plague, known as the Black Death, in 1348.

WHERE TO SEE MEDIEVAL LONDON

The Tower of London's White Tower is likely the most complete 11th-century palace in Europe, while the Museum of London (p185) contains medieval artifacts. Manuscripts, including the Domesday Book, are found at the British Library (p168). A 14th-century rose window is all that remains of Winchester Palace near the Clink (p214).

872
The Danes occupy London.

1066
Edward the Confessor buried, and William the Conqueror crowned on Christmas Day.

1209
Old London Bridge completed.

1348
The Black Death kills half of the London population.

1381
Peasants' Revolt.

Tudor London

The Tudors' reign began in 1485 with Henry VII. They established peace throughout England, allowing art and commerce to flourish. Under Elizabeth I, explorers opened up the New World, installing London as the world's foremost trade market. It was also during Elizabeth's reign that the foundations of England's great theatrical and literary traditions were firmly laid. The Globe Theatre was erected in 1576 and premiered many of Shakespeare's plays.

Religious Strife and Civil War

Just two years after Elizabeth I's death Catholic conspirators, led by Guy Fawkes, attempted to assassinate King James I by blowing him up in the Houses of Parliament. An anti-Catholic backlash followed and religious conflict, married to a power struggle between Parliament and the monarch, led to Civil War in 1642. London, a Parliamentarian stronghold, became a key battleground. Parliamentarian victory in 1649 established an English Commonwealth dominated by Puritans under Oliver Cromwell. Their rule was, however, short-lived and the monarchy was restored under Charles II in 1660.

↑ Charles I beheaded by the Parliamentarians, led by Oliver Cromwell

Timeline of events

1585
Shakespeare arrives in London.

1642
Civil War begins and Charles I decamps from London.

1649
Charles I beheaded at Whitehall, Commonwealth established.

1660
Monarchy restored under Charles II.

1665
The Great Plague kills 100,000.

Devastation and Reconstruction

On 2 September 1666 a fire broke out at a bakery in Pudding Lane, near London Bridge. It raged for five days, destroying much of the City of London. The post-fire reconstruction formed the basis of the modern-day City of London. As settlements spread beyond the original walled city, the City of London was soon stretching as far as the previously separate City of Westminster.

Expansion

The foundation of the Bank of England in 1694 spurred growth and transformed London into a global financial powerhouse. By the middle of the 18th century London was the largest city in Europe and within a hundred years had become the most populous and wealthiest in the world. The prospect of jobs and money lured millions of the dispossessed from the countryside and from abroad. They crowded into insanitary dwellings, many just east of the City, where docks provided employment. From the 1820s the fields and villages that ringed the city, places like Brompton, Islington and Battersea, filled rapidly with terraced housing for the growing numbers of people.

1 Queen Elizabeth I, who oversaw great change in the city. ↑

2 Guy Fawkes, plotting King James I's downfall.

3 The Great Fire of London, 1666.

Did You Know?
—
After the Great Fire, Sir Christopher Wren designed 51 new churches for the city, plus St Paul's Cathedral.

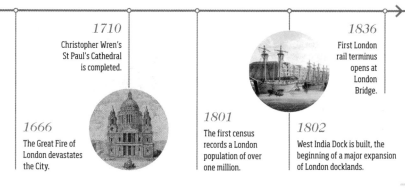

1666
The Great Fire of London devastates the City.

1710
Christopher Wren's St Paul's Cathedral is completed.

1801
The first census records a London population of over one million.

1802
West India Dock is built, the beginning of a major expansion of London docklands.

1836
First London rail terminus opens at London Bridge.

1

2

Victorian London

Much of London today is Victorian. In this golden age of British engineering, many of the city's iconic buildings and structures – the modern Houses of Parliament, Tower Bridge, St Pancras station, the Royal Albert Hall and the London Underground – were built. In 1855 the Metropolitan Board of Works was created, the beginnings of a form of local government. Its chief engineer, Joseph Bazalgette, designed a ground-breaking underground sewer system which did much to alleviate the filth and stink in the streets and the river, reducing the outbreaks of cholera that had accompanied urban expansion. By the end of the 19th century, 4.5 million people lived in inner London and another 4 million in its immediate vicinity.

World Wars and Postwar Reconstruction

During World War I, Zeppelin airships bombed the city, but the damage and number of casualties was nothing as compared to the devastation wreaked during World War II. Much of London, particularly central areas, was flattened, first by the bombing during the Blitz of 1940–41 and then towards the end of the war by V-1 and V-2 rockets, early forms of cruise missiles. The

↑ Winston Churchill, prime minister during World War II

Timeline of events

1837
Queen Victoria makes Buckingham Palace her London residence.

1858
Smelliness of the Thames forces parliament into recess.

1908
London hosts the Olympic Games.

1851
The Great Exhibition is held in Hyde Park.

1863
World's first underground railway opens between Paddington and Farringdon.

substantial rebuilding that followed the war coincided with the decline of the docks and other Victorian industries. Enormous housing estates sprung up around the city, some of which remain today. Still around too is the Royal Festival Hall, built on the banks of the Thames for the 1951 Festival of Britain, a celebration of British technology and culture, and later joined by a string of Brutalist buildings to form the Southbank Centre. Mass immigration from the former colonies of Britain's rapidly disappearing empire, and from the Indian subcontinent and the West Indies, contributed to the city's ever diverse population.

1 The Great Exhibition of 1851.

2 Sleeping in a Tube station during World War II.

3 The Festival of Britain.

4 Opening ceremony, 2012 Olympics.

London Today

The city saw in the new millennium with a swathe of grand building projects – the London Eye, Tate Modern and the ill-fated Millennium Dome – and cranes continue to dominate the skyline in a city that never seems finished. Indeed, regeneration reverberates around the city as it grapples to combat a housing crisis and toxic pollution levels. Despite a worrying spate of knife crime and this cosmopolitan city's disquiet over Britain's decision to leave the European Union, the enduring spirit of the city's inhabitants and a sense of community prevail.

Did You Know?

The Millennium Dome cost over £700 million to construct.

1951
Festival of Britain held on the South Bank.

2000
Ken Livingstone becomes London's first directly elected mayor.

2005
Major terrorist attack takes place on London's transport system.

2012
London hosts the Olympic Games for the third time.

2019
A million march through London in protest at the UK's decision to leave the EU.

EXPERIENCE

Looking towards St Paul's Cathedral

WHITEHALL AND WESTMINSTER

Whitehall and Westminster have been at the centre of political and religious power in England for a thousand years. King Canute, who ruled at the beginning of the 11th century, was the first monarch to have a palace on what was then an island in the swampy meeting point of the Thames and its vanished tributary, the Tyburn. Canute built his palace beside the church that, some 50 years later, Edward the Confessor would enlarge into England's greatest abbey, giving the area its name (a minster is an abbey church). Over the following centuries the offices of state were set up in the vicinity, many of them in Whitehall. This grand street took its name from the Palace of Whitehall that once stood there, established by Henry VIII in the early 16th century as a residence of the royal court. The palace burnt down in 1698 but Whitehall remained at the heart of government, its buildings now occupied by the Ministry of Defence, the Foreign Office, Cabinet Office and several other prestigious government departments.

WHITEHALL AND WESTMINSTER

Must Sees
1. Westminster Abbey
2. Houses of Parliament
3. Tate Britain

Experience More
4. Big Ben
5. Jewel Tower
6. St Margaret's Church
7. Parliament Square
8. Downing Street
9. Churchill War Rooms
10. Banqueting House
11. Horse Guards Parade
12. Household Cavalry Museum
13. Guards Museum
14. Westminster Cathedral
15. St John's Smith Square

Stay
① Artist Residence

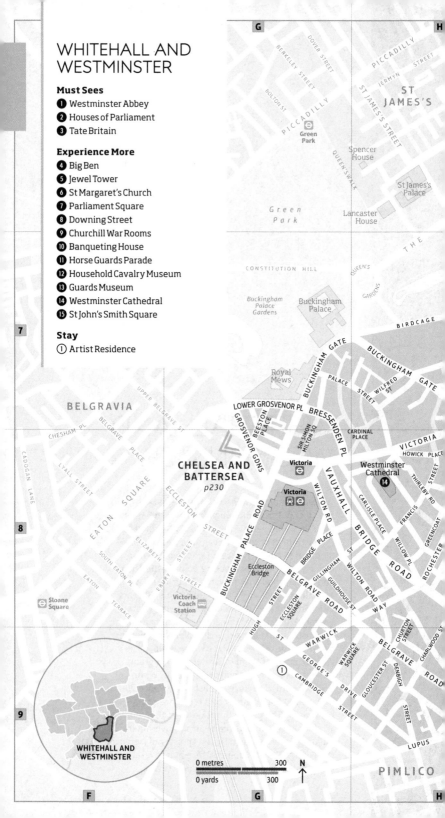

WHITEHALL AND WESTMINSTER

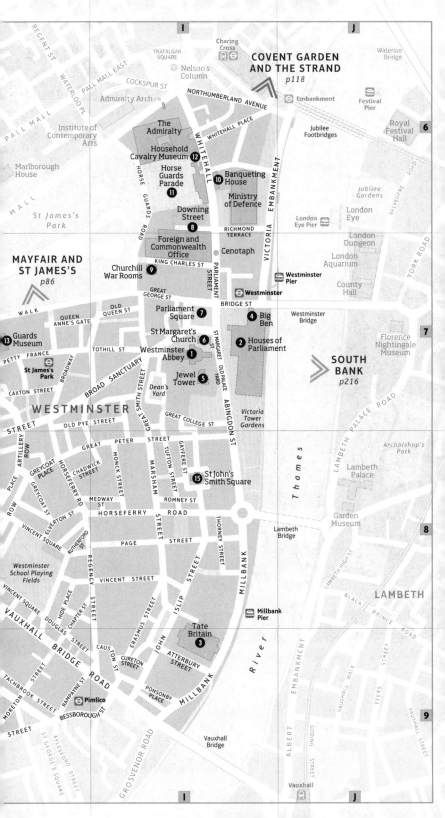

INSIDER TIP
Evensong

Attend the Evensong service to hear spell-binding choral music and get a glimpse inside the abbey - free of charge. The service, which also includes prayer and readings, takes place daily, except for Wednesday, at 5pm (3pm Sat & Sun).

The imposing façade of the West Front with its two towers ↑

①　WESTMINSTER ABBEY

📍 I7　🏠 Broad Sanctuary SW1　🚇 St James's Park, Westminster
🚆 Victoria, Waterloo　🕐 Times vary for specific parts of the church, check website　🌐 westminster-abbey.org

The glorious Gothic Westminster Abbey has some of the best examples of medieval architecture in London and one of the most impressive collections of tombs and monuments in the world.

Half national church, half national museum, the abbey is part of British national consciousness. It is the stunning setting for coronations, royal marriages and Christian worship and is the final resting place of 17 of Britain's monarchs. Many of the leading lights from British history are also buried or memorialized here, including poets and politicians, writers and scientists.

History of the Abbey

The first abbey church was established as early as the 10th century by St Dunstan and a group of Benedictine monks. The present structure dates largely from the 13th century; the new French-influenced design was begun in 1245 at the behest of Henry III. It survived Henry VIII's 16th-century onslaught on Britain's monastic buildings owing to its unique role as the royal coronation church.

←

Statue of Richard I, known as Richard the Lionheart, opposite the rear of Westminster Abbey

CORONATION

The abbey has been the fittingly sumptuous setting for all royal coronations since 1066. The last occupant of the Coronation Chair was the present monarch, Elizabeth II. She was crowned in 1953 and many watched the event on TV: this was the first televised coronation.

Inside the Abbey

The abbey's interior presents an exceptionally diverse array of architectural and sculptural styles, from the austere French Gothic of the nave, through the stunning complexity of Henry VII's Tudor chapel, to the riotous invention of the later 18th-century monuments. The Weston Tower, added in 2018, provides access to the triforium and its Queen's Diamond Jubilee Galleries, packed with historical treasures.

The West Front towers were designed by Nicholas Hawksmoor.

1 Monument to William Shakespeare in Poets' Corner.

2 Executed by Elizabeth I in 1587, Mary Queen of Scots was reburied in Henry VII's Lady Chapel by her son James I (James VI of Scotland) in 1612.

3 The Westminster Abbey choir sing from their stalls in the quire every day. The original quire stalls were medieval, but the ones you see now date from 1848.

Timeline

1050
△ New Benedictine abbey church begun by Edward the Confessor.

1245
New church begun to the designs of Henry of Reyns.

1269
△ Body of Edward the Confessor is moved to a new shrine in the abbey.

1540
△ Monastery dissolved on the orders of King Henry VIII.

The stonework here is Victorian.

The north transept's three chapels contain some of the abbey's finest monuments.

St Edward's chapel houses the shrine of Edward the Confessor.

The Queen's Diamond Jubilee Galleries are 16 m (52 ft) above the abbey floor.

The Lady Chapel, with a superb vaulted ceiling.

The Weston Tower's skillful craftmanship ensures it blends perfectly with the original structure.

The octagonal Chapter House contains 13th-century tiles.

The south transept contains Poets' Corner, where famous literary figures are commemorated.

The cloisters were built mainly in the 13th and 14th centuries.

↑ Cross-section of Westminster Abbey, revealing the interior

Massive flying buttresses help spread the weight of the nave.

The nave – 31 m (102 ft) tall – is the highest in England.

1745
△ West towers completed.

1838
△ Queen Victoria's coronation.

1953
Elizabeth II's coronation is beamed to televisions across the nation.

2011
△ Prince William and Catherine Middleton marry in the abbey.

2 ✎ Ⓜ 🖥 🏛

HOUSES OF PARLIAMENT

📍I7 🚇London SW1 🚊Westminster 🚌Victoria 🚢Westminster Pier
🕐For details of tours and to buy tickets, check website 🗓Recesses: mid-Feb,
Easter, Whitsun, summer (late Jul–early Sep), conference (mid-Sep–mid-Oct), mid-Nov, Christmas 🌐parliament.uk/visit

At the heart of political power in England is the Palace of Westminster. Built in Neo-Gothic style it lies beside the Thames near Westminster Bridge and makes an impressive sight, especially with the distinctive Elizabeth Tower.

For over 500 years the Palace of Westminster has been the seat of the two Houses of Parliament, called the Lords and the Commons. The Commons is made up of elected Members of Parliament (MPs) of different political parties; the party – or coalition of parties – with the most MPs forms the Government, and its leader becomes prime minister. MPs from the second largest party make up the Opposition. Commons debates are impartially chaired by an MP designated as Speaker. The Government formulates legislation which must be agreed to in both Houses before it becomes law.

↑ The Houses of Parliament, designed by Sir Charles Barry

→ The Gothic Revival masterpiece of the Palace of Westminster

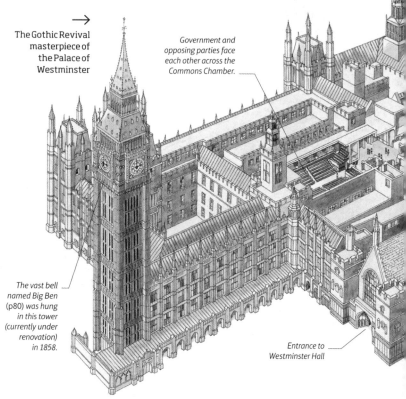

Government and opposing parties face each other across the Commons Chamber.

The vast bell named Big Ben (p80) was hung in this tower (currently under renovation) in 1858.

Entrance to Westminster Hall

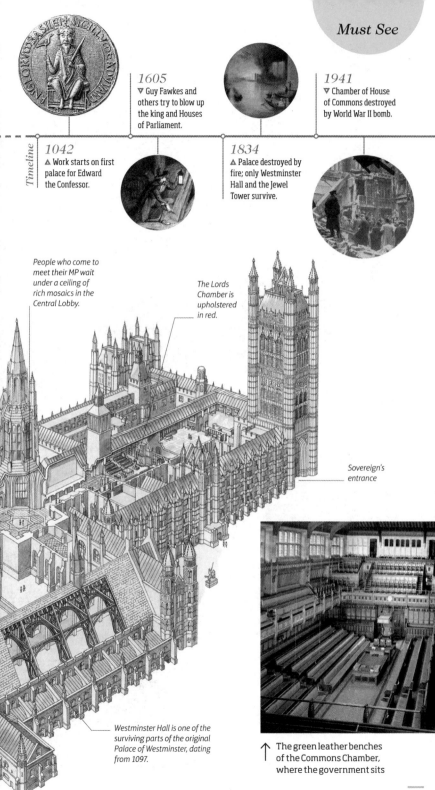

Timeline

1605
▽ Guy Fawkes and others try to blow up the king and Houses of Parliament.

1941
▽ Chamber of House of Commons destroyed by World War II bomb.

1042
△ Work starts on first palace for Edward the Confessor.

1834
△ Palace destroyed by fire; only Westminster Hall and the Jewel Tower survive.

People who come to meet their MP wait under a ceiling of rich mosaics in the Central Lobby.

The Lords Chamber is upholstered in red.

Sovereign's entrance

Westminster Hall is one of the surviving parts of the original Palace of Westminster, dating from 1097.

↑ The green leather benches of the Commons Chamber, where the government sits

The stately façade ↑
of Tate Britain, home
of British art

TATE BRITAIN

⑨ I9 ⚑ Millbank SW1 **Ⓔ** Pimlico ⚏ Victoria, Vauxhall ⛴ Millbank Pier
🕐 10am–6pm daily (to 9:30pm first Fri, every month except Jan)
🚫 24–26 Dec 🌐 tate.org.uk

The nation's largest collection of British art, spanning the 16th to the
21st centuries, is held in a fabulous Neo-Classical building facing the river.
The works include sculpture and modern installation pieces, plus a separate
wing given over to the moody paintings of British artist J M W Turner.

The gallery exhibits a broad range of British
art, from Tudor portraits and 18th-century
landscapes to a large sculpture collection and
modern art. Displays change frequently and
the gallery's broad definition of British art
stretches to work by non-British artists who
spent time in the country, such as Canaletto
and James Whistler. The gallery opened in
1897, founded on the private collection of the
sugar merchant Henry Tate and works from
the older National Gallery. The Tate includes
seven rooms added to display the paintings
of J M W Turner, one of Britain's most revered
artists. The Turner Bequest, as it is known,
was left to the nation by Turner on his death
in 1851. It is displayed in its own wing, called
the Clore Gallery, and consists of some 300 oil
paintings, 300 sketchbooks and about 20,000
watercolours and drawings. Major temporary
exhibitions here always draw huge crowds.

↑ Turner's *Peace – Burial at Sea* (1842), a
tribute to his friend and rival David Wilkie

↑ Inside the gallery, where
art graces every corner

TURNER PRIZE

Every other year, Tate Britain exhibits
the shortlisted works for the prestigious and often controversial Turner
Prize, which was established
in 1984. Representing all
visual arts, four contem-
porary artists are short-
listed annually on the
basis of their work
during the preceding
year, before a panel
of judges picks the
winner. Among the
most sensational of
the boundary-testing
winners have been
Damien Hirst's
*Mother and Child,
Divided* (1995) and
the ceramics of
Grayson Perry
(right) in 2003.

EXPERIENCE MORE

4

Big Ben

📍 I7 🏠 Bridge St SW1 🚇 Westminster 🌐 parliament.uk

Big Ben is not the name of the world-famous four-faced clock in the 96-m (315-ft) tower that rises above the Houses of Parliament, but of the resonant 13.7-tonne bell inside the tower on which the hour is struck. It is thought to be named after the First Commissioner of Works, Sir Benjamin Hall. Cast at Whitechapel Bell Foundry in 1858, it was the second giant bell made for the clock, the first having become cracked during a test ringing. The clock is the largest in Britain, its four dials 7 m (23 ft) in diameter and the minute hand 4.2 m (14 ft) long, made in hollow copper for lightness. The tower itself was renamed the Elizabeth Tower in 2012 in honour of Queen Elizabeth II in her Diamond Jubilee year.

A symbol the world over, Big Ben kept exact time for the nation more or less between 1859 and 2017, when it fell silent while the tower closed for essential building works. These are expected to be completed in 2021.

5

Jewel Tower

📍 I7 🏠 Abingdon St SW1 🚇 Westminster 🕐 Apr-Sep: 10am–6pm daily; Oct: 10am–5pm daily; Nov-Mar: 10am–4pm Sat & Sun 🗓 1 Jan & 24–26 Dec 🌐 english-heritage.org.uk

This 14th-century building and Westminster Hall (p77) are the only remaining vestiges of the old Palace of Westminster, having survived a fire in 1834. The tower was built around 1365 as a stronghold for Edward III's treasure and today houses an exhibition called "Parliament Past and Present", which relates the history of Parliament. The display on the upper floor is devoted to the history of the tower itself.

The tower served as the Weights and Measures office from 1869 until 1938 and another small display relates to that era. Alongside are the remains of the moat and a medieval quay.

6

St Margaret's Church

📍 I7 🏠 Broad Sanctuary SW1 🚇 Westminster 🕐 9:30am–3:30pm Mon-Fri, 9:30am–1:30pm Sat, 2:30–4:30pm Sun 🌐 westminster-abbey.org/st-margarets-church

This early 16th-century church has long been a favoured venue for political and society weddings, such as Winston and Clementine Churchill's. Although much restored, it retains some Tudor features,

→
Telephones in the Map Room of the Churchill War Rooms

notably a stained-glass window commemorating the marriage of King Henry VIII and his first wife, Catherine of Aragon.

7
Parliament Square

📍 I7 🏠 SW1 🚇 Westminster

Laid out in 1868 to provide a more open aspect for the new Houses of Parliament, the square today is hemmed in by heavy traffic. Statues of statesmen are dominated by Winston Churchill, glowering at the House of Commons. Standing on the west side, notable figures include Mahatma Gandhi and Nelson Mandela. Millicent Fawcett – a campaigner for women's suffrage – is the only female represented in the square.

8
Downing Street

📍 I6 🏠 SW1 🚇 Westminster 🚫 To the public

The official home and office of the UK's Prime Minister is one of four surviving houses built in the 1680s for Sir George Downing (1623–84). Downing went to America as a boy and

←
The Elizabeth Tower, seen from Albert Embankment

returned to fight for the Parliamentarians in the English Civil War. The building contains a State Dining Room and the Cabinet Room, where senior government ministers meet regularly to formulate policy. Downing Street has been closed to the public for security reasons since 1989.

9
Churchill War Rooms

📍 I7 🏠 Clive Steps, King Charles St SW1 🚇 Westminster, St James's Park 🕐 9:30am-6pm daily (last adm: 5pm; Jul & Aug: to 7pm) 🚫 24-26 Dec 🌐 iwm.org.uk

This intriguing slice of 20th-century history is a warren of

rooms below the Treasury building, where the War Cabinet met during World War II, when German bombs were falling on London. The War Rooms include living quarters for key ministers and military leaders and the Cabinet Room, where strategic decisions were taken. They are laid out as they were when the war ended, with Churchill's desk, communications equipment and maps for plotting military strategy. The Churchill Museum is a multimedia exhibit recording Churchill's life and career, and the display "Undercover: Life in Churchill's Bunker" features personal stories, objects and interviews with those who worked in the War Rooms. Booking ahead is recommended.

THE CENOTAPH

On Remembrance Sunday every year - the Sunday nearest 11 November - ceremonies held around the UK honour those who have lost their lives in conflicts since World War I. The Cenotaph, a monument on Whitehall completed in 1920 by Sir Edwin Lutyens, is the focal point of London's remembrance service, when members of the royal family and other dignitaries place wreaths of red poppies at its base.

Henry VIII's jousting grounds, now Horse Guards Parade

10 🔄 🏛

Banqueting House

📍 I6 📌 Whitehall SW1
🚇 Embankment, Charing Cross, Westminster
🕐 10am–5pm daily (last adm: 4:30pm) 🚫 24–26 Dec & 1 Jan 🌐 hrp.org.uk

This delightful building is of great architectural importance. It was the first built in central London to embody the Classical Palladian style that designer Inigo Jones brought back from his travels in Italy. Completed in 1622, its disciplined stone façade marked a startling change from the Elizabethans' fussy turrets and unrestrained external decoration.

Rubens's ceiling paintings, a complex allegory on the exaltation of James I, were commissioned by his son, Charles I, in 1630. This blatant glorification of royalty was despised by Oliver Cromwell and the Parliamentarians, who executed King Charles I on a scaffold just outside Banqueting House in 1649. Eleven years later, the English monarchy was restored with the coronation of Charles II.

The building is used today for official functions, and may close early when these are scheduled: check the website for details.

11

Horse Guards Parade

📍 I6 📌 Whitehall SW1
🚇 Westminster, Charing Cross, Embankment

This is where the Trooping the Colour ceremony (p59) takes place each year, but you can see royal pageantry in action daily: Changing the Queen's Life Guard takes place at 11am (10am on Sunday), and there's a guard inspection at 4pm.

This was Henry VIII's tiltyard (tournament ground); nearby is a trace of the "real tennis" court where the king is said to have played the precursor of modern lawn tennis. The elegant buildings, completed in 1755, were designed by William Kent. On the opposite side, the ivy-covered Citadel is a bomb-proof structure built in 1940 beside the Admiralty. During World War II, it was used as a communications headquarters by the Navy.

QUEEN ANNE'S GATE

Not far from St James's Park Tube station is Queen Anne's Gate, a well-preserved street lined with spacious terraced houses, many of which are Grade I listed. Most date from 1704 and are notable for the ornate canopies over each front door. At the east end of the street are houses built some 70 years later, some sporting blue plaques that record former residents, such as Lord Palmerston, a prime minister during the Victorian era. It is rumoured that the British Secret Service, MI5, was formerly based in this unlikely spot.

can see the working stables, and kids (big and small) can try on uniforms.

13

Guards Museum

H7 **Birdcage Walk SW1** **St James's Park** **10am-4pm daily (last adm: 3:30pm)** **Mid-Dec–end Jan & for ceremonies** **theguardsmuseum.com**

Entered from Birdcage Walk, this museum is under the parade ground of Wellington Barracks, headquarters of the five Foot Guards regiments. The museum illustrates battles in which the Guards have taken part, from the English Civil War (1642–51) to the present. Weapons, uniforms and fascinating models are on display.

14

Westminster Cathedral

H8 **Victoria St SW1** **Victoria** **Cathedral: 7am-7pm Mon-Fri, 7:30am-7pm Sat & Sun; Tower & Exhibition: 9:30am-5pm daily (to 6pm Sat & Sun)** **westminstercathedral.org.uk**

One of London's rare Neo-Byzantine buildings, this cathedral for the Catholic

diocese was completed in 1903. Its 87-m- (285-ft-) high red-brick bell tower, with horizontal stripes of white stone, has a superb viewing gallery, while the Treasures of the Cathedral exhibition displays rare ecclesiastical objects. The rich interior decoration, with marble of varying colours and intricate mosaics, makes the domes above the nave seem incongruous. They were left bare because the project ran out of money. Eric Gill's dramatic reliefs of the 14 Stations of the Cross, created during World War I, adorn the piers of the nave. The organ is superb; there are often free recitals on Sundays at 4:45pm.

15

St John's Smith Square

I8 **Smith Sq SW1** **Westminster** **For concerts only** **sjss.org.uk**

A masterpiece of English Baroque architecture, Thomas Archer's plump church looks as if it is trying to burst from the confines of the square. Today principally a concert hall, it has an accident-prone history: completed in 1728, it was burned down in 1742, struck by lightning in 1773 and destroyed by a World War II bomb in 1941. There is a basement restaurant, open 10am–5pm weekdays and on concert evenings.

12

Household Cavalry Museum

I6 **Horse Guards, Whitehall SW1** **Charing Cross, Westminster, Embankment** **Apr-Oct: 10am-6pm daily; Nov-Mar: 10am-5pm daily** **Good Fri, Marathon Day, 24-26 Dec; occasionally for ceremonies** **householdcavalrymuseum.co.uk**

A collection of artifacts and interactive displays cover the history of the senior regiments based at Horse Guards, from their role in the 1815 Battle of Waterloo to their service in Afghanistan in the early 21st century. Visitors

The Life Guards, part of the royal Household Cavalry ↑

A SHORT WALK
WHITEHALL AND WESTMINSTER

Distance 1.5 km (1 mile) **Time** 30 minutes
Nearest Tube St James's Park

London has comparatively little monumental architecture, but a stroll through the historic seat of both the government and the established church uncovers broad, stately avenues designed to overawe with pomp. On weekdays the streets are filled with members of the civil service, while at weekends they teem mainly with tourists, visiting some of London's most famous sights.

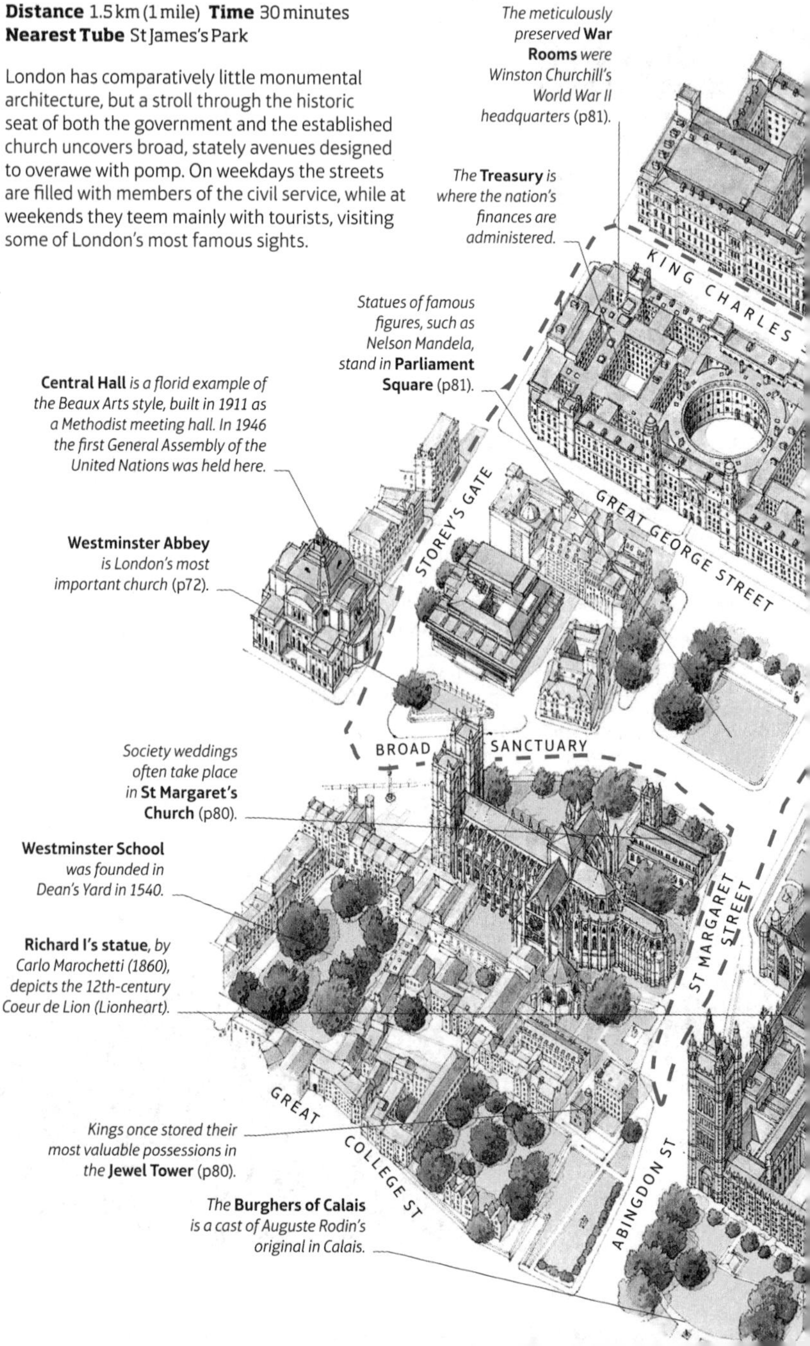

The meticulously preserved **War Rooms** were Winston Churchill's World War II headquarters (p81).

The **Treasury** is where the nation's finances are administered.

Statues of famous figures, such as Nelson Mandela, stand in **Parliament Square** (p81).

Central Hall is a florid example of the Beaux Arts style, built in 1911 as a Methodist meeting hall. In 1946 the first General Assembly of the United Nations was held here.

Westminster Abbey is London's most important church (p72).

Society weddings often take place in **St Margaret's Church** (p80).

Westminster School was founded in Dean's Yard in 1540.

Richard I's statue, by Carlo Marochetti (1860), depicts the 12th-century Coeur de Lion (Lionheart).

Kings once stored their most valuable possessions in the **Jewel Tower** (p80).

The **Burghers of Calais** is a cast of Auguste Rodin's original in Calais.

KING CHARLES

GREAT GEORGE STREET

STOREY'S GATE

ST MARGARET STREET

BROAD SANCTUARY

GREAT COLLEGE ST

ABINGDON ST

FINISH

British prime ministers have lived on **Downing Street** since 1732 (p81).

A mounted guard is ceremonially changed at **Horse Guards Parade** every day (p82).

Dover House, a stately mansion dating from 1787, now houses the Scotland Office.

Inigo Jones designed the elegant **Banqueting House**, which has a Rubens ceiling, in 1622 (p82).

Depicting wartime uniforms, the **Monument to the Women of World War II** was unveiled by the Queen in 2005.

Edwin Lutyens's **Cenotaph** dates from 1920 (p81).

DOWNING ST

WHITEHALL

RICHMOND

TERRACE

The Commons Chamber will relocate to a redesigned **Richmond House** in the mid-2020s while the Palace of Westminster undergoes renovation work.

PARLIAMENT STREET

VICTORIA EMBANKMENT

Westminster Pier is a starting point for riverboat excursions.

Portcullis House provides offices for Members of Parliament.

Boudicca, the British queen who resisted the Romans, was portrayed by Thomas Thornycroft in the 1850s.

BRIDGE

STREET

START

Westminster station

The **Houses of Parliament** and **Big Ben** were designed by Charles Barry in 1834, when the Palace of Westminster burned down (p76).

0 metres 100
0 yards 100

N

→ The *Burghers of Calais* statue, by the Houses of Parliament

WHITEHALL AND WESTMINSTER

Locator Map
For more detail see p70

Inside the decorative Fortnum & Mason's department store

MAYFAIR AND ST JAMES'S

The exclusivity of these most gentrified of London districts, with their royal connections, stretches back centuries. St James's Palace was the first royal residence to be constructed on this patch of land, built in the 1530s by Henry VIII, who also laid out the hunting grounds that would become St James's Park. During the 17th century several large mansions were added as aristocrats sought proximity to the royal court. Mayfair did not emerge as a tangible district until the late 17th century when the annual May Fair, held around present-day Shepherd Market, was moved here. The fair was abolished in 1764, having earned a reputation for debauchery and rowdiness that did not sit well with the wealthy residents moving to the area as the city expanded westwards. Three great squares were built and Mayfair became the property of a small number of landed estates, the most significant of which, the Grosvenor Estate, remains in the hands of the Grosvenor family to this day.

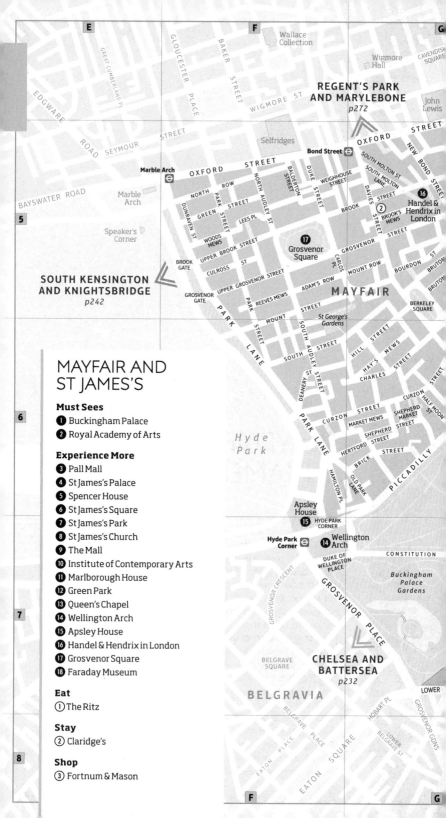

MAYFAIR AND ST JAMES'S

Must Sees

1 Buckingham Palace
2 Royal Academy of Arts

Experience More

3 Pall Mall
4 St James's Palace
5 Spencer House
6 St James's Square
7 St James's Park
8 St James's Church
9 The Mall
10 Institute of Contemporary Arts
11 Marlborough House
12 Green Park
13 Queen's Chapel
14 Wellington Arch
15 Apsley House
16 Handel & Hendrix in London
17 Grosvenor Square
18 Faraday Museum

Eat

① The Ritz

Stay

② Claridge's

Shop

③ Fortnum & Mason

REGENT'S PARK
AND MARYLEBONE
p272

SOUTH KENSINGTON
AND KNIGHTSBRIDGE
p242

CHELSEA AND
BATTERSEA
p232

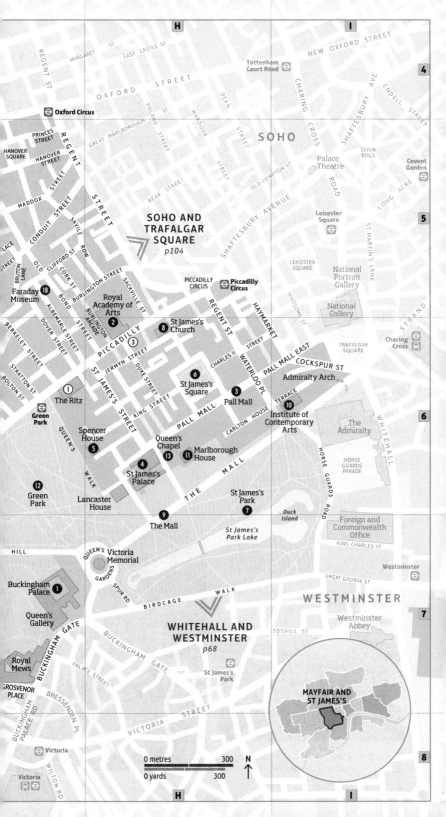

The Nash-designed Picture Gallery has works by Italian, Dutch and Flemish masters.

The Victorian Ballroom, used for state banquets and ceremonies.

② (160 m/175 yd) ①

→

Buckingham Palace, official home of the British monarch

BUCKINGHAM PALACE

⊠ G7 ⊠ SW1 ⊠ St James's Park, Victoria ⊠ Victoria ⊠ State Rooms and Garden: Jul-Oct 9:30am-6:30pm daily (last adm: 4:15pm); selected dates Dec-May, check website ⊠ rct.uk

The Queen's official London residence is one of the capital's best-recognized landmarks. Visit its opulent State Rooms for a glimpse of how the royals live.

Both administrative office and family home, Buckingham Palace is the official London residence of the British monarchy. The palace is used for ceremonial occasions for visiting heads of state as well as the weekly meeting between the Queen and Prime Minister. John Nash converted the original Buckingham House into a palace for George IV (reigned 1820–30). Both he and his brother, William IV (reigned 1830–37), died before work was completed, and Queen Victoria was the first monarch to live at the palace. She added a fourth wing to incorporate more bedrooms and guest rooms.

↑ Exhibits in the Queen's Gallery, including fine porcelain and old masters

The Throne Room holds thrones used by Queen Elizabeth II and the Duke of Edinburgh during her coronation.

Traditionally, the royal family waves to the crowds from the palace balcony during public ceremonies.

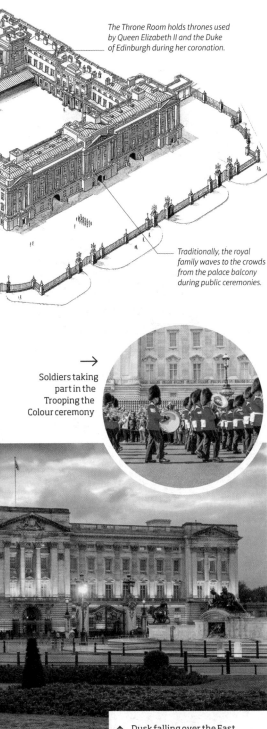

→ Soldiers taking part in the Trooping the Colour ceremony

↑ Dusk falling over the East façade, which was added to the palace in 1913

① 🖼 🛍

The Queen's Gallery

📍G7 🚇St James's Park, Victoria ⏰10am-5:30pm daily (mid-Jul-Sep: 9:30am-5:30pm; last adm: 4:15pm) 🚫Between exhibitions, check website

The royal family possesses one of the finest and most valuable art collections in the world, including works by Johannes Vermeer and Leonardo da Vinci. The Queen's Gallery hosts a rolling programme of the Royal Collection's most impressive masterpieces, with temporary exhibitions featuring fine art, porcelain, jewels, furniture and manuscripts.

② 🖼 🎭 🛍

Royal Mews

📍G7 🚇St James's Park, Victoria ⏰10am-4pm daily (Apr-Oct: to 5pm; Nov: Mon-Sat) 🚫Subject to closure at short notice, check website; Dec-Jan

Head to the Royal Mews to discover plenty of royal pomp. Stables and coach houses, designed by Nash in 1825, accommodate the horses and coaches used by the royal family on state occasions. The Mews' extensive collection of coaches, motorcars and carriages includes the Irish state coach, bought by Queen Victoria for the State Opening of Parliament; the open-topped 1902 royal landau, used to give the crowds the best view of newlywed royal couples; and the glass coach, also used for royal weddings. The newest coach is the Diamond Jubilee State Coach, built in 2012. The star exhibit is the Gold State Coach: built for George III in 1762, with panels by Giovanni Cipriani, it has been used at every coronation since 1821.

2 🍴 🖥 🛍

ROYAL ACADEMY OF ARTS

Though it holds one of the nation's great art collections, the Royal Academy of Arts is most renowned for its blockbuster temporary exhibitions, as well as its popular annual Summer Exhibition.

A storied art institution that holds one of the country's most prestigious collections of British art, the Royal Academy of Arts (RA) celebrated its 250th anniversary in 2018. It has always been led by its elected and appointed Royal Academicians, artists themselves, whose works make up the bulk of the permanent collection and who help to deliver the Royal Academy Schools' programme. The collection is displayed across two Italianate buildings, palatial Burlington House and Burlington Gardens. The two are linked by a bridge, built to mark the anniversary. Several new galleries including the Vaults and the Collection Gallery were opened for the occasion too.

↑ The exterior of Burlington House, Royal Academy of Arts

→ Installation works on display during the annual Summer Exhibition

1 Sir Joshua Reynolds attempted to rival Dutch master Rembrandt with this self-portrait painted in c 1780.

2 The only marble sculpture by Michelangelo in Britain is his *Taddei Tondo*; carved in 1504-5, it depicts the Virgin and Child with the Infant St John.

3 The Collection Gallery features Giampietrino's 16th-century copy of Leonardo da Vinci's *The Last Supper*.

THE SUMMER EXHIBITION

The highlight of the RA calendar and among the most talked-about events in British art is the Summer Exhibition, held annually since 1769. Anyone can submit their work, for a fee, to be considered for the show, making it a potentially career-changing event for unknown artists, though established artists exhibit too. Over 1,500 entries are selected, ranging from painting, printmaking and sculpture to photography, film and architecture, and displayed to the public, for an admission charge, between June and August in the main galleries and spilling out across the campus. Most of the works displayed are for sale.

Did You Know?

Famous entrants to the Summer Exhibition include Sir Winston Churchill, who submitted under a pseudonym.

EXPERIENCE MORE

❸ Pall Mall

📍 H6 🚇 SW1 🚉 Charing Cross, Piccadilly Circus, Green Park

This dignified street is named for the game of pall-mall – a cross between croquet and golf – which was played here in the 17th century. For over 200 years, Pall Mall has been at the heart of London's clubland. Exclusive gentlemen's clubs were formed here for members of the elite.

The clubhouses now amount to a textbook of the most fashionable architects of their era. At the east end, on the left is the colonnaded entrance to No 116, Nash's United Services Club (1827). This was the favourite club of the Duke of Wellington and now houses the Institute of Directors. Facing it, on the other side of Waterloo Place, is the Athenaeum (No 107), designed three years later by the architect Decimus Burton, and long the powerhouse of the British establishment. Next door are two clubs by Sir Charles Barry, mastermind of the Houses of Parliament (p76): the Travellers at No 106 and the Reform at No 104. The clubs' stately interiors are well-preserved but only members and their guests are admitted.

❹ St James's Palace

📍 H6 🚇 Pall Mall SW1 🚉 Green Park ⏰ To the public 🌐 royal.uk

Built by Henry VIII in the 1530s on the site of a former leper hospital, this palace was a primary royal residence only briefly, mainly during the reign of Elizabeth I and in the late 17th and early 18th centuries. In 1952, Queen Elizabeth II made her first speech as monarch here, and foreign ambassadors are still officially accredited to the Court of St James's. Its northern gatehouse, seen from St James's Street, is one of London's great Tudor landmarks. The palace remains a royal residence for, among others, the Princess Royal and Princess Alexandra, and its State Apartments are used during official state visits.

❺ Spencer House

📍 H6 🚇 27 St James's Pl SW1 🚉 Green Park ⏰ Sep-Jul: 10am-5:30pm Sun (last adm: 4:30pm) 🌐 spencerhouse.co.uk

This Palladian palace, built in 1766 for the first Earl Spencer,

an ancestor of the late Diana, Princess of Wales, has been completely restored to its 18th-century splendour. It contains some wonderful paintings and contemporary furniture. The house is open to the public on Sundays, for guided tours only.

❻ St James's Square

📍 H6 🚇 SW1 🚉 Green Park, Piccadilly Circus ⏰ 10am-4:30pm Mon-Fri

London's squares, quadrangles of elegant homes surrounding gated gardens, are among the city's most attractive features. St James's, one of London's earliest, was laid out in the 1670s and lined with exclusive houses for those whose business made it vital for them to live near St James's Palace. Many buildings date from the 18th and 19th centuries and have had many illustrious residents. During World War II, generals Eisenhower and de Gaulle both had headquarters here.

Today, No 10 on the north side, Chatham House (1736), is home to the Royal Institute for International Affairs. In the northwest corner, at No 14, is the **London Library**

← The elegant Spencer House, on the edge of Green Park

→ The royal St James's Park, famed for its floral displays

(1896), a private lending library that was founded in 1841 by historian Thomas Carlyle (*p237*) and others. It offers guided tours at 6pm on some weekdays. The pretty gardens in the middle contain an equestrian statue of William III, here since 1808.

London Library

⊛ 🔽 For public tours; check website 🅦 londonlibrary. co.uk

---

7 🖵

St James's Park

🔽 H6 🏠 SW1 🚇 St James's Park 🕐 5am–midnight daily 🅦 royalparks.org.uk

In summer, office workers sunbathe in between the

↑ Stained glass at the Wren-designed St James's Church

flowerbeds of the capital's most ornamental park. In winter, the sunbathers are replaced with overcoated civil servants discussing affairs of state as they stroll by the lake, eyed by its resident ducks, geese and pelicans (which are fed at 2:30pm daily).

Originally a marsh, the park was drained by Henry VIII and incorporated into his hunting grounds. On his return from exile in France, Charles II had it remodelled in the more continental style as pedestrian pleasure gardens, with an aviary along its southern edge (hence Birdcage Walk, the name of the street that runs alongside the park where the aviary once was).

It is a hugely popular place to escape the city's hustle and bustle, with an appealing view of Whitehall rooftops and Buckingham Palace, a café that is open daily and an attractive lake.

---

8 🖵

St James's Church

🔽 H6 🏠 197 Piccadilly W1 🚇 Piccadilly Circus 🕐 8am–7pm daily 🅦 sjp.org.uk

Among the many churches Christopher Wren designed, this is said to be one of his favourites. It has been altered

over the years and was half-wrecked by a bomb in 1940, but it maintains its essential features from 1684 – the tall, arched windows and a thin spire (a 1966 replica of the original). The ornate screen behind the altar is one of the finest works of the 17th-century master carver Grinling Gibbons. The artist and poet William Blake and Georgian prime minister Pitt the Elder were both baptized here.

The church hosts concerts, talks and events, and houses a popular café. The outer courtyard hosts a food market on Monday and Tuesday, an antiques market on Tuesday and a crafts market from Wednesday to Saturday.

Tourists thronging the Mall en route to Buckingham Palace ↑

⑨ The Mall

📍H6 🚇SW1 🚉Charing Cross, Piccadilly Circus, Green Park

This broad triumphal approach to Buckingham Palace was created by Aston Webb when he redesigned the front of the palace and the Victoria Memorial in 1911. It follows the course of the old path at the edge of St James's Park, laid out in the 1660s during the reign of Charles II, when it became London's most fashionable promenade. Down both sides of the Mall the national flags of foreign heads of state fly during their official visits. The annual London Marathon finishes on the Mall, amid a mass of crowds who cheer as enthusiastically for the weary stragglers at the end as they do for the elated runners at the front.

---

⑩ Institute of Contemporary Arts

📍I6 🚇The Mall SW1 🚉Charing Cross, Piccadilly Circus ⏰Noon–11pm Tue–Sun; exhibition space: noon–9pm Tue–Sun 🚫Public hols 🌐ica.art

The Institute of Contemporary Arts (ICA) was established in 1946 to offer British artists some of the facilities available to artists at the Museum of Modern Art in New York. It has been situated in John Nash's Neo-Classical Carlton House Terrace (1833) since 1968. With its entrance on the Mall, this extensive warren contains exhibition spaces, a cinema, auditorium, bookshop, bar and restaurant. It also hosts concerts, theatre and dance performances, and lectures. A modest fee applies to non-members, providing all-day access to most exhibitions and events, though access to exhibitions is free on Tuesdays.

⑪ Marlborough House

📍H6 🚇Pall Mall SW1 🚉St James's Park, Green Park ⏰Only for pre-booked group tours 🌐thecommon wealth.org/about-us/marlborough-house

Marlborough House was designed by Christopher Wren for the Duchess of Marlborough and completed

EAT

Afternoon Tea at the Ritz

The poshest afternoon tea in town is accompanied by a pianist and harpist. Expect sandwiches, scones and dainty pastries. Men must wear jacket and tie.

📍G6 🚇150 Piccadilly W1 🌐theritz london.com

£££

in 1711. It was substantially enlarged in the 19th century and used by members of the royal family. From 1863 until he became Edward VII in 1901, it was the home of the Prince and Princess of Wales and the social centre of London. The building now houses the Commonwealth Secretariat.

12

Green Park

G6 **SW1** **Green Park, Hyde Park Corner** **royal parks.org.uk**

Once part of Henry VIII's hunting grounds, this was, like St James's Park, adapted for public use by Charles II in the 1660s and is a natural, undulating landscape of grass and trees (with a fine spring show of daffodils). It was a favourite site for duels during the 18th century: in 1771 the poet Alfieri was wounded here by his mistress's husband, Viscount Ligonier, but then rushed back to the Haymarket Theatre in time to catch the last act of a play. Today the park is a popular place to take a breather from the city.

13

Queen's Chapel

H6 **Marlborough Rd SW1** **Green Park** **royal.uk**

This chapel by architect Inigo Jones was built for Charles I's French wife, Henrietta Maria, in 1627. Originally intended to be part of St James's Palace, it was the first Classical church to be built in England, and features contributions by both Grinling Gibbons and Christopher Wren. George III married Charlotte of Mecklenburg-Strelitz here in 1761. The chapel is only open for Sunday services from Easter to the end of July, at 8:30am and 11:15am.

SHOPPING ARCADES

On and around Piccadilly are four arch-fronted shopping arcades built in the 19th and early 20th centuries. These elegant covered walkways were the luxury shopping malls of their day, and are still home to the same kinds of top-drawer retailers. The first one to open, in 1819, was the Burlington Arcade, setting the template for the other three: the Royal, Princes and Piccadilly Arcades.

← Relaxing in shady, picturesque Green Park

14

Wellington Arch

📍 F7 🚇 Hyde Park Corner SW1 🚉 Hyde Park Corner ⏰ Apr–Sep: 10am–6pm daily; Oct: 10am–5pm daily; Nov–Mar: 10am–4pm daily 🚫 1 Jan, 24–26 & 31 Dec 🌐 english-heritage.org.uk

After nearly a century of debate about what to do with the patch of land in front of Apsley House, Wellington Arch was erected in 1828. It was moved to its current position, and the equestrian statue of the Duke dismantled in the 1880s. The sculpture by Adrian Jones of Nike, winged goddess of Victory, was added in 1912. Before it was installed Jones seated three people for dinner in the body of one of the horses.

Exhibitions are held in the inner rooms of the arch, while a viewing platform beneath the sculpture has great views over the royal parks and the gardens of Buckingham Palace.

AUCTION HOUSES

Venerable Sotheby's, Bonhams and Christie's head the list of auction houses dotted around Mayfair and St James's. All three were founded in the 18th century and have overseen the sale of many of the most treasured and expensive antiques and works of art on the planet. In 1836 Bonhams sold a collection of furniture from Buckingham Palace; Van Gogh's *Sunflowers* sold at Christie's in 1987 for £24.75 million; and in 2016 Sotheby's New Bond Street auction rooms sold David Bowie's art collection for almost £33 million.

15

Apsley House

📍 F7 🚇 Hyde Park Corner W1 🚉 Hyde Park Corner ⏰ Apr–Oct: 11am–5pm Wed–Sun; Nov & Dec: 10am–4pm Wed–Sun; Jan–Mar: 10am–4pm Sat & Sun 🚫 Christmas wk 🌐 wellingtoncollection.co.uk

Apsley House, or Number One London, as it is also known, at the southeast corner of Hyde Park, was completed by Robert Adam for Baron Apsley in 1778.

Fifty years later it was enlarged and altered by the architect Benjamin Dean Wyatt to provide a grand home for the Duke of Wellington. His dual career as both soldier and politician brought him victory against Napoleon at Waterloo (1815) and two terms as prime minister (1828–30 and 1834). Set against sumptuous silk hangings and gilt decoration is the duke's art collection: works by Goya, Velázquez, Titian and Rubens hang alongside displays of porcelain, silver and furniture. Ironically,

the duke's memorabilia is dominated by Canova's colossal statue of Napoleon.

Handel & Hendrix in London

📍 G5 🏠 25 Brook St W1 🚇 Bond Street 🕐 11am–6pm Mon-Sat 🌐 handelhendrix.org

A pair of Georgian houses on Brook Street have a couple of notable, very different, musical connections. The composer George Frideric Handel lived at No 25 from 1723 until his death in 1759, and his rooms have been restored to the early Georgian appearance they would have had during the composer's time, with portraits and musical instruments on display. The museum hosts changing exhibitions and regular recitals in an intimate performance space. In 1968, Jimi Hendrix moved into the

↑ A bust of Handel at the Handel & Hendrix in London museum

attic apartment next door, which has also been lovingly restored to resemble his former apartment, complete with 1960s decor. Check the website for late-night openings and Hendrix-themed events.

⑰

Grosvenor Square

📍 F5 🏠 W1 🚇 Bond Street

Mayfair has long been home to some of the grandest addresses in all of London, most notably in a series of prestigious squares, originally laid out in the early 18th century and still retaining many Georgian buildings. Grosvenor Square is the

← Londoners enjoying the sun in Grosvenor Square; a portico *(inset)* providing shade

largest, and has had ongoing political connections with the USA since John Adams – the second US president – lived at No 9 between 1785 and 1789. The west side is dominated by the former US Embassy. Having closed in 2017, the Eero Saarinen-designed Brutalist building is being redeveloped as a luxury 137-room hotel by lauded David Chipperfield Associates, slated to open in 2023. A statue of Franklin D Roosevelt – the 32nd US president – stands at the centre of the square.

⑱

Faraday Museum

📍 G5 🏠 The Royal Institution, 21 Albemarle St W1 🚇 Green Park 🕐 9am–5pm Mon-Fri ✕ Christmas wk & public hols 🌐 rigb.org

Michael Faraday was one of the 19th-century pioneers of the uses of electricity. Part of the Royal Institution, a body dedicated to scientific study, the museum includes a recreation of Faraday's laboratory and some of his scientific apparatus, as well as exhibits on the work of other great scientists.

A SHORT WALK
ST JAMES'S

Distance 2.5 km (1.5 miles) **Time** 35 minutes
Nearest Tube Green Park

After Henry VIII built St James's Palace in the 1530s, the area around it became the centre of fashionable London, and it has remained so ever since. Its historic streets, squares and arcades attract a thoroughly international – and extremely wealthy – set. A walk through the district will take you past the flagship stores of exclusive global brands and classic British names that have served royalty and aristocracy for centuries, as well as the Royal Academy and many independent art galleries.

The **Albany** mansion has been one of London's smartest addresses since it opened in 1803.

Sir Joshua Reynolds founded the **Royal Academy of Arts** in 1768. Now it mounts large popular exhibitions (p92).

Uniformed beadles discourage unruly behaviour in the **Burlington Arcade**, a 19th-century mall (p97).

Fortnum & Mason was founded in 1707 by one of Queen Anne's footmen (p95).

Named after César Ritz, and opened in 1906, the **Ritz Hotel** still lives up to his name.

Ryder Street is lined with art galleries.

An ancestor of Princess Diana built **Spencer House** in 1766 (p94).

Clarence House was designed by John Nash for William IV, and is now Prince Charles's London home.

Did You Know?

Hatchards on Piccadilly is London's oldest bookshop, opened in 1797.

0 metres   100
0 yards   100

N ↑

START

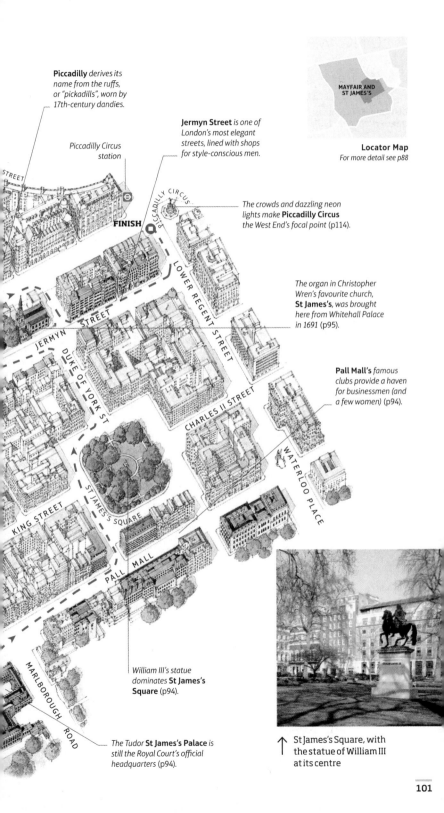

Piccadilly derives its name from the ruffs, or "pickadills", worn by 17th-century dandies.

Piccadilly Circus station

Jermyn Street is one of London's most elegant streets, lined with shops for style-conscious men.

Locator Map
For more detail see p88

MAYFAIR AND ST JAMES'S

FINISH

The crowds and dazzling neon lights make **Piccadilly Circus** the West End's focal point (p114).

The organ in Christopher Wren's favourite church, **St James's**, was brought here from Whitehall Palace in 1691 (p95).

Pall Mall's famous clubs provide a haven for businessmen (and a few women) (p94).

LOWER REGENT STREET

JERMYN STREET

DUKE OF YORK ST

CHARLES II STREET

WATERLOO PLACE

KING STREET

ST JAMES'S SQUARE

PALL MALL

MARLBOROUGH ROAD

William III's statue dominates **St James's Square** (p94).

The Tudor **St James's Palace** is still the Royal Court's official headquarters (p94).

↑ St James's Square, with the statue of William III at its centre

A LONG WALK
MAYFAIR TO BELGRAVIA

Distance 5 km (3 miles) **Time** 70 minutes
Nearest Tube Green Park

This picturesque walk takes you from Green Park to Hyde Park, through the hearts of Mayfair and Belgravia, two of London's most elegant Georgian residential districts. It includes a bracing stroll through Hyde Park and, if you're feeling more energetic, you can rent a rowing boat on the Serpentine. You'll spot a number of cosy pubs and pretty cafés along the way where you can pop in for a break.

Park Lane, *once the city's most desirable residential street, is home to some of London's priciest hotels.*

Enter Hyde Park and look out for **Speaker's Corner** *(p257), where on Sundays anyone can make a speech on any topic.*

Cross the park, enjoying the view on all sides, and make for the **Boat House** *where you can rent a rowing boat from April to October.*

Turn left and follow the path beside the lake to the **Serpentine Bar and Kitchen** *for refreshments.*

Pass the **Pantechnicon**, *an eccentric 1830 structure fronted by colossal Doric columns. It is now a fashion and culinary hub.*

Cross Knightsbridge and stroll over to one of the city's most famous department stores, **Harrods** *(p254). Alternatively, Harvey Nichols is just by Knightsbridge station.*

As you wander into Belgravia, stop by the **Nag's Head**, *one of London's smallest pubs. A pretty mews also runs off the same street as the pub.*

MARBLE ARCH — OXFORD ST — NORTH ROW — GREEN STREET — UPPER BROOK ST — CULROSS ST — GROSVENOR GATE — PARK LANE — BAYSWATER ROAD — THE RING — Speaker's Corner — Hyde Park — Boat House — Serpentine Bar and Kitchen — SERPENTINE ROAD — ROTTEN ROW — SOUTH CARRIAGE DRIVE — KNIGHTSBRIDGE — TREVOR SQUARE — SLOANE STREET — Nags Head — Pantechnicon — MOTCOMB ST — BROMPTON RD — BASIL STREET — Harrods — BEAUCHAMP PL — BELGRAVIA — PONT STREET

Locator Map
For more detail see p88 and p244

Offfice workers
enjoying the
sunshine in
Berkeley Square

Make your way north to the
peaceful haven of **Mount
Street Gardens**, which backs
on to the Jesuit Church of the
Immaculate Conception.

DUKE STREET
BALDERTON STREET

GROSVENOR SQUARE

GROSVENOR STREET
MOUNT ROW
BOURDON ST
BRUTON ST

MAYFAIR

BERKELEY SQUARE

OLD BOND STREET

Leafy **Berkeley Square**,
*is home to some splendid
18th-century houses.*

*Keep to the south of
the square and turn
into* **Charles Street**,
*noting the evocative
lampholders at
Nos 40 and 41.*

MOUNT ST
Mount Street Gardens
HILL STREET
SOUTH STREET
CHARLES STREET
CURZON STREET
HERTFORD STREET
BRICK ST
OLD PARK LANE

PARK ST
SOUTH AUDLEY ST

BERKELEY STREET
DOVER ST
ST JAMES'S STREET

CURZON ST
HALF MOON ST
MARKET MEWS
SHEPHERD MARKET

START
Green Park
The Ritz

QUEEN'S WALK

PARK LANE

PICCADILLY

Green Park

*Hop off at Green Park
Station and pause at
the beautiful* **Ritz** *hotel
(p96), then take a left
up Berkeley Street.*

Apsley House

Hyde Park Corner
FINISH
Wellington Arch

GROSVENOR CRESCENT
GROSVENOR PLACE
CHAPEL ST
BELGRAVE SQUARE

Grab a bite to eat in
Shepherd Market,
*which was laid out by
Edward Shepherd who
also built the nearby
Crewe House in 1730.*

Finish your walk at
Hyde Park Corner
*station. Here you can
choose to spend more
time in either of the
nearby Royal Parks.*

0 metres	400	N ↑
0 yards	400	

↑ Alfresco dining at the stylish cafés
found in Shepherd Market

The celebrated Kingly Court food market in Soho

SOHO AND TRAFALGAR SQUARE

Formerly used as royal hunting grounds, Soho was first developed in the late 17th century by wealthy landowners. Its aristocratic residents, in contrast to those in neighbouring Mayfair, soon moved on and their influence on the character of the area went with them. Instead, the district became synonymous with bohemians and immigrants. French Huguenots, Jews, Greeks, Italians, Maltese, Chinese and others all came to Soho in significant numbers between the end of the 17th and the mid-20th centuries. Artists, writers and musicians flocked here too, as did gangsters and prostitutes, and the area retained an edgy, alternative air until the late 1980s. In contrast, Trafalgar Square, with its grandiose buildings and proximity to Whitehall, has always had closer ties to the establishment, though it has also long been a place of protest. For centuries the site of the royal stables (or mews), the square itself is a 19th-century construct, given its name in 1830.

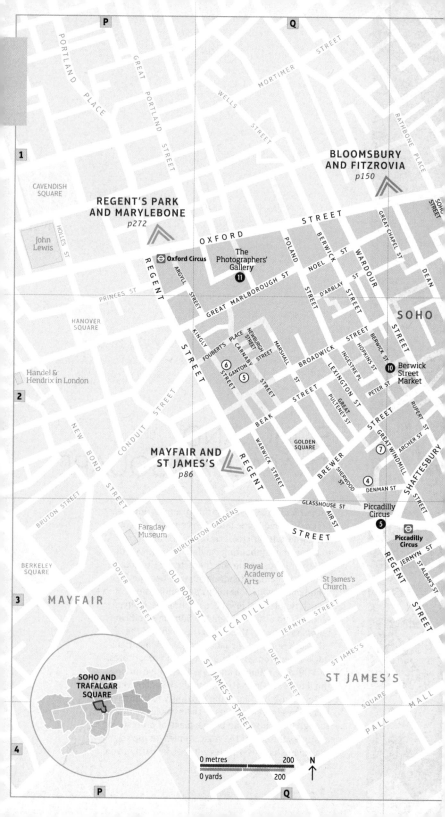

SOHO AND TRAFALGAR SQUARE

Must Sees
1. National Gallery
2. Chinatown

Experience More
3. Trafalgar Square
4. St Martin-in-the-Fields
5. Piccadilly Circus
6. Leicester Square
7. National Portrait Gallery
8. Charing Cross Road
9. Shaftesbury Avenue
10. Berwick Street Market
11. The Photographers' Gallery

Eat
1. Café in the Crypt
2. Barrafina
3. Ceviche Soho
4. Kricket
5. Pastaio

Drink
6. Ain't Nothin' But
7. The Lyric

COVENT
GARDEN AND
THE STRAND
p122

WHITEHALL AND
WESTMINSTER
p68

① 🅼 🍴 🖥 🛍

NATIONAL GALLERY

📍S3 🏛Trafalgar Sq WC2 🚇Charing Cross, Leicester Sq, Piccadilly Circus 🚆Charing Cross 🕙10am–6pm daily (to 9pm Fri) 🚫24–26 Dec, 1 Jan 🌐nationalgallery.org.uk

Erected in the heart of the West End in order to be accessible by all, the National Gallery houses some of the most famous paintings in the world, by masters such as Rubens, Velázquez, Monet and Van Gogh.

The National Gallery has flourished since its inception. In 1824 the House of Commons was persuaded to buy 38 major paintings, including works by Raphael and Rubens, and these became the start of a national collection. Today the gallery has more than 2,300 paintings produced in the Western European painting tradition. The main gallery building, designed in Greek Revival style by William Wilkins, was built between 1833 and 1838. It was subsequently enlarged and the dome added in 1876. To its left lies the Sainsbury Wing, financed by the grocery family and completed in 1991.

The Collection

The National Gallery's paintings are mostly kept on permanent display. The collection spans late-medieval times to the early 20th century, including Renaissance Italy and the French Impressionists. There are works by artists such as Botticelli, Leonardo, Monet and Goya, and highlights include Van Eyck's *Arnolfini Portrait*, Velázquez's *Rokeby Venus*, Raphael's *The Madonna of the Pinks* and Van Gogh's *Sunflowers*.

→

The National Gallery, overlooking Trafalgar Square

←

Groups of visitors studying works by the masters in the airy galleries

GALLERY GUIDE

Most of the collection is housed on one floor divided into four wings. The paintings hang chronologically, with the earliest works (1200–1500) in the Sainsbury Wing. The West, North and East Wings cover 1500–1600, 1600–1700 and 1700–1930. Lesser paintings from all periods are on the lower floor.

Did You Know?

Turner's *The Fighting Temeraire* is featured, alongside the artist's self-portrait, on the UK's £20 note.

↑ Pausing for thought in front of some of the gallery's masterpieces

↑ Dating from 1437, Piero della Francesca's *The Baptism of Christ*

The Sainsbury Wing: 1200-1500

Three lustrous panels from the *Maestà*, Duccio's great altarpiece in Siena cathedral and his outstanding *Virgin and Child with Saints Dominic and Aurea* are among the earliest paintings here. The fine *Wilton Diptych* portraying England's Richard II may be by a French artist. It displays the lyrical elegance of the International Gothic style. Italian masters of this style include Pisanello and Gentile da Fabriano, whose *Madonna*

TOP 5 PAINTINGS NOT TO MISS

The Arnolfini Portrait
Jan van Eyck
Room 63

The Rokeby Venus
Diego Velázquez
Room 30

The Hay Wain
John Constable
Room 34

The Fighting Temeraire
J M W Turner
Room 34

Sunflowers
Vincent Van Gogh
Room 43

hangs beside another, by Masaccio – both from the 1420s. Also shown are works by Masaccio's pupil, Fra Filippo Lippi, Botticelli and Uccello. Raphaels include the famous *Madonna of the Pinks*, displayed near Piero della Francesca's *Nativity* and *Baptism*. There is also a fine collection of Mantegna, Bellini and other great works from the Venetian, Paduan and Ferrarese schools. Antonello da Messina's *Saint Jerome in his Study* has been mistaken for a Van Eyck; it is not hard to see why when you compare it with Van Eyck's *Arnolfini Portrait*. Other Netherlandish artists on display include Rogier van der Weyden and his followers. There is also a Hieronymus Bosch of *Christ Mocked* (sometimes known as *The Crowning with Thorns*). Room 66 is largely devoted to Leonardo da Vinci's second *Virgin of the Rocks*, which is hung alongside the preparatory charcoal *Virgin and Child*.

The West Wing: 1500-1600

Sebastiano del Piombo's *The Raising of Lazarus* was painted, with Michelangelo's help, to rival Raphael's *Transfiguration*, which hangs in the Vatican in Rome. Other highlights of the High (or Late) Renaissance include Agnolo Bronzino's mysterious, erotic *Venus and*

INSIDER TIP
Get a Guide

If you are short of time join a one-hour guided tour that takes place daily at 2pm. These informative tours take in the gallery's most iconic works.

Cupid, Raphael's original portrait of Pope Julius II and several Titians, including *Bacchus and Ariadne* – which the public found too garish when it was cleaned in the 1840s. The Netherlandish and German collections include *The Ambassadors*, a fine double portrait by Holbein; and Altdorfer's superb *Christ Taking Leave of his Mother*. There are also several Bruegels, including *The Adoration of the Kings*.

The North Wing: 1600-1700

The superb Dutch and Flemish collection includes the largest number of works by Rembrandt outside of Amsterdam, including his poignant *Self-Portrait at the Age of 63*. Van Dyck and the prolific Rubens, too, are each amply represented, and there are also works by Vermeer and Franz Hals. French works include a grand portrait of Cardinal Richelieu by Philippe

↑ The luminous, classical landscape of Turner's *Dido building Carthage*, which is one of his most important works of art

↑ Examining Canaletto's famous work, *The Stonemason's Yard*

de Champaigne. Claude's seascape *Seaport with the Embarkation of the Queen of Sheba* hangs beside Turner's rival painting *Dido building Carthage*. The glorious Spanish collection has works by Murillo, Velázquez and Zurbarán, and Italians Caravaggio and Carracci are well represented, though Guido Reni's vast *Adoration of the Shepherds* dominates all else.

The East Wing: 1700–1930

One of the gallery's most famous 18th-century works is Canaletto's *The Stonemason's Yard*, which shows a tradi-tional Venetian view, and was thought to have been commissioned by a local patron. Other Venetians here are Longhi and Tiepolo. The French collection includes Rococo masters Chardin, Watteau and Boucher. Gainsborough's early work *Mr and Mrs Andrews* and *The Morning Walk* are popular; his rival, Sir Joshua Reynolds, is represented by several of his portraits. Hogarth's satirical *Marriage à-la-mode* series is another highlight.

The great age of 19th-century landscape painting is amply represented as well, with fine works by Turner and Constable, including Constable's moody *The Hay Wain* and Turner's late-career painting *The Fighting Temeraire*. There are also works by the French artists Corot and Daubigny, which are often displayed downstairs.

Of Romantic art, there is Géricault's vivid work, *Horse Frightened by Lightning* and *A Shipwreck*, which possibly prefigures his *The Raft of the Medusa*. In contrast, the society portrait of *Madame Moitessier* by Ingres, though Romantic, is restrained and Classical. Impressionists and other French avant-garde artists are well represented. Among the highlights are *The Water-Lily Pond* by Monet, Renoir's *At the Theatre*, Van Gogh's *Sunflowers*, and Rousseau's *Surprised!* In Seurat's *Bathers at Asnières* he did not originally use his pointillist technique, but only later reworked areas of the picture using dots of colour.

→ One of the highlights of the collection, Van Gogh's *Sunflowers*

❷ 🍴 🥤 🛍

CHINATOWN

📍R2 🏛Gerrard St and around W1 🚇Leicester Sq,
Piccadilly Circus 🌐chinatown.co.uk

Though much smaller than its equivalents in New York
City and San Francisco, London's Chinatown packs a
punch. There are restaurants aplenty and a constant
buzz that attracts countless locals and visitors.

Chinatown occupies the small network of pedestrianized
streets north of Leicester Square and revolves around the
main drag, Gerrard Street. Historically, the Chinese community
in London, who total more than 120,000, came predominantly
from Hong Kong and were concentrated initially in Limehouse,
in the East End. The current base in Soho was established in the
1960s, though the Chinese population is now widely dispersed
across the city. Today, Chinatown is an intense little precinct
marked by ornamental archways and, more often than not,
strewn with paper lanterns. It is packed overwhelmingly with
authentic restaurants and Chinese supermarkets, with bakeries
and bubble tea shops, and herbal medicine, acupuncture and
massage centres filling the gaps.

CHINESE NEW YEAR

Based on lunar cycles,
Chinese New Year falls
between 21 January
and 20 February. It is
raucously celebrated in
Chinatown in a sea of
red paper lanterns, to
the noise of firecrackers
and the aromas of
Chinese street food.
Though celebrations
last for a fortnight, the
main event usually
falls on a Sunday when
a parade makes its way
through Chinatown.
Shaftesbury Avenue
is closed to traffic and
stages are erected
there and in Trafalgar
Square for dance and
martial arts shows.

↑ Gerrard Street, at the heart
of Chinatown, during
Chinese New Year

① Ornate Chinese arches stand over the area of Chinatown in Soho.

② There are many authentic places to try a variety of Chinese cuisines from all over China.

③ Traditional Chinese goods are on sale in the shops around Chinatown.

Did You Know?

There are nearly 80 restaurants packed into Chinatown.

EAT

Shu Xiangge
Specialists in traditional Sichuan hotpot, with 80 different ingredients to add to their fragrant, communal broths. The authentic interior has a hand-painted mural.

📍 10 Gerrard St W1

£ £ £

XU
Atmospheric Taiwanese restaurant which re-creates the look of a 1930s Taipei social club, with wood panelling, hand-painted murals and a tea room on the ground floor. The food is modern, a fusion of Taiwanese and Cantonese cuisine.

📍 30 Rupert St W1
🌐 xulondon.com

£ £ £

EXPERIENCE MORE

❸ Trafalgar Square

🚇 S3 📍 WC2 🚈 Charing Cross

London's main venue for rallies and outdoor public meetings was conceived by John Nash and was mostly constructed during the 1830s. The 52-m (169-ft) column commemorates Admiral Lord Nelson, Britain's most famous sea lord, who died heroically at the Battle of Trafalgar in 1805. It dates from 1842; 14 stonemasons held a dinner on its flat top before the statue of Nelson was finally installed. Edwin Landseer's four lions guard its base. The north side of the square is now taken up by the National Gallery *(p108)*, with Canada House on the west side and South Africa House on the east. Three plinths support statues of the great and the good; funds ran out before the fourth plinth, on the northwest corner, could be filled. It now hosts one of London's most idiosyncratic art displays, as artworks are commissioned specially for it, and change every year or two.

❹ St Martin-in-the-Fields

🚇 S3 📍 Trafalgar Sq WC2 🚈 Charing Cross ⏰ 8:30am–6pm Mon–Fri, 9am–6pm Sat & Sun 🌐 stmartin-in-the-fields.org

There has been a church on this site since the 13th century. Famous people buried here include Charles II's mistress Nell Gwyn, and the painters William Hogarth and Joshua Reynolds. The present church was designed by James Gibbs and completed in 1726. In architectural terms it was one of the most influential ever built; it was much copied in the US, where it became a model for the Colonial style of church architecture. An unusual feature of the interior is the royal box at gallery level to the left of the altar.

From 1914 until 1927, the crypt was used as a shelter for homeless soldiers and others; during World War II it was an air-raid shelter. It is still today well known for its work on behalf of the homeless and vulnerable. The crypt also contains a café, a gift shop and a brass rubbing centre, which is open daily. Lunchtime (free) and evening concerts (tickets required) are held in the church and weekly jazz evenings in the café. All are welcome at the daily services; check the website for times.

❺ Piccadilly Circus

🚇 Q3 📍 W1 🚈 Piccadilly Circus

For years people have been drawn to gather beneath Piccadilly Circus's centrepiece, the statue of Eros, originally intended as an angel of mercy but renamed in the public imagination after the Greek god of love. Poised delicately

Looking across Trafalgar Square to St Martin-in-the-Fields ↓

↑ The bustling pavements of Piccadilly Circus, overseen by the statue of Eros

with his bow, Eros has become almost a trademark of the capital. It was erected in 1892 as a memorial to the Earl of Shaftesbury, the Victorian philanthropist. Part of Nash's master plan for Regent Street, Piccadilly Circus has been considerably altered over the years and consists for the most part of shops selling souvenirs for visitors and high-street chains. The huge and gaudy, curved digital advertising screen marks the entrance to the city's lively entertainment district with its cinemas, theatres, nightclubs, pubs and restaurants.

Leicester Square

R2 **WC2** **Leicester Sq, Piccadilly Circus**

It is hard to imagine that this, the perpetually animated heart of the West End entertainment district, was once a fashionable place to live. Laid out in 1670 south of Leicester House, a long-gone royal residence, the square numbered among its occupants the scientist Sir Isaac Newton and the artists Joshua Reynolds and William Hogarth.

In Victorian times, several popular music halls were established here, including the Empire (today the cinema on the same site perpetuates the name) and the Alhambra, replaced in 1937 by the Art Deco Odeon. The TKTS booth, located in the square, is a must-visit for cut-price theatre tickets. There is also a statue of Charlie Chaplin, which was unveiled in 1981, while the statue of William Shakespeare dates from 1874.

The area around the Tube station here can be very congested at any time of the day or night; the streets of Soho and Chinatown to the north (p112) can be a better bet for a meal or drink.

National Portrait Gallery

S3 **2 St Martin's Place WC2** **Leicester Sq, Charing Cross** **For refurbishment until 2023** **npg.org.uk**

Set somewhat unfairly in the shadow of the more popular National Gallery (p108) next door, the National Portrait Gallery, with over 215,000 separate works spanning six centuries, holds one of the world's greatest collection of portraits. In June 2020, the gallery closed its doors for a

EAT

Café in the Crypt
Popular, licensed canteen with simple food under the arches of a church crypt.

S3 **St Martin-in-the-Fields, Trafalgar Sq WC2** **stmartin-in-the-fields.org**

££££

Barrafina
Ultracool Spanish joint with industrial modern decor.

R2 **26 Dean St W1** **barrafina.co.uk**

££££

Ceviche Soho
Stylish Peruvian restaurant; try the sea bass ceviche washed down with a Pisco Sour.

R2 **17 Frith St W1** **cevichefamily.com**

££££

Kricket
Gourmet Indian food served in tapas-style portions.

Q2 **12 Denman St W1** **kricket.co.uk**

££££

Pastaio
Trendy pasta specialist with communal seating.

Q2 **19 Ganton St W1** **pastaio.co.uk**

££££

major refurbishment; it is scheduled to re-open in 2023. During the closure, artworks from the collection will be displayed in the National Gallery, as well as at various locations across the UK.

Trafalgar Square, overlooked by Nelson's Column and surrounded by grand buildings

Shaftesbury Avenue, the heart of London's theatre district ↑

8 Charing Cross Road

📍 S2 🚇 WC2 🔵 Leicester Sq

Once London's favourite street with book lovers, with a clutch of shops able to supply just about any recent volume, Charing Cross Road has seen many of its independent bookshops forced to shut due to rising rents. However, you will find the flagship store of the venerable Foyles bookshop located here; founded in 1903, it is the largest in the UK. At the junction with New Oxford Street rises the 1960s Centre Point tower. This junction is one of the key sites for the huge Crossrail underground rail project, so expect traffic disruption.

DRINK

Ain't Nothin' But

Popularly referred to simply as the Blues Bar, this London stalwart always has an enthusiastic crowd in its dimly lit room, rarely failing to get the party cookin'.

📍 Q2 🏠 20 Kingly St W1
🌐 aintnothinbut.co.uk

The Lyric

This snug, ever-lively Victorian boozer pulls in hop lovers with the widest range of beers in Soho, including some unusual brews.

📍 R2 🏠 37 Great Windmill St W1
🌐 lyricsoho.co.uk

---

9 Shaftesbury Avenue

📍 R2 🚇 W1 🔵 Piccadilly Circus, Leicester Sq

The main artery of London's theatreland, Shaftesbury Avenue has six theatres and three cinemas, all but one on its north side. It is also packed with restaurants, bars and clubs, making it a go-to destination of an evening. This street, cut through an area of slums between 1877 and 1886, is named after the Earl of Shaftesbury (1801–85), whose attempts to improve housing conditions had helped some of the local poor.

→

Installation images from Deutsche Börse Photography Foundation Prize 2018 at the Photographers' Gallery

10 Berwick Street Market

📍 R2 🚇 W1 🔵 Piccadilly Circus 🕐 8am–6pm Mon–Sat 🌐 thisissoho.co.uk/the-market

There has been a market here since the late 18th century. It was a Berwick Street trader, Jack Smith,

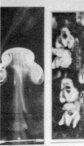

who introduced grapefruit to London in 1890. Today this remains the West End's best street market, despite the encroachment of development on its western side, where you'll find sizzling street food alongside the fresh produce and flowers. Long a destination for vinyl lovers – with Reckless Records at No 30, and Sister Ray at No 75 – it also has a growing number of cafés and restaurants. At its southern end the street narrows into an alley on which the famous strip club Raymond Revuebar (once the comparatively respectable face of Soho sleaze) presented its "festival of erotica" from 1958 to 2004.

THE HEART OF SOHO

Beating a path through Soho is Old Compton Street, a busy thoroughfare of restaurants, bars, clubs and shops. Home for centuries to poets, writers and musicians, it's now an LGBT+ hub, the Admiral Duncan pub leading a pack of popular bars and clubs. Turn off on Frith Street to see iconic jazz club Ronnie Scott's and Bar Italia; above the latter, John Logie Baird first demonstrated TV in 1926.

The Photographers' Gallery

Q1 16-18 Ramillies St W1 Oxford Circus 10am-6pm Mon-Sat, 11am-6pm Sun thephotographersgallery.org.uk

This forerunning gallery exhibits work from both new and well-known photographers, as well as staging regular talks, workshops (especially for young photographers) and film screenings. Entry is free after 5pm, and when exhibitions are staged, the gallery stays open late (until 8pm) on Thursdays. There's a café, and the bookshop also sells cameras and prints.

A SHORT WALK

SOHO AND TRAFALGAR SQUARE

Distance 1.5 km (1 mile) **Time** 20 minutes
Nearest Tube Leicester Square

Soho is London's most animated quarter, with crowds enjoying the numerous restaurants, cinemas, theatres and bars. Walk along broad avenues lined with regal office buildings and wander through Trafalgar Square, a hub of the West End and popular meeting place for visitors to the city.

Charing Cross Road (p118) *is famous for specialist and second-hand bookshops.*

START

CHARING

GERRARD PLACE

GERRARD STREET

LISLE STREET

CRANBOURN

LEICESTER SQUARE

WARDOUR STREET

Shaftesbury Avenue (p118), *lined with theatres boasting popular permanent and new shows, is the heart of London's Theatreland.*

SHAFTESBURY AVENUE

RUPERT STREET

Chinese lanterns adorn **Chinatown** (p112), *a small district packed with colourful restaurants and shops.*

COVENTRY STREET

OXENDON ST

PANTON STREET

ORANGE STREET

WHITCO

Notre Dame, *once a theatre, was converted into a church in 1855. The Jean Cocteau murals inside date from 1960.*

HAYMARKET

A 19th-century statue of William Shakespeare overlooks **Leicester Square** (p115), *the city's cinema district.*

Theatre Royal Haymarket *is graced by a John Nash portico.*

People gathering near the central fountain at Leicester Square

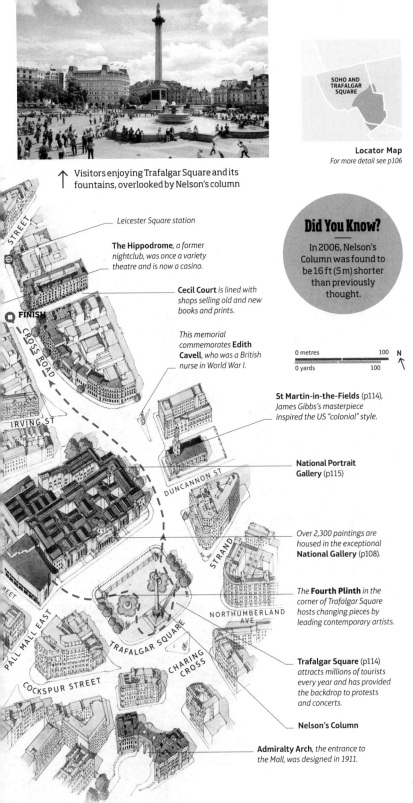

Visitors enjoying Trafalgar Square and its fountains, overlooked by Nelson's column

Locator Map
For more detail see p106

Leicester Square station

The Hippodrome, *a former nightclub, was once a variety theatre and is now a casino.*

Cecil Court *is lined with shops selling old and new books and prints.*

FINISH

This memorial commemorates **Edith Cavell**, *who was a British nurse in World War I.*

Did You Know?

In 2006, Nelson's Column was found to be 16 ft (5 m) shorter than previously thought.

St Martin-in-the-Fields (p114), *James Gibbs's masterpiece inspired the US "colonial" style.*

0 metres 100
0 yards 100
N

National Portrait Gallery (p115)

Over 2,300 paintings are housed in the exceptional **National Gallery** (p108).

The **Fourth Plinth** *in the corner of Trafalgar Square hosts changing pieces by leading contemporary artists.*

Trafalgar Square (p114) *attracts millions of tourists every year and has provided the backdrop to protests and concerts.*

Nelson's Column

Admiralty Arch, *the entrance to the Mall, was designed in 1911.*

STREET

CROSS ROAD

IRVING ST

DUNCANNON ST

STRAND

NORTHUMBERLAND AVE

PALL MALL EAST

TRAFALGAR SQUARE

CHARING CROSS

COCKSPUR STREET

SOHO AND TRAFALGAR SQUARE

COVENT GARDEN AND THE STRAND

The site of a convent garden in medieval times, Covent Garden was laid out as an Italianate piazza in the 1630s by Inigo Jones, whose St Paul's Church still dominates the west side. It was initially among the city's most fashionable addresses, then coffee houses, brothels and an increasing number of market stalls transformed the area's reputation and the wealthier residents trickled away. To accommodate the expansion of the market a permanent market building was commissioned and constructed in the 1830s, the elegant Neo-Classical structure dominating the centre of the piazza today. It housed a produce market until 1974 when the market moved to a larger site in Nine Elms, between Vauxhall and Battersea, better able to cope with its inflated size. Traders still occupy the building in Covent Garden but cater mostly to tourists now, operating from shops, craft stalls and restaurants.

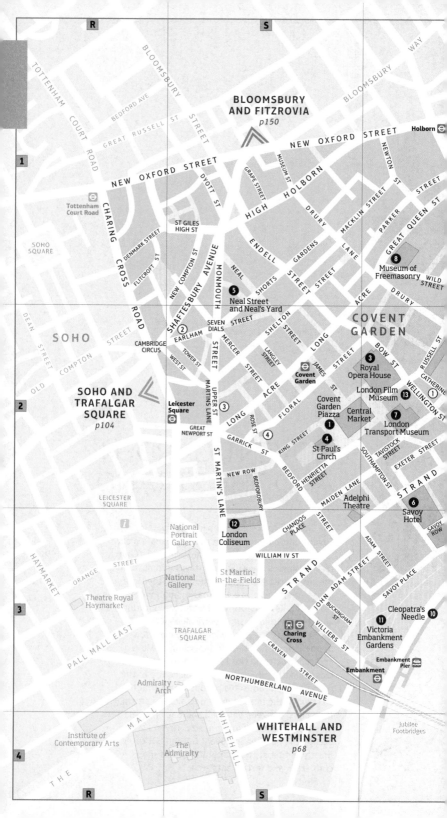

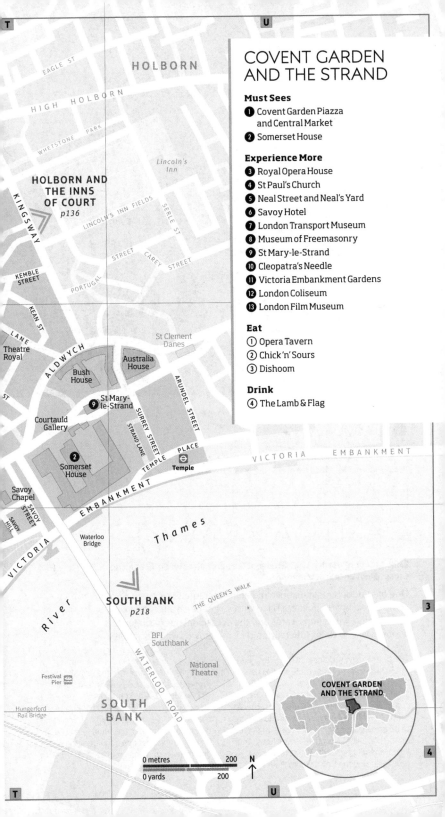

COVENT GARDEN AND THE STRAND

Must Sees
1. Covent Garden Piazza and Central Market
2. Somerset House

Experience More
3. Royal Opera House
4. St Paul's Church
5. Neal Street and Neal's Yard
6. Savoy Hotel
7. London Transport Museum
8. Museum of Freemasonry
9. St Mary-le-Strand
10. Cleopatra's Needle
11. Victoria Embankment Gardens
12. London Coliseum
13. London Film Museum

Eat
1. Opera Tavern
2. Chick 'n' Sours
3. Dishoom

Drink
4. The Lamb & Flag

HOLBORN

EAGLE ST

HIGH HOLBORN

WHETSTONE PARK

Lincoln's Inn

HOLBORN AND THE INNS OF COURT
p136

KINGSWAY

LINCOLN'S INN FIELDS

SERLE ST

STREET

CAREY STREET

PORTUGAL STREET

KEMBLE STREET

KEAN ST

LANE

Theatre Royal

ALDWYCH

St Clement Danes

Australia House

Bush House

9 St Mary-le-Strand

Courtauld Gallery

SURREY STREET

STRAND LANE

ARUNDEL STREET

TEMPLE PLACE

Temple

2 Somerset House

Savoy Chapel

EMBANKMENT

VICTORIA EMBANKMENT

SAVOY STREET

SAVOY HILL

VICTORIA

Waterloo Bridge

Thames

River

SOUTH BANK
p218

THE QUEEN'S WALK

BFI Southbank

National Theatre

WATERLOO ROAD

Festival Pier

Hungerford Rail Bridge

SOUTH BANK

COVENT GARDEN AND THE STRAND

0 metres 200
0 yards 200

N

Strolling and snacking under the iron and glass roof of the Apple Market ↑

1 🍴 🖥 🛍

COVENT GARDEN PIAZZA AND CENTRAL MARKET

📍 S2 🏠 Covent Garden WC2 🚇 Covent Garden, Leicester Sq 🚆 Charing Cross 🌐 coventgarden.london

One of London's most distinct and animated squares, Covent Garden comprises a bustling piazza filled with street performers and a market alive with shops, cafés and the occasional opera singer. It is a must-visit – a claim substantiated by the crowds who flock here.

The central, covered Apple Market, designed in 1833 for fruit and vegetable wholesalers, today houses an array of stalls and small shops selling designer clothes, books, arts and crafts, decorative items and antiques. The 17th-century architect Inigo Jones planned this area to be an elegant residential square, modelled on the piazza of Livorno in central Italy, but the Victorian buildings on and around the piazza now, including the Royal Opera House, are almost entirely commercial. The market stalls continue south into the neighbouring Jubilee Hall, which was built in 1903. The colonnaded Bedford Chambers on the north side give a hint of Inigo Jones's plan, although these buildings are not original either, having been rebuilt and partially modified in 1879. Despite the renovations, the tradition of street entertainers in the piazza has endured since at least the 17th century.

EAT

The Ivy Market Grill
The first of the once-exclusive Ivy restaurant's offshoots. Smart Art Deco interior and a menu heavy on seafood and steaks.

🏠 1a Henrietta St WC2
🌐 theivymarket
grill.com

€€€€

Tuttons
Sit out on the piazza or in the refined dining area in this Covent Garden stalwart. Serves classic English food.

🏠 11/12 Russell St WC2
🌐 tuttons.com

€€€€

1 The Punch & Judy is a popular market pub with tables inside the Apple Market and outside on the terrace overlooking the piazza.

2 Street entertainers are a much-loved tradition in the piazza. These days musicians, circus performers and magicians must pass an audition in order to perform here.

3 Jubilee Market offers mainly souvenirs, jewellery and cheaper items, though on Mondays here and in the Apple Market antiques and vintage collectables are on sale.

Courtyard of Somerset House with fountains and café tables ↑

2 🖼 🍴 💻 🛍

SOMERSET HOUSE

📍 T2 🏛 Strand WC2 🚇 Temple, Charing Cross
🚆 Charing Cross ⛴ Embankment Pier ⏰ 8am-11pm daily
📷 Courtauld Gallery: until 2021 🌐 Somerset House:
somersethouse.org.uk; Courtauld Gallery: courtauld.ac.uk

This grand Georgian building, with four Neo-Classical wings around a huge stone courtyard, is an innovative arts and cultural centre offering a range of events and exhibitions in a marvellous riverside location.

Somerset House is best known as the home of the Courtauld Gallery, the city's premiere collection of Impressionist paintings. It is also a unique and popular venue for outdoor summer cinema and eclectic festivals, art fairs and installations.

It was built in the 1770s and its first resident was the Royal Academy of Arts. Later tenants included the Navy Board at the end of the 1780s. The building retains some striking architectural features, including the classical grandeur of the Seamen's Waiting Hall and the spectacular five-storey rotunda staircase called Nelson's Stair, both in the South Wing. Strolling through the wing from the courtyard leads to a riverside terrace featuring a restaurant and an open-air bar, which is perfect for a sundowner. Below are the modern Embankment Galleries with a range of contemporary arts exhibitions, including photography, design and fashion.

EAT

Bryn Williams at Somerset House
Top-notch modern seasonal British cuisine with an emphasis on salads and grilled vegetables.

🏛 South Wing
🌐 bryn-somerset house.co.uk

£££

Watch House
This artisan brew bar serves superb coffee alongside sweet treats, small plates and gut-busting all-day brunches.

🏛 East Wing
🌐 watchhouse.com

£££

EXPERIENCE MORE

3 (M) (Ⅱ) (⌸) (⌂)

Royal Opera House

📍T2 🏠Bow St WC2
🚇Covent Garden 🕐From
10am daily; closing times
vary, check website 🌐roh.
org.uk

Built in 1732, the first theatre
on this site served as more of
a playhouse, although many
of Handel's operas and
oratorios were premiered
here. Like its neighbour, the
Theatre Royal Drury Lane,
the building proved prone to
fire and burned down in 1808
and again in 1856. The present
opera house was designed
in 1858 by E M Barry. John
Flaxman's portico frieze,
depicting tragedy and
comedy, survived from the
previous building of 1809.

Today, it is home to the
Royal Opera and Royal Ballet
companies – the best tickets
can cost over £200 (though
restricted-view tickets up in the
"slips" can be had for as little
as £10). The opera house has
become less exclusive, opening up its spaces to daytime
visitors. The foyer café-bar is
a peaceful escape from the
Covent Garden bustle, while
the fifth-floor terrace provides
views across the piazza. Backstage tours are available.

4

St Paul's Church

📍S2 🏠Bedford St WC2
🚇Covent Garden 🕐8:30am-
5pm Mon-Fri, 9am-1pm Sun
🌐actorschurch.org

St Paul's is the "Actors' Church"
and plaques commemorate
famed men and women of the
theatre. Inigo Jones designed
the altar at the west end to
allow his grand portico to face
east into Covent Garden Piazza.
When clerics objected to this
unorthodox placement, the
altar was moved to its conven-
tional position at the east end,
but Jones went ahead with his
original exterior design. Thus
the church is entered from the
west, and the east portico
is a fake door.

The church grounds are a
particularly pleasant place
to pause – and surprisingly
quiet in contrast to the hustle
and bustle of neighbouring
Covent Garden.

Did You Know?

The courtyard is turned
over to a glittering
tree and an ice rink
at Christmas time.

Courtauld Gallery

Scheduled to reopen in 2021
following a £50 million refurbishment, the Courtauld is
most famous for its exquisite
collection of Impressionist and
Post-Impressionist paintings
but also has works by Botticelli,
Bruegel, Bellini and Rubens.
World-famous paintings by
Monet, Gauguin, Pissarro,
Modigliani and Renoir are
here, as are Manet's *A Bar at
the Folies-Bergères*, Van Gogh's
*Self-Portrait with Bandaged
Ear*, Cézanne's *The Card Players*
and studies of dancers by
Degas. Extended exhibition
spaces will broaden the range
on show, including galleries on
the late medieval period and
the Bloomsbury Group.

↑ The Floral Hall - now the Paul
Hamlyn Hall - at the Royal
Opera House

↑ The brightly painted former warehouses of Neal's Yard and the original branch of Neal's Yard Remedies

PICTURE PERFECT
Neal's Yard

A riot of rainbow-coloured walls, window frames and flower baskets, Neal's Yard – secreted in the triangle between Monmouth St, Neal St and Shorts Gardens – is the perfect subject to use for a striking shot.

5 🍴 🖥 🛍

Neal Street and Neal's Yard

📍S1 🚇WC2 🚊Covent Garden

In this attractive street, former warehouses dating from the 19th century can be identified by the hoisting mechanisms high on their exterior walls. Most buildings have been converted into shops and restaurants. Off Neal Street is Neal's Yard, a bright and cheerful courtyard of independent restaurants and shops, most displaying vividly painted façades. Seek out Homeslice for a 20" pizza

or try veggie delights at Wild Food Café; either will set you up for an afternoon of shopping. Neal's Yard Remedies offers potions and lotions, while Neal's Yard Dairy is one of London's best cheese shops.

6 🍴 🖥 🛍

Savoy Hotel

📍T2 🚇Strand WC2 🚊Charing Cross, Embankment 🌐thesavoylondon.com

Pioneer of en-suite bathrooms and electric lighting, the grand Savoy was built in 1889 on the site of the medieval Savoy Palace. The Gatsbyesque forecourt, leading up to the Art Deco façade, is the only street in Britain where traffic drives on the right. The glorious American Bar, one of the first to introduce cocktails to Europe, was voted the world's best bar in 2017.

Attached to the hotel are the Savoy Theatre, built for the D'Oyly Carte opera and famed for performing the operas of Gilbert and Sullivan, and the Simpson's in the Strand English restaurant, where traditional roasts are served ceremoniously from silver carving trolleys.

SEVEN DIALS

The pillar at this junction of seven streets features six sundials, the central spike forming the seventh. In the 19th century this was a slum area and a nexus for street thieves; with a choice of seven escape routes, pickpockets often evaded their pursuers. Today Seven Dials is a vibrant shopping and dining area that's perfect for strolling, its cobbled streets and charming hidden courtyards filled with one-off shops, boutiques, high-end cosmetics stores, bars and restaurants.

7 ⊘ 🅜 🖵 🏛

London Transport Museum

📍 T2 🏠 The Piazza WC2
Ⓔ Covent Garden 🕐 10am–
6pm daily (last adm: 5:15pm)
🌐 ltmuseum.co.uk

You don't have to be a train spotter to enjoy this intriguing collection, housed in the picturesque Victorian Flower Market, which features public transport from the past and present. The history of London's transport is in essence a social history of the capital, reflecting the city's growth.

The museum houses a fine collection of 20th-century commercial art. London's bus and train companies have long been prolific patrons of contemporary artists, and copies of some of the finest posters on display can be bought at the museum shop. They include the innovative Art Deco designs of E McKnight Kauffer, as well as work by renowned artists of the 1930s, such as Graham Sutherland and Paul Nash.

There are plenty of engagingly hands-on exhibits, including a London bus and an Underground train that children can climb aboard and pretend to drive.

The museum also offers Hidden London, a programme of events in disused stations across the city; check the website for more information. Those aged 17 and under can enter for free and all tickets allow unlimited admission for a year.

---

8 🅜 🏛

Museum of Freemasonry

📍 T1 🏠 Freemasons' Hall, 60 Great Queen St WC2
Ⓔ Covent Garden 🕐 10am–
5pm Mon–Sat (to 10pm first Thu of month) 🌐 museum freemasonry.org.uk

Looming over a corner on Great Queen Street, the Art Deco Freemasons' Hall was built in 1933 as a memorial to some 3,000 freemasons who died in active service in World War I. The headquarters of English freemasonry, the cultish traditions of this secretive organization are in evidence in the building's museum. Ceremonial objects are displayed around the centrepiece exhibit, an oversized Grand Master's throne made for George I in 1791, topped with globes and a crown and still used today. Peek into one of the lodge rooms where masons meet; it looks like a courtroom, and is hung with portraits of previous Grand Secretaries (leaders of this Masonic lodge).

EAT

Opera Tavern
Succulent slow-cooked octopus is among the flavoursome tapas here.

📍 S2 🏠 23 Catherine St
WC2 🌐 saltyard
group.co.uk

£££

Chick 'n' Sours
Deep-fried chicken, cocktails and a thumping soundtrack. This is fried chicken, but not as you know it.

📍 T2 🏠 1a Earlham St
WC2 🌐 chickn
sours.co.uk

£££

Dishoom
Bombay brasserie serving Irani delights.

📍 T2 🏠 12 Upper St
Martin's Lane WC2
🌐 dishoom.com

£££

←
Early motor buses on show in the London Transport Museum

9

St Mary-le-Strand

T2 **Strand WC2**
Temple

Now beached on a road island at the east end of the Strand, this pleasing church was consecrated in 1724. It was the first public building by James Gibbs, who also designed the church of St Martin-in-the-Fields on Trafalgar Square *(p114)*.

Gibbs was influenced by one of his early supporters, Sir Christopher Wren, but the exuberant external decorative detail here was inspired by the Baroque churches of Rome, where Gibbs studied. Its multi-arched tower is layered like a wedding cake, and culminates in a cupola and lantern. The interior is richly decorated in white and gold.

There are plans to develop this whole area, which could threaten the church, but they are unlikely to come to fruition for a long time.

10

Cleopatra's Needle

T3 **Embankment WC2**
Embankment, Charing Cross

Erected in Heliopolis in about 1500 BC, this incongruous pink granite monument is much older than London itself. Presented to Britain by the then Viceroy of Egypt, Mohammed Ali, in 1819 and erected in 1878, its inscriptions celebrate the deeds of the pharaohs of ancient Egypt.

11

Victoria Embankment Gardens

T3 **WC2** **Embankment, Charing Cross**
7:30am–dusk daily

This narrow sliver of a public park, which was created when the Embankment was built, boasts well-kept flowerbeds, a clutch of statues of British worthies and, in summer, a season of concerts.

Its main historical feature is the York water gate at its northwest corner, which was built as a triumphal entry from (now demolished) York House to the Thames for the Duke of Buckingham in 1626.

DRINK

The Lamb & Flag
This popular pub sits in an alley linking Garrick and Floral streets. Punters often spill out onto the street. It vies for the title of oldest pub in London - an inn has stood here since the 16th century.

T2 **33 Rose St WC2**
lambandflag coventgarden.co.uk

← Tulips encircling the Robert Burns statue in Victoria Embankment Gardens

← Aston Martin V12 from *Die Another Day*, London Film Museum

 12

London Coliseum

S3 **St Martin's Lane WC2** **Leicester Sq, Charing Cross** **For guided tours; check website** **londoncoliseum.org**

London's largest theatre and one of its most elaborate, this flamboyant building, topped with a large globe, was designed in 1904 by Frank Matcham and was equipped with London's first revolving stage. It was also the first theatre in Europe to have lifts. A former variety house, today it is the home of the English National Opera and stages innovative productions sung in English. It is well worth visiting for a guided tour, if only for the Edwardian interior with its gilded cherubs and heavy purple curtains. The original glass roof provides dramatic views over Trafalgar Square.

13

London Film Museum

T2 **45 Wellington St WC2** **Covent Garden** **10am–6pm daily (last adm: 5pm)** **londonfilmmuseum.com**

Though previously an actual museum of film, this now misleadingly named place is really a James Bond museum, the Bond in Motion exhibition having effectively become the permanent and only display. The Bond memorabilia on show includes outfits and posters, but the exhibition revolves around an impressive collection of the original vehicles featured in the films. There are aircraft, boats, sleds and motorcycles, but it's the cars, many of them set against a moving backdrop from their respective movie, that usually attract the most excitement. Among the highlights are the unmistakable submersible white Lotus Esprit S1 from *The Spy Who Loved Me*, the "Little Nellie" Wallis WA-116 Agile Autogyro flown in 1967's *You Only Live Twice* and the quintessential Bond car, the Aston Martin DB5, first seen in 1964's *Goldfinger*.

THEATRELAND

So choc-a-bloc with theatres is the West End that it has earned the moniker Theatreland, which you will see written on street signs, particularly around Soho and Covent Garden. Theatre first took off in London in the late 16th century, and in 1663 the West End had its first playhouse, the Theatre Royal, a previous incarnation of the theatre that stands on Drury Lane, Covent Garden, today. The present structure was completed in 1812, in a century when Theatreland really began to boom; the nearby Adelphi, on the Strand, had been built in 1806 and then, after the Theatres Act of 1843, dozens more followed to cater for the Victorian appetite for music hall. Today the West End has around 50 working theatres.

A SHORT WALK
COVENT GARDEN

Distance 1.5 km (1 mile) **Time** 25 minutes
Nearest Tube Leicester Square

Although it is no longer alive with the calls of fruit and vegetable market traders going about their business, visitors, residents and street entertainers throng Covent Garden Piazza, much as they would have done centuries ago. Pause to people-watch as you stroll through this buzzing area, popping into vibrant boutiques and historic pubs along the way.

Bright and colourful **Neal Street and Neal's Yard** *are home to lots of charming shops and cafés (p130).*

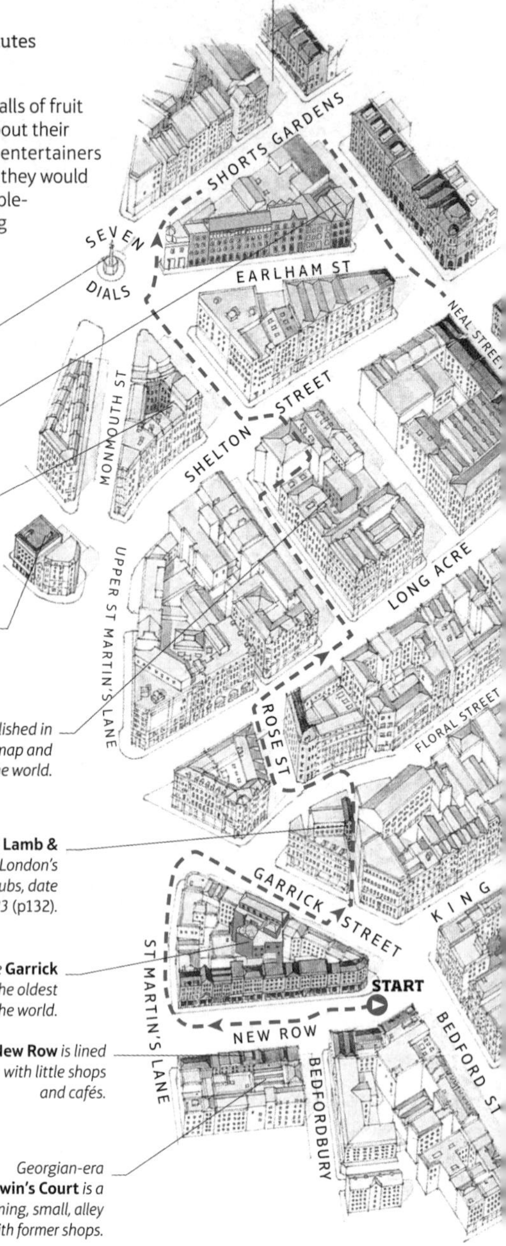

A replica of a 17th-century monument marks the junction at **Seven Dials**.

The airy **Thomas Neal's** *complex houses designer shops and the Donmar Warehouse theatre.*

Ching Court *is a Post-Modernist courtyard by architect Terry Farrell.*

St Martin's Theatre *is home to the world's longest-running play: The Mousetrap.*

Stanfords, *established in 1852, is the largest map and guide retailer in the world.*

Parts of the **Lamb & Flag**, *one of London's oldest pubs, date from 1623 (p132).*

The exclusive **Garrick Club** *is one of the oldest in the world.*

New Row *is lined with little shops and cafés.*

Georgian-era **Goodwin's Court** *is a charming, small, alley lined with former shops.*

Did You Know?

Eliza Doolittle, of George Bernard Shaw's *Pygmalion* (1913), was a flower seller in Covent Garden.

SHORTS GARDENS
SEVEN DIALS
EARLHAM ST
NEAL STREET
MONMOUTH ST
SHELTON STREET
UPPER ST MARTIN'S LANE
LONG ACRE
FLORAL STREET
ROSE ST
GARRICK STREET
KING
ST MARTIN'S LANE
START
NEW ROW
BEDFORD ST
BEDFORDBURY

↑ Street cafés line the cobbled streets of atmospheric Covent Garden

Covent Garden station

Many of the world's greatest classical singers and dancers have appeared on the **Royal Opera House's** stage (p129).

Bow Street Police Station housed London's first police force, the Bow Street Runners, in the 18th century. It is now the NoMad hotel.

A theatre has stood on the site of the **Theatre Royal Drury Lane** since 1663, making it London's oldest theatre. It is owned by composer Andrew Lloyd Webber and stages popular musicals.

8 Russell Street is where Dr Johnson first met his biographer, James Boswell.

The history of the city's historic public transport system is brought to life in the **London Transport Museum** (p131).

Performers of all kinds – jugglers, clowns, acrobats and musicians – entertain the crowds in **Covent Garden Piazza** and under cover in the **Central Market** (p126).

Jubilee Market sells clothes and bric-a-brac.

Despite appearances, **St Paul's Church** faces away from the Piazza. Its grand portico serves as a stage for a colourful cast of street performers (p125).

Rules restaurant is frequented by the rich and famous for its typically English food.

JAMES ST.
FLORAL STREET
BOW STREET
COVENT GARDEN
RUSSELL STREET
WELLINGTON ST.
STREET
FINISH
SOUTHAMPTON ST.
HENRIETTA ST.
MAIDEN LANE

0 metres 100
0 yards 100

N ↑

A stained-glass window in St Etheldreda's Church

HOLBORN AND THE INNS OF COURT

Holborn has been the home of the legal profession in London since the 13th century. The sprawling Royal Courts of Justice, the country's central civil courts, were built here, where the Strand meets Fleet Street, between 1873 and 1882. Much older are the Inns of Court, dating from the medieval period, which supply the courts here and elsewhere with their barristers and judges. Though the exact foundation dates for all four Inns of Court are uncertain, the reason for their location can be traced to a decree of Henry III, from 1234.
It stated that no body providing legal education could be located in the City of London, forcing the legal profession to move just outside the boundary of the City to Holborn. Though student barristers can now study elsewhere, to graduate they must still belong to one of the Inns.

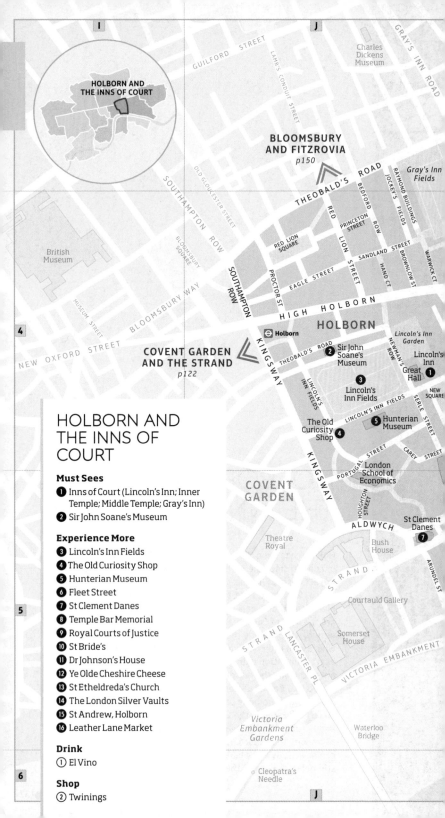

HOLBORN AND THE INNS OF COURT

Must Sees

1. Inns of Court (Lincoln's Inn; Inner Temple; Middle Temple; Gray's Inn)
2. Sir John Soane's Museum

Experience More

3. Lincoln's Inn Fields
4. The Old Curiosity Shop
5. Hunterian Museum
6. Fleet Street
7. St Clement Danes
8. Temple Bar Memorial
9. Royal Courts of Justice
10. St Bride's
11. Dr Johnson's House
12. Ye Olde Cheshire Cheese
13. St Etheldreda's Church
14. The London Silver Vaults
15. St Andrew, Holborn
16. Leather Lane Market

Drink

1. El Vino

Shop

2. Twinings

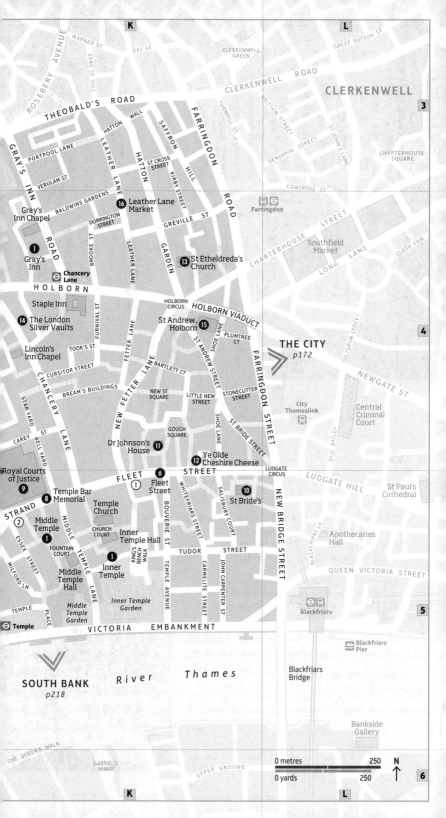

Well-tended, pretty gardens in front of Middle Temple ↑

Did You Know?

The Inns have starred as locations in such films as *The Da Vinci Code* and *Pirates of the Caribbean*.

❶ Ⓜ

INNS OF COURT

Resembling the colleges of Oxford or Cambridge University, the four Inns of Court – Lincoln's Inn, Gray's Inn, Inner Temple and Middle Temple – are oases of calm in the middle of London and perfect sites for a relaxing and intriguing wander through history.

The Inns of Court are the centuries-old homes of the Bar in England and Wales, and every barrister must belong to one of the four Inns. Established in the late medieval period, barristers have long used the Inns for training and study and as accommodation. The leafy precincts, each with their own chapel, historic hall and landscaped gardens, make great places for a lunchtime picnic, and their jumble of passageways, hidden corners and courtyards are well worth exploring. Temple, the joint campus of Inner and Middle Temples, was first home to the Knights Templar, who were based here in the 13th century, and a rebuilt version of their church is a highlight of all four Inns.

It is among the most historic churches in London and one of only four medieval "round churches" in England.

→

A perfect place to relax, on the grass of Lincoln's Inn Fields

Lincoln's Inn

📍 J4 🏛 Lincoln's Inn Fields WC2 🚇 Holborn, Chancery Lane 🕐 7am–7pm Mon-Fri 🌐 lincolnsinn.org.uk

Some of the buildings in Lincoln's Inn, the most well preserved of London's Inns of Court, date back to the late 15th century. The coat of arms above the arch of the Chancery Lane gatehouse is Henry VIII's, and the heavy oak door is from the same time. Shakespeare's contemporary, Ben Jonson, is believed to have laid some of the bricks of Lincoln's Inn during the reign of Elizabeth I. The chapel is early 17th-century Gothic. Lincoln's Inn has its share of famous alumni: Oliver Cromwell, John Donne, the 17th-century poet, and William Penn, founder of the US state of Pennsylvania, were all students here.

INSIDER TIP
Summer Spot

The best time to visit the Inns of Court is in the summer for a picnic. The gardens are open on weekdays at lunchtime (opening times vary for each individual garden).

Inner Temple and Middle Temple

📍 K5 🏛 Temple EC4 🚇 Temple 🌐 innertemple. org.uk; middletemple. org.uk

Temple's series of courtyards and buildings comprise two of the four Inns of Court: Middle Temple and Inner Temple. The name derives from the Knights Templar, a chivalrous order based here in medieval times, whose initiations probably took place in the crypt of **Temple Church**. Built in the 12th century, and maintained by the Inns since 1608, the circular Temple Church boasts an impressive Elizabethan organ and 13th-century effigies of the Knights Templar in its nave.

Among Temple's other ancient buildings is the Elizabethan Middle Temple Hall, open to non-members for lunch during term-time (check website). Behind Temple, peaceful lawns stretch down towards the Embankment.

Temple Church

⬦ 🕐 Times vary, check website 🌐 templechurch.com

Gray's Inn

📍 K4 🏛 High Holborn WC1 🚇 Holborn, Chancery Lane 🕐 6am–8pm Mon-Fri, by prior arrangement 🌐 graysinn.org.uk

This ancient legal centre and law school dates to the 14th century, though it was largely rebuilt after damage inflicted during World War II. The Shakespeare play *A Comedy of Errors* was first performed in Gray's Inn Hall in 1594 and the hall's 16th-century interior screen still survives. The young Charles Dickens was employed as a clerk here between 1827 and 1828. The lovely gardens known as "the Walks", once a convenient site for staging duels, are open to lunchtime strollers during the week (except public holidays).

THE KNIGHTS TEMPLAR

The Knights Templar, who founded Temple and built Temple Church, was a religious order established to protect pilgrims on their way to and from Jerusalem in the 12th century. The Holy City had been seized in the late 11th century by Christian crusaders but pilgrimage routes were fraught with danger. The order was dissolved in 1312.

② Ⓜ 🛍

SIR JOHN SOANE'S MUSEUM

📍J4 🏠13 Lincoln's Inn Fields WC2 ⊖Holborn ⏰10am–5pm Wed–Sun; advance booking online required ⏱25 & 26 Dec & a week in Jan for conservation ⓦsoane.org

One of the most delightful and unusual museums in London, this extraordinary house, filled to bursting with an eclectic gathering of beautiful and peculiar objects, was left to the nation by the architect Sir John Soane in 1837.

Though laden with Classical statuary and other eye-catching and unusual artifacts, it is the interior design of the building itself that makes this place unlike any other museum. The house abounds with architectural surprises and illusions. Cunningly placed mirrors play tricks with light and space, and in the centre of the basement an atrium stretches up to the roof, the glass dome of which illuminates the galleries on every floor. In the picture gallery on the ground floor, walls turn out to be folding panels which knowledgeable curators open to reveal further paintings and, most unexpectedly, a floorless extension to the room itself, hung with yet more pictures.

↑ The museum, made up of three houses that Soane bought one by one

↑ Rooms filled with an eclectic array of ancient statuary

WHO WAS SIR JOHN SOANE?

Born in 1753, the son of a bricklayer, John Soane eventually became one of Britain's leading architects of the 19th century. Most of his buildings were Neo-Classical in style and he was responsible for designing Dulwich Picture Gallery *(p325)*, Pitzhanger Manor *(p330)* and the Bank of England *(p186)*.

EXPERIENCE MORE

3 Lincoln's Inn Fields

J4 WC2 Holborn 7:30am-dusk daily

A former public execution site, many religious martyrs and those suspected of treachery to the Crown perished here under the Tudors and Stuarts. When the developer William Newton wanted to build on this site in the 1640s, students at Lincoln's Inn and other residents made him undertake that it would remain a public area forever. Thanks to this early protest, tennis is played on the public courts here year-round, while lawyers read their briefs in the fresh air.

4 The Old Curiosity Shop

J4 13-14 Portsmouth St WC2 Holborn the-old-curiosity-shop.com

Whether it inspired Charles Dickens's 19th-century novel of the same name or not, the Old Curiosity Shop is a genuine 16th-century building. With its wooden beams and overhanging first floor, it gives a rare impression of a London streetscape from before the Great Fire of 1666. The shop is still trading, currently as a handmade-shoe shop.

5 Hunterian Museum

J4 35-43 Lincoln's Inn Fields WC2 Holborn, Chancery Lane For refurbishment until 2022 rcseng.ac.uk

Inside the Royal College of Surgeons, the Hunterian Museum started life as the personal collection of John Hunter (1728–93), one of the leading teachers of surgery in his day, who amassed a large collection of human and animal anatomical specimens to aid his teaching. Most famously the skeleton of Charles Byrne, the "Irish Giant" at 2.31 m (7 ft 7 in) tall, is here. It is not a museum for the squeamish, but the surgical instruments and interactive displays on modern surgery are fascinating for those with an interest in the subject.

↑ The Old Curiosity Shop provides a glimpse of London as it looked before 1666

↑ Fleet Street, one of the oldest streets in the City of London, which once rang with the sounds of printing presses

6 Fleet Street

K5 EC4 Temple, Blackfriars, St Paul's

England's first printing press was set up by William Caxton in the late 15th century. In around 1500, his assistant began his own business in Fleet Street, and the area grew to become the centre of London's publishing industry. Playwrights Shakespeare and Ben Jonson were patrons of the old Mitre Tavern, now No 37 Fleet Street. In 1702, England's first daily newspaper, *The Daily Courant*, was issued from Fleet Street – conveniently placed for the City and Westminster, which were the main sources of news. Later the street became synonymous with the Press. The grand Art Deco building with Egyptian-style detail at No 135 is the former headquarters of the *Daily Telegraph*. Next to the church of St-Dunstan-in-the-West (which largely dates from the 1830s) is a building adorned with the names of former newspapers.

The printing presses underneath the newspaper offices were abandoned in 1987, when new technology rendered Fleet Street presses obsolete and production shifted to Wapping and the Docklands. Today the newspaper offices have also left Fleet Street, even though some of the journalists' traditional watering holes remain, such as Ye Olde Cheshire Cheese public house *(p146)*, and the legendary El Vino wine bar *(p145)*, found at the western end.

Did You Know?

Sweeney Todd, the "Demon Barber of Fleet Street", is said to have had his parlour at 152 Fleet St.

7 St Clement Danes

J5 Strand WC2 Temple 9am-4pm Mon-Fri, 10am-3pm Sat, 9:30am-3pm Sun 26 Dec-3 Jan, public hols stclementsdanesraf.org

Sitting proudly isolated on a traffic island, this wonderful church was designed by Christopher Wren in 1680. Its name derives from an earlier church built here by the descendants of Danish invaders, whom Alfred the Great had allowed to remain in London in the 9th century. From the 17th to the 19th centuries many people were buried here, and their memorial plaques are now in the crypt. Outside, to the east, is a statue (1910) of Dr Johnson *(p146)*, who often came to services here.

Nearly destroyed during World War II, the church was rebuilt and became the central church of the Royal Air Force (RAF). The interior is dominated by RAF symbols, memorials and monuments. Housed in elaborate glass cabinets along the aisles, remembrance books record the names of over 150,000 men and women who died while serving the RAF.

The church bells ring to various tunes, including that of the old nursery rhyme *Oranges and Lemons*, in whose lyrics the church features. Free lunchtime recitals are put on every Tuesday.

8 Temple Bar Memorial

K5 Fleet St EC4 Temple, Chancery Lane

In the middle of Fleet Street stands a monument looking somewhat like a giant sentry box, with Queen Victoria and her son, the Prince of Wales,

DRINK

El Vino

Immortalized as "Pomeroys" in John Mortimer's Rumpole of the Bailey stories, wood-panelled wine bar El Vino is famous for the lengthy lunches enjoyed here by both barristers and, in the past, journalists.

⊙ K5 ⌂ 47 Fleet St EC4 ⊞ elvino.co.uk

standing guard on either side. Dating from 1880, it marks the spot where Temple Bar, a magnificent gateway by Sir Christopher Wren, used to stand. This was the principal entrance to the City of London, where by tradition the monarch, when in State procession to the Tower of London or St Paul's Cathedral, had to pause and ask permission of the Lord Mayor to enter. The original gateway was dismantled when it began to cause traffic congestion, and spent over a century in the grounds of a country estate in Hertfordshire before being erected at the entrance of Paternoster Square near St Paul's (p176) in 2004.

Royal Courts of Justice (the Law Courts)

⊙ K5 ⌂ Strand WC2 ⊖ Holborn, Temple, Chancery Lane ⊙ 9:30am–4:30pm Mon-Fri ⊗ Public hols ⊞ theroyalcourtsof justice.com

Knots of demonstrators and television cameras can often be seen outside this sprawling and fanciful Victorian Gothic building, waiting for the verdict of a contentious case. These are the nation's main civil courts, dealing with such matters as divorce, libel, civil liability and appeals. Cases involving criminal offences are dealt with at the Old Bailey (p189), ten minutes' walk to the east. The public are admitted to all the courtrooms and a list details which case is being heard in which one. The massive building was completed in 1882 and is said to contain 1,000 rooms and 5.6 km (3.5 miles) of corridors.

St Bride's

⊙ K5 ⌂ Fleet St EC4 ⊖ Blackfriars ⊙ 8am-6pm Mon-Fri, 10am-3:30pm Sat, 10am-6:30pm Sun ⊗ Public hols ⊞ stbrides.com

St Bride's is one of Wren's best-loved churches. Its position just off Fleet Street has made it the traditional venue for memorial services to departed journalists, and wall plaques commemorate notable pressmen and women and printers. The marvellous octagonal layered spire has been the model for tiered wedding cakes since shortly after it was added in 1703, and although the church was bombed during World War II, its interior had been faithfully restored by 1957. The crypt contains remnants of earlier churches on the site, and a section of Roman pavement. Tours lasting 90 minutes are led at 2:15pm on Tuesdays.

↑ The Royal Courts of Justice, one of Britain's key courts of law

Ye Olde Cheshire Cheese, an icon of London's pub scene ↑

11 🎨 🏛

Dr Johnson's House

📍K4 🏠17 Gough Sq EC4 ⊖Blackfriars, Chancery Lane, Temple 🕐May-Sep: 11am-5:30pm Mon-Sat; Oct-Apr: 11am-5pm Mon-Sat 🔒Public hols 🌐drjohnsonshouse.org

The oft-quoted Dr Samuel Johnson was an 18th-century scholar famous for the many witty (and often contentious) remarks that his biographer, James Boswell, recorded and published. Johnson lived at 17 Gough Square from 1748 to

Hodge looking out towards the famed Dr Johnson's House ↑

1759. He compiled the first definitive English dictionary (published in 1755) in the attic, where six scribes and assistants stood all day at high desks.

The house, built before 1700, retains some period features and is furnished with 18th-century pieces. There is a small collection of exhibits relating to Dr Johnson and the times in which he lived, including a tea set belonging to his friend Mrs Thrale and pictures of Johnson and his contemporaries. There are also replica Georgian costumes for children to try on. A statue of one of Johnson's favourite cats, Hodge, stands outside.

12 🍽

Ye Olde Cheshire Cheese

📍K4 🏠145 Fleet St EC4 ⊖Blackfriars 🕐Noon-11pm Mon-Sat

There has been an inn here for centuries and parts of this building date back to 1667, when rebuilding took place after the Great Fire of 1666. The diarist Samuel Pepys

often drank here in the 17th century, but it was Dr Samuel Johnson's association with "the Cheese" that made it a place of pilgrimage for the 19th-century literati. Novelists Mark Twain and Charles Dickens were frequent visitors. In recent years it has been argued that Johnson may never have drank here; nevertheless, this is a great old pub, one of few to have kept the 18th-century arrangement of small rooms with fireplaces,

SHOP

Twinings
The oldest tea shop in London. Learn about the history of Britain's favourite drink, and try (and buy) a variety of brews from the world-famous brand.

📍K5 🏠216 Strand WC2 🌐twinings.co.uk

↑ The stained-glass west window of St Etheldreda's Church

tables and benches, rather than knocking through the walls to make larger bars.

13
St Etheldreda's Church

📍 K4 🏛 14 Ely Place EC1
🚇 Farringdon ⏰ 8am–5pm Mon–Sat, 8am–12:30pm Sun 🔒 Public hols 🌐 stetheldreda.com

Built in 1290, this rare survivor is the oldest Catholic church in England. First the town chapel of the Bishops of Ely, it passed through various hands over the centuries, including those of Sir Christopher Hatton, an Elizabethan courtier, who built Hatton House in the grounds and used the church crypt as a tavern. Rebuilt and restored several times, the church has some stunning stained glass.

14
The London Silver Vaults

📍 K4 🏛 53-64 Chancery Lane WC2 🚇 Chancery Lane ⏰ 9am–5:30pm Mon–Fri, 9am–1pm Sat 🔒 Public hols 🌐 silvervaultslondon.com

These silver vaults began life as the 19th-century Chancery Lane Safe Deposit Company. Visitors are led downstairs, then through steel security doors to reach a nest of underground shops shining with antique and modern silverware. Prices range from modest to eye-watering.

15
St Andrew, Holborn

📍 K4 🏛 5 St Andrew St EC4 🚇 Chancery Lane, Farringdon ⏰ 9am–5pm Mon–Fri 🌐 standrewholborn.org.uk

A site of worship for over 1,000 years, the medieval church that stood here survived the Great Fire, but in 1668 renowned architect Christopher Wren was asked to redesign it. The lower part of the tower is virtually all that remains of the earlier church. One of Wren's most spacious churches, it was gutted during World War II but faithfully restored and then further renovated in 2019.

Benjamin Disraeli, the Jewish-born prime minister, was baptized here in 1817, at the age of 12. In the 19th century, a charity school was attached to the church.

16
Leather Lane Market

📍 K4 🏛 Leather Lane 🚇 Farringdon, Chancery Lane ⏰ 10am–2pm Mon–Fri

Running parallel to Hatton Garden is Leather Lane Market. This traditional London market sells a bit of everything, including some tasty street food, and is a perfect place to pick up a treat or two.

↑ The impressive silverware and antiques in the London Silver Vaults

A SHORT WALK
INNS OF COURT

Distance 2 km (1.25 miles) **Time** 30 minutes
Nearest Tube Holborn

This is calm, dignified, legal London, packed with history and interest. Lincoln's Inn, adjoining one of the city's first residential squares, has buildings dating back to the late 15th century. Suited lawyers carry bundles of briefs between their offices here and the Neo-Gothic Law Courts. Nearby is Temple, another historic legal district, which has a famous 13th-century round church.

The **Sir John Soane's Museum** *was the home of the Georgian architect. It was left, with his collection, to the nation (p142).*

LINCOLN'S INN FIELDS

LINCOLN'S INN FIELDS

LINCOLN'S INN FIELDS

Lincoln's Inn *(p141)*

The mock-Tudor archway, leading to Lincoln's Inn and built in 1845, overlooks the **Lincoln's Inn Fields** *(p143).*

SERL

START

PORTSMOUTH ST

PORTUGAL STREET

CAREY

The **Old Curiosity Shop** *is a rare 16th-century, pre-Great Fire building (p143).*

↑ A circular pergoda at the centre of the peaceful green haven of Lincoln's Inn Fields

0 metres 100
0 yards 100

N ↑

FINISH

The **Gladstone statue** *was erected in 1905 to commemorate William Gladstone, the Victorian statesman who served four terms as prime minister.*

↑ The imposing façade of the Royal Courts of Justice, the nation's main civil courts

Locator Map
For more detail see p138

HOLBORN AND THE INNS OF COURT

Did You Know?

Lincoln's Inn Fields is the largest public square in London.

*The opening scene of Charles Dickens' Bleak House was set in **Lincoln Inn's Old Hall,** which dates back to 1490.*

*Look for the gold lions on the railings of the **Law Society's headquarters**.*

*For two centuries **Fleet Street** was the centre of the national press. The newspaper offices left in the 1980s (p144).*

El Vino is a wine bar where Fleet Street's journalists once mingled with barristers (p145).

No 17 Fleet Street has a superb half-timbered façade (1610) that survived the Fire. James I's eldest son, Prince Henry, had a room on the first floor of this former tavern.

STREET

BELL YARD

CHANCERY LANE

FETTER LANE

FLEET STREET

Temple was first home to the Knights Templar, who were based here in the 13th century.

*A dragon sculpture marks where the City of London meets Westminster at the **Temple Bar Memorial** (p144).*

STRAND

MIDDLE TEMPLE LANE

*Designed by Wren (1679), **St Clement Danes** is the Royal Air Force's church (p144).*

*The **Royal Courts of Justice**, the country's main court for civil cases and appeals, was built in 1882. It is made out of 35 million bricks faced with Portland stone (p145).*

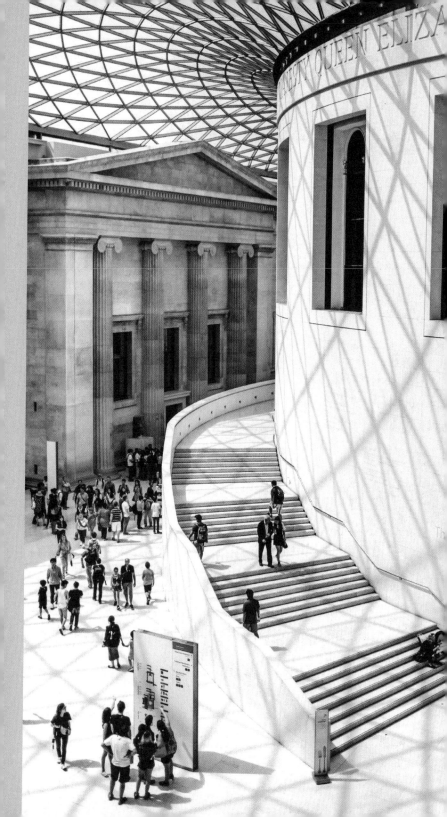

BLOOMSBURY AND FITZROVIA

The handsome garden squares of Fitzrovia and Bloomsbury date mainly from the late 18th and early 19th centuries, but it wasn't until the early 20th century that the area became inseparably connected with the cultural and intellectual elite of London. By that time Bloomsbury was already established as a place of learning, home to the British Museum, founded in 1753, and the University of London, founded in 1826. Along with Fitzrovia it was an apt location, therefore, for the homes and haunts of the avant-garde set known as the Bloomsbury Group, a network of mostly upper-middle-class, learned and artistic friends and associates. Since the Bloomsbury Group's heyday the university has expanded significantly, adding the monolithic Senate House – now home to the School of Oriental and African Studies and central library – to its collection of campuses, and cementing the area's place as the student capital of central London.

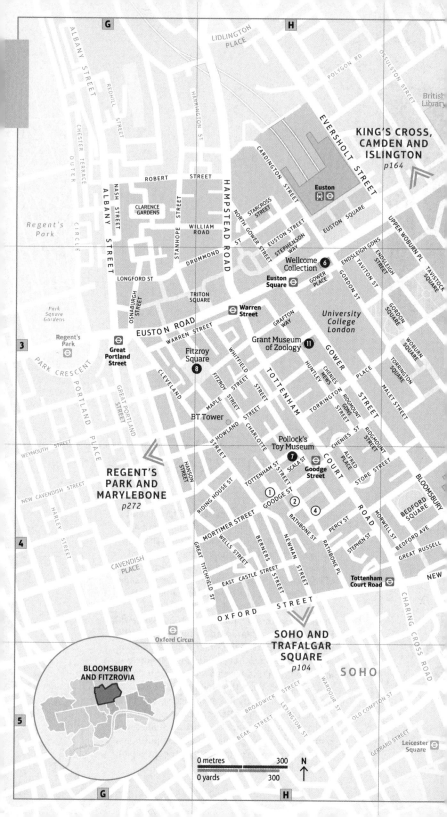

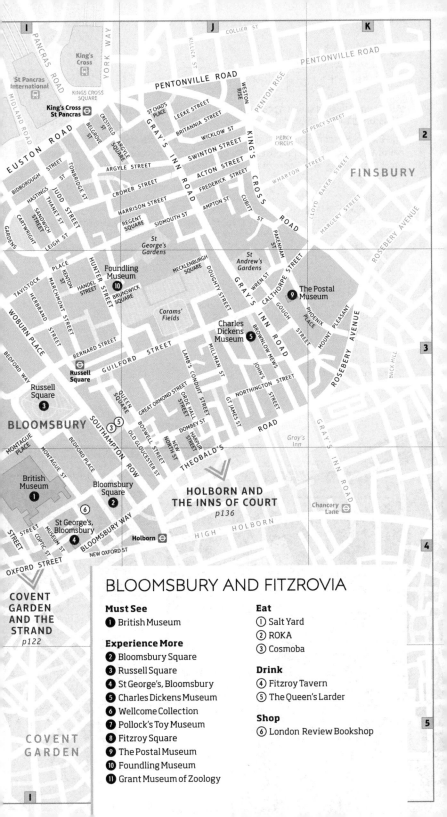

BLOOMSBURY AND FITZROVIA

Must See
1 British Museum

Experience More
2 Bloomsbury Square
3 Russell Square
4 St George's, Bloomsbury
5 Charles Dickens Museum
6 Wellcome Collection
7 Pollock's Toy Museum
8 Fitzroy Square
9 The Postal Museum
10 Foundling Museum
11 Grant Museum of Zoology

Eat
1 Salt Yard
2 ROKA
3 Cosmoba

Drink
4 Fitzroy Tavern
5 The Queen's Larder

Shop
6 London Review Bookshop

1 (M) (Y) (⊡) (⊓)

BRITISH MUSEUM

📍I4 🏠Great Russell St WC1 🚇Tottenham Court Road, Holborn, Russell Square
🚂Euston 🕐10am–5:30pm daily, till 8:30pm Fri 🚫1 Jan, 24–26 Dec 🌐britishmuseum.org

The British Museum holds one of the world's greatest collections of historical and cultural artifacts. This immense hoard of treasure comprises over eight million objects spanning the history of mankind, from prehistoric times to today.

> 💬 INSIDER TIP
> **Eye Openers**
>
> The museum offers an excellent set of free tours. There are over a dozen daily "eye-opener tours" of individual rooms; and on Friday evenings the "spotlight tours" focus on specific exhibits such as the Rosetta Stone. There's no need to book, simply check the website for where and when to meet.

The oldest public museum in the world, the British Museum was established in 1753 to house the books, antiquities, and plant and animal specimens of the physician Sir Hans Sloane (1660–1753). The collection expanded rapidly and during the 19th century the museum acquired a mass of Classical and Middle Eastern antiquities, some of which still make up the top attractions here, such as the Rosetta Stone and the Parthenon sculptures. You can now see items drawn from a dizzying number of cultures and civilizations, from Stone Age Europe and Ancient Egypt to modern Japan and contemporary North America. There are sculptures and statues, mummies and murals, coins and medals, ceramics, gold and silver, prints, drawings and innumerable other man-made objects from every corner of the globe and every period of history.

1 The Rosetta Stone was the key to interpreting Egyptian hieroglyphs.

2 The museum holds the largest collection of Egyptian mummies outside of Egypt.

3 Beautiful statues from the Parthenon in Ancient Greece.

The Greek Revival-style main entrance to the British Museum on Great Russell Street ↓

A World of Treasures

There are 95 galleries covering 4 km (2.5 miles) over three floors and eight levels of the museum, though the majority of exhibits are on the ground and upper floors. Ancient Egyptian artifacts are on the upper floor in Rooms 61 to 66 and in Room 4, beside the Great Court. The Greece, Rome and Middle East collections are also spread across the two main floors, though major items such as the Parthenon sculptures are in the large rooms of the ground floor to the west of the Great Court. The Africa collection is on the lower floor, while Asia exhibits are on the ground and upper floors on the north side. The Americas collection is located in the north-east corner of the main floor. The Sainsbury Gallery hosts major temporary exhibitions.

←

The world-famous Reading Room, designed by Sir Norman Foster, at the centre of the museum's Great Court

Did You Know?

The Reading Room roof is made up of 3,312 panes of glass, and takes two weeks to clean.

Inside the Enlightenment gallery, formerly the library of King George III ↑

GREAT COURT AND READING ROOM

The architectural highlight of the building is the Great Court, a breathtaking conversion of the original 19th-century inner courtyard. Opened in 2000, the court is now covered by a tessellated glass roof, creating Europe's largest indoor public square. At the centre of the Great Court is the glorious dome-roofed Reading Room of the former British Library where figures such as Mahatma Gandhi and Karl Marx studied.

Top Collections

Prehistoric and Roman Britain

▷ Highlights among the relics of ancient Britain on display include the gold "Mold Cape", a ceremonial Bronze Age cape found in Wales; an antlered headdress worn by hunter-gatherers 9,000 years ago; and "Lindow Man", a 1st-century AD victim of sacrifice who was preserved in a bog until 1984.

Europe

Sutton Hoo's treasure, the burial hoard of a 7th-century Anglo-Saxon king, is in Room 41. The artifacts include a helmet and shield, Celtic bowls, and gold and garnet jewellery. Exquisite timepieces include a 400-year-old clock from Germany, designed as a model galleon; in its day it pitched, played music and even fired a cannon. Nearby are the famous 12th-century Lewis chessmen. Baron Ferdinand Rothschild's (1839–98) Renaissance treasures are in Room 2a.

Middle East

Galleries devoted to the Middle East collections cover 7,000 years of history, with famous items such as 7th-century BC Assyrian reliefs from King Ashurbanipal's palace at Nineveh, two large human-headed bulls from 7th-century BC Khorsabad and the Black Obelisk of Shalmaneser III, an Assyrian king. The upper floors contain pieces from ancient Sumeria, part of the Oxus Treasure (which lay buried for over 2,000 years) and the diverse new Islamic World galleries.

Egypt

Egyptian sculptures in Room 4 include a fine red granite head of a king, thought to be Amenhotep III, and a huge statue of King Rameses II. Here too is the Rosetta Stone, used as a key for deciphering Egyptian hieroglyphs. An array of mummies, jewellery and Coptic art is upstairs.

Greece and Rome

◁ The Greek and Roman collections include the controversial Parthenon sculptures. These 5th-century BC reliefs decorated the temple to Athena on the Acropolis, Athens. Much of it was ruined, and what survived was removed by the British diplomat Lord Elgin. There is also the Nereid Monument and sculptures from the Mausoleum at Halicarnassus.

Asia

Fine porcelain, Shang bronzes (c 1500–1050 BC) and ceremonial bronze vessels are in the Chinese Collection. In the Sir Percival David Collection the Chinese ceramics date from the 3rd to early 20th centuries. There is a fine collection of sculpture from the Indian subcontinent, including sculpted reliefs that once covered the walls of the Buddhist temple at Amaravati. A Korean section contains works of Buddhist art, and there is a traditional Japanese teahouse in Room 92.

Africa

African sculptures, textiles and graphic art are in Room 25. Famous bronzes from the Kingdom of Benin, set to be loaned on a rotating basis back to Nigeria, stand alongside modern African prints, paintings, drawings and colourful fabrics.

EXPERIENCE MORE

THE BLOOMSBURY GROUP

The Bloomsbury Group was an informal set of writers, artists and intellectuals who lived in and around Bloomsbury at the beginning of the 20th century. The group, with its passionate belief in the "aesthetic experience and the pursuit of knowledge", and modern attitudes towards feminism, sexuality and politics, first gathered at No 46 Gordon Square, home of the Stephen sisters, Virginia (later Woolf) and Vanessa (later Bell). Other key members included novelist E M Forster, economist John Maynard Keynes, the biographer Lytton Strachey and artists Duncan Grant and Dora Carrington.

2

Bloomsbury Square

📍 I4 🚇 WC1 🚇 Holborn

Considered to be London's oldest square, it was laid out in 1661 by the 4th Earl of Southampton, who owned the land. None of the original buildings survive and the square's shaded garden is encircled by a busy one-way traffic system. (There is a car park below the square that, unusually for central London, nearly always has a free space or two.)

From this square, the entire Bloomsbury area was gradually developed. Noted for the brilliance of many of its inhabitants, it gave its name most famously to the avant-garde Bloomsbury Group. Look out for their individual plaques throughout the area.

3

Russell Square

📍 I3 🚇 WC1 🚇 Russell Sq

One of London's largest squares, Russell Square is a lively place, with a fountain, café and traffic roaring around its perimeter. The east side boasts perhaps the best of the Victorian grand hotels to survive in the capital. Designed by Charles Doll and opened in 1898, the former Russell Hotel – now the Kimpton Fitzroy London – remains a wondrous

→
The austere but bright interior of St George's, Bloomsbury

↑ Russell Square, an oasis in a whirl of busy traffic

confection of red terracotta, with colonnaded balconies and prancing cherubs beneath the main columns.

The poet T S Eliot worked at the west corner of the square from 1925 until 1965, in what were the offices of publisher Faber & Faber.

---

 ④ Ⓜ️

St George's, Bloomsbury

📍I4 🏛️Bloomsbury Way WC1 🚇Holborn, Tottenham Court Rd, Russell Sq 🕐Times vary, check website 🌐stgeorges bloomsbury.org.uk

St George's was designed by Nicholas Hawksmoor, a pupil of Christopher Wren, and completed in 1730. It was built as a place of worship for the residents of fashionable Bloomsbury. In 1913, the funeral of Emily Davison, the suffragette killed by King George V's racehorse at the Epsom Derby, was held here. The crypt is the unlikely home of the **Museum of Comedy**,

---

the first of its kind in the UK. Attached is a venue that hosts stand-up comedy performances in the evenings.

Museum of Comedy
🌐 🕐Times vary, check website 🌐museumof comedy.com

---

 ⑤

Charles Dickens Museum

📍J3 🏛️48 Doughty St WC1 🚇Chancery Lane, Russell Sq 🕐10am–5pm Tue–Sun (last adm: 4pm; Dec: also Mon); check website for monthly late opening 🕐1 Jan, 25 & 26 Dec, and occasionally for events 🌐dickens museum.com

The novelist Charles Dickens lived in this early-19th-century terraced house for three of his most productive years (from 1837 to 1839); *Oliver Twist* and *Nicholas Nickleby* were entirely written here, and the *Pickwick Papers* was finished. Although Dickens had a number of London homes throughout his lifetime, this is the only one to have survived.

In 1923, it was acquired by the Dickens Fellowship and it is now a well-conceived museum with some of the principal rooms laid out exactly as they were in Dickens's time. Others have been adapted to display a varied collection of articles associated with him.

The museum's collection spans over 100,000 exhibits, including manuscripts, paintings and personal items, papers and pieces of furniture from his other homes, and first editions of many of his best-known works. As well as its permanent collection, the museum puts on special exhibitions and events, and

→ A bust of the great chronicler of London, at the Charles Dickens Museum

---

runs a monthly "Housemaid's Tour". The garden café (no entry fee) provides respite from the busy city centre and has a decent selection of drinks and treats.

The cheerful home of Pollock's Toy Museum ↑

Wellcome Collection

⑥ 🏠 H3 🏛 183 Euston Rd NW1 🚇 Euston, King's Cross, Warren St ⏰ 10am-6pm Tue-Sat (to 9pm Thu), 10am-6pm Sun, times vary on public hols 🚫 1 Jan, 24-26 Dec 🌐 wellcome collection.org

Sir Henry Wellcome (1853–1936) was a pharmacist, entrepreneur and collector. His passionate interest in medicine and its history, as well as archaeology and ethnography, led him to gather more than one million objects from around the world, now housed in this building.

As well as temporary exhibitions, there are two permanent displays: Medicine Man has objects from Wellcome's diverse collection, including Napoleon's toothbrush and Florence Nightingale's moccasins, while Being Human uses art to explore human health and identity in the 21st century. Visitors can also discover the reimagined Reading Room – a hybrid area bridging library, exhibition and event space – relax in the café or enjoy afternoon tea in the restaurant.

The Wellcome Library, which occupies the upper floors, is the world's largest collection of books devoted to the history of medicine.

Pollock's Toy Museum

⑦ 🏠 H4 🏛 1 Scala St W1 (entrance on Whitfield St) 🚇 Goodge St, Warren St, Tottenham Court Rd ⏰ 10am-5pm Mon-Sat 🚫 Sun & public hols 🌐 pollockstoys.com

Named for Benjamin Pollock, a renowned maker of toy theatres in the late 19th and early 20th centuries, this is a child-sized museum created in two 18th- and 19th-century houses. The small rooms have been filled with a fascinating assortment of historic toys from all over the world. There are dolls, puppets, trains, cars, construction sets, a fine rocking horse and a splendid collection of mainly Victorian doll's houses. Parents beware – the exit leads you through a toyshop.

Fitzroy Square

⑧ 🏠 H3 🏛 W1 🚇 Warren St, Great Portland St

Designed by Robert Adam in 1794, the square's south and east sides survive in their original form, built in dignified Portland stone. Blue plaques record the homes of many artists,

writers and statesmen: writers George Bernard Shaw and Virginia Woolf both lived at No 29 – although not at the same time. Shaw gave money to the artist Roger Fry to establish the Omega workshop at No 33 in 1913. Here young artists were paid a fixed wage to produce Post-Impressionist furniture, pottery, carpets and paintings for sale to the public.

The Postal Museum

⑨ 🏠 J3 🏛 15-20 Phoenix Pl WC1 🚇 Farringdon ⏰ 10am-5pm daily 🚫 24-26 Dec 🌐 postalmuseum.org

Just over the road from the Mount Pleasant Royal Mail Sorting Office, once the largest sorting office in the world, the Postal Museum charts the 500 years of Britain's postal service in a series of interactive and child-friendly exhibits. The star attraction is Mail Rail, a 15-minute miniature train ride through tunnels that once formed part of the postal service's underground railway. The at-times pitch-black, narrow, atmospheric tunnels feature audiovisual displays along the way and deposit you in the original engineering depot. The museum itself contains exhibits spanning the full life of the oldest postal service in the world.

Foundling Museum

⑩ 🏠 I3 🏛 40 Brunswick Sq WC1 🚇 Russell Sq ⏰ 10am-5pm Tue-Sat, 11am-5pm Sun 🚫 1 Jan, 24-26 & 31 Dec 🌐 foundlingmuseum.org.uk

In 1722, Captain Thomas Coram, a retired sailor and shipbuilder recently returned from the Americas and quite horrified by the poverty on London's streets, vowed to set up a refuge for abandoned children. Assisted by two friends, the artist William Hogarth and the composer George Frideric Handel, Coram worked tirelessly to raise funds. Hogarth donated paintings to the hospital and other artists followed suit. The wealthy were encouraged to view the works of art and visit the children, in the hope that they would donate money to the cause.

On the ground floor, the story of the many children cared for here is told. The collection of 18th-century paintings, sculpture, furniture and interiors is displayed, with one room dedicated to Handel, on the upper floors.

Next to the museum, with its entrance on Guilford Street, is Coram's Fields, a unique park for children and young-sters (all adults must be accompanied by children). It includes a youth centre, a city farm and a café.

Grant Museum of Zoology

📍 H3 🏠 21 University St WC1 🚇 Warren St, Euston Square, Russell Square 🕐 1-5pm Mon-Sat 🖥 ucl. ac.uk/culture/grant-museum-zoology

The heart of Bloomsbury's university district is Gower Street: on one side is the Neo-Classical main building of University College London, designed by William Wilkins in 1826, and opposite is the original terracotta building of University College Hospital. UCL owns several museum collections, including the Grant Museum of Zoology, established in 1827. It houses around 68,000 specimens – animal skeletons, taxidermy, mounted insects and other creatures preserved in jars (including one containing 18 preserved moles) – in crowded wooden cases, making it an atmospheric, occasionally gruesome, insight into the world of 19th-century science and collecting.

Unusual exhibits at the Grant Museum of Zoology *(inset and below)*

EAT

Salt Yard
Excellent tapas combining Spanish and Italian cuisines.

📍 H4 🏠 54 Goodge St W1 🖥 saltyard group.co.uk

💷💷⒠

ROKA
Japanese *robatayaki* (barbecue) specialist, which serves a variety of sublime dishes including crab, black cod and prawn dumplings.

📍 H4 🏠 37 Charlotte St W1 🖥 rokarestaurant. com

💷💷💷

Cosmoba
Authentic, family-run Italian restaurant with an extensive menu featuring antipasti, pasta, salads, fresh fish and more.

📍 I3 🏠 9 Cosmo Pl WC1 🖥 cosmoba.co.uk

💷💷⒠

DRINK

Fitzroy Tavern
Award-winning, beautifully restored Victorian pub.

📍 H4 🏠 16 Charlotte St W1 ☎ 020 7580 3714

The Queen's Larder
Olde-worlde Bloomsbury pub with decent ales.

📍 I3 🏠 1 Queen Sq WC1 🖥 queenslarder. co.uk

A SHORT WALK
BLOOMSBURY

Distance 2 km (1.5 miles) **Time** 25 minutes
Nearest Tube Holborn

This so-called "brainy quarter" is dominated by the grand British Museum and, to its north, the main campus of University College London. A walk through the area will take you past Georgian buildings (formerly the homes of some of London's most prolific writers and greatest minds) and pretty squares, as well as a good handful of bookshops to browse.

Senate House *(1932), the administrative headquarters of the University of London, holds a priceless library.*

↑ Bedford Square, one of London's best-preserved Georgian squares

0 metres 100
0 yards 100

N ↑

Bedford Square

An embarrassment of riches, the vast **British Museum** *(p154) attracts almost six million visitors a year.*

Museum Street *is lined with small cafés and shops selling old books, prints and antiques.*

Pizza Express *occupies a charming, little-altered Victorian dairy.*

Did You Know?

Bloomsbury is older than you think – the area is mentioned in the 1086 Domesday Book as a "wood for 100 pigs".

Russell Square (p158), once part of the Duke of Bedford's estate, is now a shady retreat on a hot day.

Locator Map
For more detail see p152

BLOOMSBURY AND FITZROVIA

The **Duke of Bedford's statue** commemorates the fifth duke, Francis Russell (1765–1805). An avid farmer, he is shown with sheep and a plough.

SOUTHAMPTON ROW

BEDFORD PLACE

MONTAGUE ST

↑ Bloomsbury Square, laid out in 1661

Bloomsbury Square

USSELL STREET

BURY PLACE

BLOOMSBURY SQUARE

LITTLE RUSSELL STREET

BLOOMSBURY WAY

○ START

○ FINISH

Sicilian Avenue is a small and unexpected pedestrian precinct dating from 1905, with colonnades that evoke Roman architecture.

The tower on the typically flamboyant Hawksmoor church of **St George's** (p159) is modelled on the tomb of 4th-century Greek king Mausolus.

KING'S CROSS, CAMDEN AND ISLINGTON

King's Cross was predominantly rural until the late 18th century. It was commonly referred to as Battle Bridge, after a mythical battle said to have taken place here between Boudicca and the Romans, until the new name was adopted following the erection of a memorial to George IV in 1830 at the local crossroads. By this time King's Cross was becoming increasingly industrial, driven partly by the completion of the Regent's Canal in 1820, connecting it to the manufacturing cities of the north of England, and then by the construction of train depots, goods stations and passenger service termini. Decades of decline followed World War II but were reversed in the first years of this century when St Pancras Station became the terminus for international train routes to the rest of Europe, kick-starting a multi-billion-pound investment in the area. The urbanization of neighbouring Camden and Islington, connected to King's Cross by the canal, did not set in until the 19th century. With industrialization came social decline, which lasted through much of the last century, but since the 1980s both areas have seen remarkable regeneration.

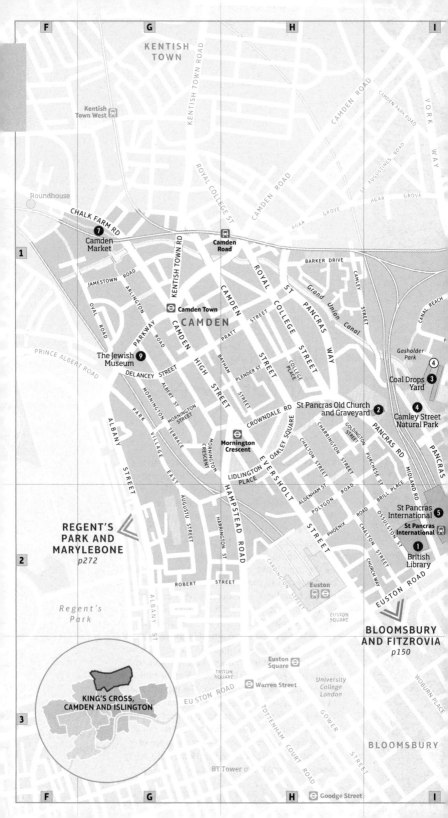

KENTISH TOWN

Kentish Town West

Roundhouse

CHALK FARM RD

7 Camden Market

Camden Road

CAMDEN ROAD

BARKER DRIVE

Camden Town

CAMDEN

Grand Union Canal

Gasholder Park

4

The Jewish Museum **9**

Coal Drops Yard **3**

4 Camley Street Natural Park

St Pancras Old Church and Graveyard **2**

Mornington Crescent

PRINCE ALBERT ROAD

REGENT'S PARK AND MARYLEBONE
p272

St Pancras International **5**

St Pancras International

1 British Library

Regent's Park

Euston

EUSTON SQUARE

BLOOMSBURY AND FITZROVIA
p150

KING'S CROSS, CAMDEN AND ISLINGTON

Euston Square

Warren Street

University College London

TRITON SQUARE

EU STON ROAD

BT Tower

BLOOMSBURY

Goodge Street

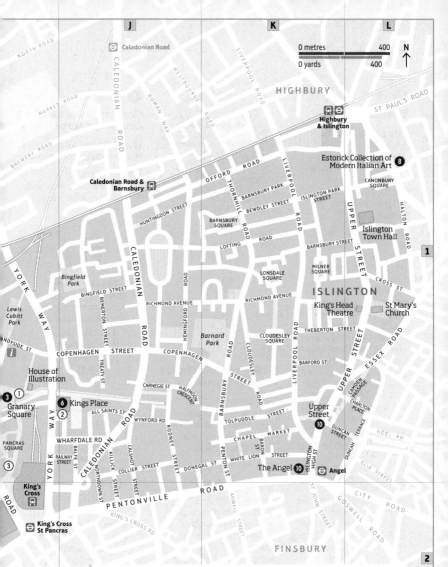

KING'S CROSS, CAMDEN AND ISLINGTON

Experience

① British Library
② St Pancras Old Church and Graveyard
③ Granary Square and Coal Drops Yard
④ Camley Street Natural Park
⑤ St Pancras International
⑥ Kings Place
⑦ Camden Market
⑧ Estorick Collection of Modern Italian Art
⑨ The Jewish Museum
⑩ The Angel, Islington and Upper Street

Eat

① The Lighterman
② Rotunda
③ German Gymnasium
④ Vermuteria

EXPERIENCE

① Ⓜ ⓨ ⓓ ⓐ
British Library

📍I2 🏠96 Euston Rd
NW1 🚇King's Cross
St Pancras 🕐9:30am–
8pm Mon–Thu, 9:30am–
6pm Fri, 9:30am–5pm
Sat, 11am–5pm Sun
🚫1 Jan, 24–26 Dec
🌐bl.uk

Designed by Sir Colin St John Wilson and opened in 1997 after nearly 20 years of construction, this controversial Grade I listed red-brick building houses the national collection of books, manuscripts and maps. There are a staggering 170 million items in total, which include a copy of nearly every printed book in the UK is held here – more than 14 million – and these can be consulted by those with a Reader Pass (you can pre-register for one online). The real highlight, though, is the Treasures of the British Library, which holds some extraordinary items, such as the Magna Carta, a Gutenberg Bible, Shakespeare's First Folio and lyrics by the Beatles. There are other free exhibitions, which change regularly (these often close earlier than the main building during the week), plus talks, discussions and workshops.

Did You Know?

The Soane mausoleum in the Old Church graveyard inspired the design of the iconic red telephone box.

The superb special exhibitions, held throughout the year, usually have an entry charge. Tours are highly recommended and include a visit to the Viewing Gallery; it's advisable to book at least two weeks in advance.

②
St Pancras Old Church and Graveyard

📍I1 🏠Pancras Rd
NW1 🚇King's Cross
St Pancras 🕐9am–dusk
daily (church closes at
4pm) 🌐posp.co.uk

This site is thought to have been a place of Christian worship since the 4th century – there are fragments of Roman tiles in one of the walls, and some Norman masonry – though much of the building dates to 1847. The graveyard was until the 1850s one of the largest burial sites in London. With the arrival of the railways, half the site was built over, and gravestones were moved – hence the remarkable sight of closely packed gravestones embedded into the base of a tree. This is the Hardy Tree, named after author Thomas Hardy, who was in charge of excavating this part of the site.

←

Café tables set below towering shelves of books at the British Library

③ ⓨ ⓓ ⓐ
Granary Square and Coal Drops Yard

📍I1 🚇King's Cross St
Pancras 🌐kingscross.co.uk

Urban regeneration has transformed this area behind King's Cross station into a

EAT

The Lighterman
Modern British food in a first-floor dining room with a spacious terrace.

📍I1 🏠3 Granary
Sq N1 🌐thelighter
man.co.uk

£££££

Rotunda
Enjoy the plant-filled terrace on the canal, perfect on a sunny day.

📍J1 🏠Kings Pl, 90
York Way N1
🌐 rotundabar
andrestaurant.co.uk

£££££

German Gymnasium
Hearty German food in a modern continental grand café.

📍I1 🏠1 King's Blvd N1
🌐german
gymnasium.com

£££££

Vermuteria
Artisanal vermouths and flavoursome cicchetti in a bijou café lined with vintage cycling memorabilia.

📍I1 🏠38/39 Coal Drops
Yard N1 🌐vermuteria.cc

£££££

Visitors admiring the sparkling fountains of Granary Square at night

cultural and social hub, with major building projects still ongoing. The focus of the area is attractive Granary Square, which leads down to Regent's Canal. It is dominated by magnificent fountains that dance to a changing pattern of lights, a magnet for small children on hot days. Granary Square sweeps down into Coal Drops Yard, a smart shopping development converted from two Victorian coal sheds linked by Thomas Heatherwick's "kissing" roof, a striking 25-m-(82-ft-) high steel structure. Good restaurants and bars are dotted across the area, and there's an excellent weekend food market. On a sunny day, grab some food and head to one of the green spaces dotted around Coal Drops Yard.

PLATFORM 9¾

Wannabe witches and wizards flock to King's Cross station to find the elusive Platform 9¾, from where Harry Potter and his fellow students catch the Hogwarts Express. Though there's little to be found between platforms 9 and 10, a luggage trolley embedded into a concourse wall (conveniently, next to the Harry Potter Shop) provides a perfect photo op for those waiting for their owl from Hogwarts.

④ Camley Street Natural Park

🚇 I1 🏠 12 Camley St N1
🚉 King's Cross St Pancras
🕐 Daily; times vary, check website 🌐 wildlondon.org.uk

Linked to Coal Drops Yard by a footbridge and reopened in 2020 with an upgraded visitor centre, this is a lovable little nature reserve run by the London Wildlife Trust. It packs in grassland, woodland and wetland habitats for birds, butterflies, bats and frogs in a small space; the best time to see wildlife is between April and August. Paths wind around the reserve and there are some lovely places to sit and picnic.

⑤ St Pancras International

🚇 I2 🏠 Euston Rd NW1
🚉 King's Cross St Pancras
🌐 stpancras.com

St Pancras, London's terminus for Eurostar rail services to continental Europe, is hard to miss, thanks to the extravagant frontage, in red-brick gingerbread Gothic, of the former Midland Grand Hotel. Opened in 1874 it was one of the most sumptuous hotels of its time, and although threatened with demolition in the 1960s, it was saved by a campaign led by the poet John Betjeman (there is a statue of him on the upper level of the station concourse). The hotel has since been magnificently restored and has a swish cocktail bar.

⑥ Kings Place

🚇 J1 🏠 90 York Way N1
🚉 King's Cross St Pancras
🕐 Galleries: 10am–6pm Mon–Sat 🌐 kingsplace.co.uk

This concert and arts venue is perched on the edge of the Battlebridge Basin and Regent's Canal, a small wharf whose moorings are usually full of attractive narrowboats. Performances of classical, jazz, folk or world music are regularly staged, and there are two commercial art galleries; one of these, the Pangolin Gallery, is dedicated to modern and contemporary sculpture. The open spaces are dotted with sculpture and art.

Camden Market

7 📍G1 🚇NW1 🚇Camden Town, Chalk Farm 🕐10am–6pm daily; some cafés and bars open later 🌐camdenmarket.com

The huge Camden Market is really a series of interconnected markets running along Chalk Farm Road and Camden High Street. Packed at the weekends, most of the shops and some of the stalls are also open on weekdays.

The first market here was a small crafts market set up at Camden Lock in 1975, and today the lock, crossing the Regent's Canal, is the focus of this sprawling agglomeration.

Independently trading on an industrial scale, the warren of hundreds of stalls, units and shops occupy a network of restored and converted Victorian warehouses.

The market has been at the forefront of alternative fashion since the days of punk, and the current jumble of handmade and vintage clothes and jewellery, arts and crafts, records and music memorabilia, and all kinds

of quirky one-offs maintain the market's place among the most original shopping destinations in the city. This is also street food heaven, with scores of stalls, cafés and wonderfully inelegant restaurants dishing out authentic nosh from all over the world.

Some of the more interesting stalls are in the Stables Market towards the Chalk Farm end, where you will also find a statue of Camden habituée, the late singer-songwriter Amy Winehouse.

Estorick Collection of Modern Italian Art

8 📍L1 🚇39a Canonbury Sq N1 🚇Highbury & Islington 🕐11am–6pm Wed-Sat (to 9pm 1st Thu of month), noon–5pm Sun 🌐estorick collection.com

Based on American and Anglo-German couple Eric and Salome Estorick's collection of modern Italian art, this is one of the more surprising of Islington's assets. It is housed in an unpretentious Georgian building with a delightful garden, partly occupied by an inviting café. At the core of the collection are important works of the Italian Futurism movement: paintings and drawings by the likes of Umberto Boccioni, Carlo Carrà, Luigi Russolo and Giuditta Scalini. Spread over six galleries on three floors, there is plenty of striking modern Italian art of other genres, including sculpture.

← Bronze statue of the late Amy Winehouse

←

Victorian industrial
heritage buildings
at Camden Lock

The Jewish Museum

📍G1 🏠129-131 Albert
St NW1 🚇Camden
Town 🕐10am-5pm
Sat-Thu, 10am-2pm
Fri 🚫Jewish hols,
25 & 26 Dec 🌐jewish
museum.org.uk

London's Jewish Museum
was founded in 1932 in
Bloomsbury, and it has
occupied several locations –
at one point it was split
between two sites, in Finchley
and Camden. In 2010, it
brought the two collections
together in a single building
and today the museum
has four permanent galleries
celebrating Jewish life in
Britain from the Middle
Ages onwards. Among
the many highlights is a
Mikveh – a medieval ritual
bath – and a re-creation of
a Jewish East End street.

There is also an important
collection of Jewish ceremonial objects that are displayed
in the Judaism gallery and,
in the Holocaust Gallery,
a moving exhibition is dedicated to Auschwitz survivor
Leon Greenman.

The Angel, Islington and Upper Street

📍K1 🏠Islington N1
🚇Angel, Highbury &
Islington

One of the destination high
streets in north London,
Upper Street runs for 1.5 km
(1 mile) between Angel and
Highbury & Islington tube
stations. Lively day and night,
the street is one long parade
of restaurants, cafés, pubs,
bars, fashion boutiques and
a contrasting mix of civic
buildings, churches, an
arthouse cin ema and a live
music and clubbing venue.

Parallel to the main drag is
Camden Passage, an alleyway
even more densely packed
with shops, cafés and covered
markets. It's a popular place

A 15
Cam
Jewi
delig
Climb
grassy promontory for
spectacular views of
the city skyline - look
out for the London Eye
and St Paul's Cathedral.

for antiques hunters looking
for the latest bargain.

The area to the south
of the high street, known as
Angel, takes its name from
a 17th-century coaching inn
on the corner of Pentonville
Road, since replaced by the
current sand-coloured
structure, crowned with
an elegant domed cupola.
Built in 1903 as the Angel
Hotel, it now houses a bank
and offices.

Shops and restaurants
(inset and below) line
popular Upper Street ↓

THE CITY

The capital's financial district, the City, was built on the site of the original Roman settlement. It was, for many centuries, London in its entirety – its full name remains the "City of London". Royal government was moved from the City of London to the City of Westminster by Edward the Confessor in the 11th century, but the area's importance as a centre of trade remained and indeed grew. In the 12th century, the City was granted autonomous self-government, a privilege it has retained, and dozens of tradesmen's guilds, known as livery companies, were set up. Much of the early City, including many of the grand halls of the liveries, was obliterated by the Great Fire of 1666, but the jumbled street plan, with names like Cheapside and Poultry, stand as testament to the City's medieval past. After the fire, Christopher Wren rebuilt dozens of the city's churches, with his magnificent dome for St Paul's Cathedral rising above them all. Now the spires and financial institutions stand alongside dour postwar office blocks and an ever-expanding array of skyscrapers.

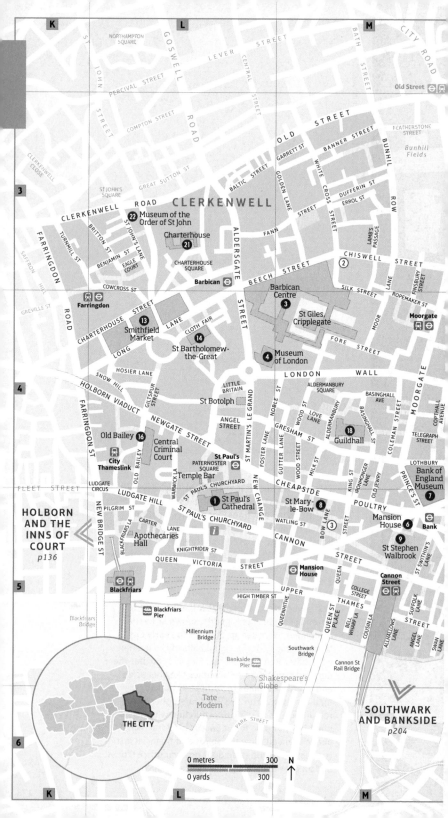

THE CITY

Must Sees
1. St Paul's Cathedral
2. Tower of London
3. Barbican Centre

Experience More
4. Museum of London
5. The Royal Exchange
6. Mansion House
7. Bank of England Museum
8. St Mary-le-Bow
9. St Stephen Walbrook
10. Monument
11. All Hallows by the Tower
12. Tower Bridge
13. Smithfield Market
14. St Bartholomew-the-Great
15. The Sky Garden
16. Old Bailey
17. Leadenhall Market
18. Guildhall
19. St Katharine Docks
20. St Katharine Cree
21. Charterhouse
22. Museum of the Order of St John

Eat
1. José Pizarro
2. The Jugged Hare

Drink
3. Merchant House

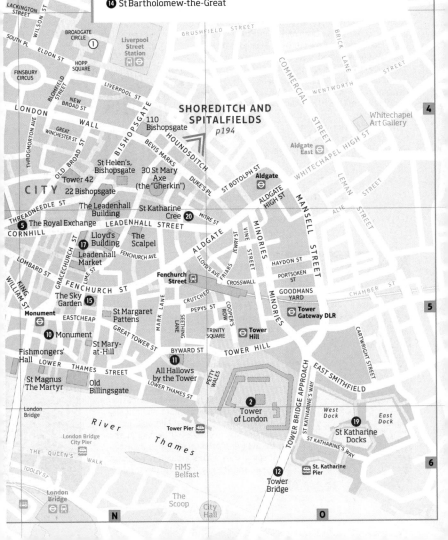

ST PAUL'S CATHEDRAL

⦿ L5 ⌂ Ludgate Hill EC4 ⊖ St Paul's, Mansion House ⊞ City Thameslink, Blackfriars ⏱ 8:30am–4:30pm Mon–Sat (also 7–9pm Thu; Aug: to 5:30pm); Galleries: 9:30am–4:15pm Mon–Sat (Aug: to 5:15pm) ⓦ stpauls.co.uk

Holding its own against the towering skyscrapers of the City, the enormous dome of St Paul's Cathedral stands out as the star of the area's churches. Completed in 1711, Sir Christopher Wren's Baroque masterpiece was England's first purpose-built Protestant cathedral, and has many similarities with St Peter's in Rome, notably in its ornate dome.

Following the Great Fire of London in 1666, the medieval cathedral of St Paul's was left in ruins. The authorities turned to Christopher Wren to rebuild it, but his ideas met with considerable resistance from the conservative Dean and Chapter. Wren's 1672 Great Model plan was rejected and a watered-down plan was finally agreed in 1675. Wren's determination paid off, though: the cathedral is considered his greatest masterpiece. Its dome is one of the largest in the world, standing 111 m (365 ft) high and weighing 65,000 tonnes.

The cathedral has a strong choral tradition and is famed for its music, with regular concerts and organ recitals.

→

The cathedral's imposing west front, dominated by its two huge towers

CHRISTOPHER WREN

Sir Christopher Wren (1632–1723) played an integral part in the restoration of London after the Great Fire of 1666. He devised a new city plan, replacing the narrow streets with wide avenues radiating from piazzas. His plan was rejected, but he was commissioned to build 52 new churches; 31 have survived various threats of demolition and the bombs of World War II, although six have only partial remains. Wren's great masterpiece is the massive St Paul's, while nearly as splendid is St Stephen Walbrook, his domed church of 1672–7. Other landmarks are St Bride's, off Fleet Street, said to have inspired the traditional shape of wedding cakes, and St Mary-le-Bow in Cheapside.

GREAT VIEW
Vista of St Paul's

Cross the Millennium Bridge to Bankside and look back to capture a great view of the famous cathedral.

↑ The elegant dome of St Paul's, viewed from the Millennium Bridge

Majestic Interior

Visitors to St Paul's will be immediately impressed by its cool, beautifully ordered and extremely spacious interior. The nave, transepts and choir are arranged in the shape of a cross, as in a medieval cathedral, but Wren's Classical vision shines through this conservative floorplan, which was forced on him by the cathedral authorities. Aided by some of the finest craftsmen of his day, he created an interior of grand majesty and Baroque splendour, a worthy setting for the many great ceremonial events that have taken place here. These include the funeral of Sir Winston Churchill in 1965 and the wedding of Prince Charles and Lady Diana Spencer in 1981.

→
Illustration of St Paul's Cathedral and its interior *(below)*

The lantern weighs a massive 700 tonnes.

The Golden Gallery is at the highest point of the dome.

Completed in 2020, a fully accessible entrance to the North Transept door was the cathedral's first major external construction in 300 years.

The brick cone located inside the outer dome supports the heavy lantern.

The Stone Gallery offers a splendid view over London.

The balustrade was added against Wren's wishes.

Flying buttresses support the nave walls and the dome.

Carvings on the pediment depict the Conversion of St Paul.

The main entrance is through the West Portico, approached from Ludgate Hill.

Wren intended a single colonnade along the West Portico, but it now has two tiers of columns.

The North and South Transepts cross the nave in a medieval style that contrasts with Wren's original plan.

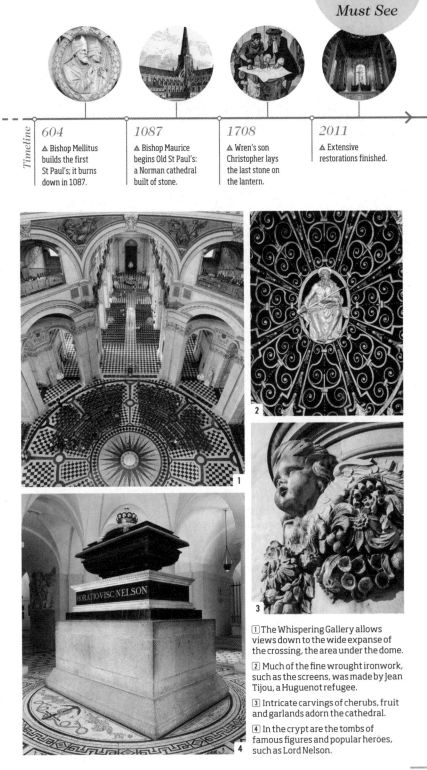

604
△ Bishop Mellitus builds the first St Paul's; it burns down in 1087.

1087
△ Bishop Maurice begins Old St Paul's: a Norman cathedral built of stone.

1708
△ Wren's son Christopher lays the last stone on the lantern.

2011
△ Extensive restorations finished.

1 The Whispering Gallery allows views down to the wide expanse of the crossing, the area under the dome.

2 Much of the fine wrought ironwork, such as the screens, was made by Jean Tijou, a Huguenot refugee.

3 Intricate carvings of cherubs, fruit and garlands adorn the cathedral.

4 In the crypt are the tombs of famous figures and popular heroes, such as Lord Nelson.

HORATIO VISC. NELSON

The imposing walls ↑
of the historic
Tower of London

② 🤿 ⛷ 🍴 🖥 🛍

TOWER OF LONDON

📍 O5 🏰 Tower Hill EC3 🚇 Tower Hill, Tower Gateway DLR
🚉 Fenchurch Street 🕐 9am-5:30pm Tue-Sat, 10am-5:30pm
Sun & Mon (Nov-Feb: to 4:30pm) 🚫 1 Jan, 24-26 Dec
🌐 hrp.org.uk

A former fortress, palace and prison, the Tower of
London attracts nearly three million visitors a year,
who come to see the Crown Jewels and to hear tales
of its dark and intriguing history.

For much of its 900-year history, the
Tower was somewhere to be feared.
Those who had committed treason or
threatened the throne were held within
its dank walls – many did not get out
alive, and some were tortured before
meeting violent deaths on Tower Hill.
   The Tower has been a tourist
attraction since the reign of Charles II
(1660–85), when both the Crown
Jewels and the collection of armour
were first shown to the public, and it
remains popular today. Come to
discover the brutality of royal regimes,
the curious menagerie that once called
the Tower home and the regalia of
Britain's kings and queens.

💬 INSIDER TIP
**Tour with a
Beefeater**

Join a Yeoman Warder,
or Beefeater, on a tour
of the Tower. A lively
retelling of tales of
executions, plots and
prisoners, it's an enter-
taining way to explore
the Tower's history.
Tours are included in
the entry fee and set off
every 30 minutes from
near the main entrance,
lasting for an hour.

Timeline

1066
△ William I erects a
temporary castle.

1534–5
△ Thomas More
imprisoned and
executed.

Did You Know?
—
The Tower has a colony of ravens. Legend has it that if they leave the Tower, the kingdom will fall.

↑ Yeoman Warders guarding the Tower

↑ King Edward I's bedchamber inside St Thomas's Tower

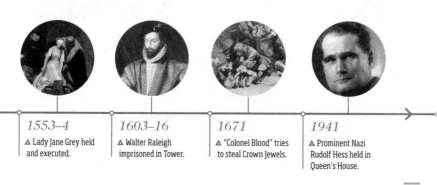

1553–4
△ Lady Jane Grey held and executed.

1603–16
△ Walter Raleigh imprisoned in Tower.

1671
△ "Colonel Blood" tries to steal Crown Jewels.

1941
△ Prominent Nazi Rudolf Hess held in Queen's House.

Life Within the Tower

The area within the mighty walls houses the remaining parts of the Medieval Palace built by Henry III, as well as several towers that held prisoners, including Anne Boleyn, Thomas Cromwell and Catherine Howard. High-ranking prisoners could live in some comfort with their own servants but the rest suffered hardship, torture and, ultimately, death.

The White Tower

The Crown Jewels are kept in the Jewel House.

The aristocratic prisoners were executed on Tower Green.

Beauchamp Tower held high-ranking prisoners.

Edward V and his brother, Richard, are said to have been murdered in the Bloody Tower.

Did You Know?

In 1952, London gangsters the Kray twins were among the last to be held at the Tower.

Main entrance

1 A sentry from the Tower Guard stands on duty outside the Jewel House.

2 Many were imprisoned in the Tower, some tortured or held in solitary confinement.

3 The Tower of London enclosure is on the edge of the city beside the Thames and Tower Bridge. There are several towers, a palace, residences and a chapel.

The beautiful Chapel of St John is made from stone brought from France.

Gallery Rooms

Wakefield Tower was part of the Medieval Palace.

Prisoners entered the Tower by boat through Traitors' Gate.

Henry III created the Medieval Palace in 1220. His son Edward I enlarged it.

← The walls enclose towers, residences and open areas

THE PRINCES IN THE TOWER

One of the Tower's darkest mysteries concerns two boy princes, sons and heirs of Edward IV. They were put into the Tower by their uncle, Richard of Gloucester, when their father died in 1483. Neither was seen again and Richard was crowned later that year. In 1674, the skeletons of two children were found nearby.

The Crown Jewels

Comprising crowns, sceptres and orbs used at coronations and other state occasions, the priceless Crown Jewels *(below)* have enormous historical significance. They mostly date from 1661 when a new set was created for the coronation of Charles II.

Coronation Regalia

Apart from the crowns, other items used during coronation ceremonies *(left)* include the Orb, the jewelled State Sword and the Sceptre with the Cross containing the world's biggest cut diamond.

Royal Armouries

On the ground floor of the White Tower, admire suits of armour from Tudor and Stuart times *(right)*, including a gargantuan set made for Henry VIII, famed for its impressive codpiece. The armour collection incorporates the famed Line of Kings, a visitor attraction for at least 350 years.

Graffiti in the Beauchamp Tower

Surprisingly elaborate carvings grace the walls of this tower, poignant messages from 16th- and 17th-century prisoners facing execution. One shows the family crest of Lord Dudley, teenage husband of the ill-fated Lady Jane Grey, imprisoned with his three brothers.

The Barbican's concrete Brutalist architecture with lake and fountains ↑

3 (🎬)(🍴)(🖥)(🎭)

BARBICAN CENTRE

📍 M4 🏠 Barbican Estate EC2 🚇 Barbican, Moorgate 🚆 Moorgate, Liverpool St 🕐 9am-11pm daily (from 11am Sun, from noon public hols); Art gallery: 10am-6pm Sun-Wed, 10am-9pm Thu-Sat; Conservatory: selected Sat & Sun, check website 🌐 barbican.org.uk

A Brutalist masterpiece, this residential, commercial and cultural complex is a formidable, fabulous anomaly in the City: an oasis of culture and community in London's largest financial district. Look out for world-class theatrical performances and concerts here.

The soul at the concrete heart of the Barbican Estate, the Barbican Centre is one of London's largest and most complete arts institutions, with two cinemas, a concert hall, two theatres and gallery spaces all celebrating the arts. The centre is also home to a public library, three restaurants, several cafés and bars and a tropical conservatory. A dynamic programme of events typically includes seasons of plays by the Royal Shakespeare Company, concerts by the resident London Symphony Orchestra, and plenty of independent cinema. The centre has always made room for experimental, genre-defying performers and artists, so expect anything from multimedia art exhibitions to street dance operas. Jazz and world music also feature frequently, with musicians and singers from Latin American, Asia and Africa often on the bill, but at any time you will find a broad range of one-off shows and events.

↑ The Barbican Hall, well known for its world music performances

THE BARBICAN ESTATE

Housing over 4,000 residents in its Brutalist tower and terrace blocks, this ambitious piece of postwar city planning was designed by Chamberlin, Powell & Bon and built on a site devastated by World War II bombs. It is a maze of concrete pavements, overhead walkways, stone staircases and looming tower blocks, but it is softened considerably by islands of green – small gardens dotted around the estate – and by an ornamental lake and fountains.

EXPERIENCE MORE

④ Ⓜ Ⓨ Ⓓ Ⓐ

Museum of London

◉ L4 ⬛ 150 London Wall EC2 ⊖ Barbican, St Paul's, Moorgate ◷ 10am-6pm daily Ⓦ museumoflondon. org.uk

Opened in 1976 on the edge of the Barbican Estate, this museum provides a lively account of London life from prehistoric times to the present day. The eclectic set of displays, which are laid out chronologically, range from detailed models and life-sized sets to items recovered from archaeological digs, photographs and recordings of Londoners talking about their lives.

Prehistory exhibits, such as flint hand axes found in the gravels under the modern city, begin on the entrance level and visitors can walk through Roman and medieval London galleries to the War, Plague and Fire exhibit, which includes a display on the Great Fire of 1666.

On the museum's lowest level, the history of London after the disastrous fire up to the present day is explored. Pride of place here, though, goes to the Lord Mayor of London's spectacular State Coach; dating from 1757, this beautifully gilded coach is still paraded once a year during the Lord Mayor's Show. The Victorian Walk uses several original shopfronts to re-create the atmosphere of late-19th-century London. There are also the Art Deco Edgar Brandt lifts from Selfridges department store on Oxford Street (1928) and unusual items such as a 1964 Beatles dress printed with the faces of the Fab Four.

Another of the permanent galleries is the London 2012 Cauldron, the centrepiece of the opening and closing ceremonies at the London Olympics. Photographs, videos, diagrams and the copper petal elements which rose together to form the Olympic Flame combine to describe the spectacle and the ingenuity of the design.

↑ Visitors examining exhibits at the fascinating Museum of London

5 🍴 🖥 🛍

The Royal Exchange

📍 N5 🚇 EC3 🚉 Bank
🌐 theroyalexchange.co.uk

Sir Thomas Gresham, an Elizabethan merchant and courtier, founded the Royal Exchange in 1565 as a centre for commerce of all kinds. The original building was centred on a vast courtyard where merchants and tradesmen did business. Queen Elizabeth I gave it its royal title and it is still one of the sites from which a new monarch is announced. Dating from 1844, this is the third splendid building on the site since Gresham's. The building is now a luxurious shopping centre with designer stores and a branch of Fortnum & Mason (p95) with an elegant central bar and café.

6 🚴 🏍

Mansion House

📍 M5 🚇 Walbrook EC4
🚉 Bank, Mansion House
🕐 2pm Tue, by prebooked guided tour 🌐 cityof london.gov.uk

The official residence of the Lord Mayor was designed by George Dance the Elder and completed in 1758. The Palladian front with its six Corinthian columns is a very familiar City landmark. Guided tours take in the state rooms, which have a dignity appropriate to the office of mayor, one of the most spectacular being the 27-m (90-ft) Egyptian Hall, and the Harold Samuel Collection, one of the most important collections of 17th-century Dutch art anywhere in the country; in particular, look out for several pieces by Frans Hals.

7 🛍

Bank of England Museum

📍 M5 🚇 Bartholomew Lane EC2 🚉 Bank 🕐 10am–5pm Mon–Fri 🚫 Public hols
🌐 bankofengland.co.uk

The Bank of England was set up in 1694 to raise money for foreign wars. It grew to become Britain's central bank, and also issues currency notes. Sir John Soane (p143) was the architect of the 1788 bank building on this site, but only the exterior wall of his design has survived. The rest was destroyed in the 1920s and 1930s when the building was enlarged by Sir Herbert Baker. The only part of Soane's design left today is the curtain wall around the outside of the building. There is now a reconstruction of Soane's stock office of 1793 in the museum. As well as images illustrating the architectural history of the building, the museum reveals the work of the Bank and financial system, and there is an interactive exhibit where visitors can set monetary policy.

Glittering gold bars (which you can touch), silver-plated decorations and a Roman mosaic floor, which was discovered during the rebuilding, are among the items on display, along with a unique collection of banknotes.

🔍 HIDDEN GEM
London Mithraeum

Beneath Bloomberg's London headquarters on Walbrook, a 2-minute walk from the Mansion House, the London Mithraeum preserves the remains of a 3rd-century temple built by followers of a bizarre Roman god cult. A sound-and-light show brings one of the secret ceremonies to life. Book ahead online (www. londonmithraeum.com).

↓ The Neo-Classical façade of the Royal Exchange

↑ St Mary-le-Bow's steeple, housing Bow bells

> **Bow bells have significance for Londoners: traditionally only those born within their sound can claim to be true Cockneys.**

⑧ St Mary-le-Bow

📍M5 🏠 Cheapside EC2
🚇 St Paul's, Mansion House
🕐 7am–6pm Mon–Fri
🌐 stmarylebow.org.uk

The church takes its name from the bow arches in the Norman crypt. When Wren rebuilt the church (in 1670–80) after the Great Fire, he continued this pattern through the arches on the steeple. The weathervane is an enormous dragon.

The church was bombed in 1941, leaving only the steeple and two walls standing, and when it was restored in 1956–62, the bells were recast and rehung. Bow bells have significance for Londoners: traditionally only those born within their sound can claim to be true Cockneys. Tours of the church are offered by arrangement, and there are free lunchtime recitals on Tuesdays.

⑨ St Stephen Walbrook

📍M5 🏠 39 Walbrook EC4
🚇 Bank, Cannon St
🕐 10am–4pm Mon, Tue & Thu, 11am–3pm Wed, 10am–3:30pm Fri
🌐 ststephenwalbrook.net

The Lord Mayor's parish church was built by architect Christopher Wren in 1672–9 and it is considered the finest of his City churches. Indeed, the deep, coffered dome, with its ornate plasterwork, was a forerunner of St Paul's Cathedral.

St Stephen's airy columned interior comes as a surprise after its plain exterior. The font cover and pulpit canopy are decorated with exquisite carved figures that contrast strongly with the stark simplicity of Henry Moore's massive white stone altar (1972), installed in 1987.

However, perhaps the most moving monument of all is a telephone in a glass box. This is a tribute to Rector Chad Varah who, in 1953, founded the Samaritans, a volunteer-staffed telephone helpline for people in emotional need.

The church is also the home of the London Internet Church, which brings together people from all over the world to worship and discuss Christianity. There are free lunchtime music recitals on Tuesdays (1pm) and Fridays (12:30pm), to which you are welcome to bring and eat a packed lunch.

THE CITY'S LIVERY HALLS

There are around 110 livery companies in London, each traditionally representing a specific profession or trade. They were first created by groups of medieval tradesmen who formed associations, or guilds, to protect, promote and regulate their trades, setting up headquarters in large houses or halls around the City. Though many did not survive the Great Fire, several dozen companies maintain their own hall to this day, while blue plaques mark former halls. Some have grand, ornate interiors worthy of a palace, but they are difficult places to visit - a few allow group tours, others are not publicly accessible.

10 Monument

N5 **Monument St EC3**
Monument **Platform:**
9:30am–6pm daily (last
adm: 5:30pm) **24–26 Dec**
themonument.org.uk

The column designed by Wren to commemorate the Great Fire of London of 1666 is the tallest isolated stone column in the world. It is 61.5 m (202 ft) high and is said to be 61.5 m west of where the fire started, in Pudding Lane. Reliefs around the column's base show Charles II restoring the city. It's a tough climb up 311 steps to the top of the column, but the views are spectacular.

11 All Hallows by the Tower

N5 **Byward St EC3**
Tower Hill **8am–6pm**
Mon–Fri (Nov–Mar: to 5pm),
10am–5pm Sat & Sun
Public hols **ahbtt.org.uk**

The oldest church in the city retains some original Saxon features and a Roman tessellated floor, discovered in 1926, on display in the Crypt Museum, along with other Roman and Saxon artifacts. The church carried out the temporary burials of those executed on nearby Tower Hill, including Thomas More, and it was from the church tower that Samuel Pepys watched the Great Fire consume London in 1666.

12 Tower Bridge

06 **SE1** **Tower Hill**
9:30am–5pm daily
24–26 Dec **tower bridge.org.uk**

Completed in 1894, this flamboyant piece of Victorian engineering is a symbol of London. Its pinnacled towers and linking catwalk support the mechanism for raising the roadway when big ships have to pass through, or for special occasions; check the website for details. When raised, the bridge is 40 m (135 ft) high.

Walking across the bridge is free but access to the elevated walkways, which includes a glass section from which you can peer vertiginously down to the traffic below, requires a ticket. This includes entry to the exhibition in the North Tower and the Engine Rooms, reached via the South Tower, and a look at the steam engine that powered the lifting machinery until 1976, when the system was electrified.

13 Smithfield Market

L4 **Charterhouse St EC1** **Farringdon,**
Barbican **2–9am**
Mon–Fri **Public hols**
smithfieldmarket.com

Animals have been traded here since the 12th century, but the site was granted its first official charter in 1400.

In 1648, Smithfield was officially established as a cattle market, and live cattle continued to be sold here until the mid-19th century. Today, it confines itself to wholesale trading in meat

↓ Tower Bridge, an enduring symbol of London

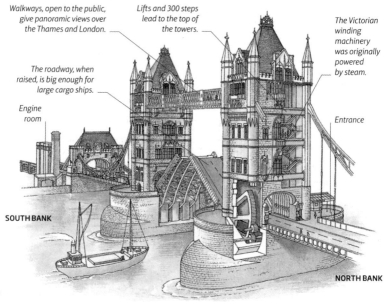

Walkways, open to the public, give panoramic views over the Thames and London.

Lifts and 300 steps lead to the top of the towers.

The Victorian winding machinery was originally powered by steam.

The roadway, when raised, is big enough for large cargo ships.

Engine room

Entrance

SOUTH BANK

NORTH BANK

EXPERIENCE The City

↑ The Sky Garden, top deck of the "Walkie-Talkie" building

and poultry. It was originally sited in Smithfield, outside the City walls and, although moved to its present location in Charterhouse Street in the 1860s and called the London Central Meat Market, the original name stuck. The old buildings are by Victorian architect Horace Jones, but there are 20th-century additions. Some pubs in the area keep market hours, serving hearty breakfasts from dawn. Now modernized, the market is one of the best-equipped meat markets in the world. Visitors should aim to arrive by 7am.

⑭ St Bartholomew-the-Great

🚇 L4 🏛 West Smithfield EC1 🚇 Barbican 🕐 8:30am-5pm Mon-Fri (mid-Nov-mid-Feb: to 4pm), 10:30am-4pm Sat, 8:30am-8pm Sun
🌐 greatstbarts.com

One of London's oldest churches, St Bart's was founded in 1123 by a courtier of Henry I.

The 13th-century arch used to be the door; the gatehouse above it is from a later period. The crossing and chancel are original, with fine Norman detailing. There are also some Tudor monuments. In the south transept is a gilded statue of St Bartholomew by Damien Hirst. In 1725, US statesman Benjamin Franklin worked for a printer in the Lady Chapel. The church also featured in the films *Four Weddings and a Funeral*, *Shakespeare in Love* and *The Other Boleyn Girl*.

⑮ The Sky Garden

🚇 N5 🏛 20 Fenchurch St EC3 🚇 Bank, Monument 🕐 10am-6pm Mon-Fri (last adm: 5pm), 11am-9pm Sat & Sun (last adm: 8pm)
🌐 skygarden.london

The Rafael Viñoly-designed 20 Fenchurch Street is commonly known as the "Walkie-Talkie", thanks to its unusual shape. Not without controversy (its shape and position make it particularly obtrusive on the city skyline), it is one of a few skyscrapers with free public access, provided that you book ahead for the Sky Garden, a three-level viewing deck. Tickets are released each Monday for bookings up to three weeks ahead and go quickly. The bars and restaurants here stay open till late.

This is a perfect place from which to view London's other mega-structures. To the south is the Shard (p214); north are Tower 42, the "Gherkin" and the Leadenhall Building, aka the "Cheesegrater", "The Scalpel" and 22 Bishopsgate, the City's tallest skyscraper.

⑯ Old Bailey

🚇 L4 🏛 EC4 🚇 St Paul's 🕐 9:55am-12:40pm & 1:55-3:40pm Mon-Fri (reduced times Aug; hours vary from court to court) 🚫 Public hols 🌐 cityof london.gov.uk

The new Central Criminal Courts opened here in 1907 on the site of the infamous and malodorous Newgate prison. Across the road, the Magpie and Stump pub served "execution breakfasts" until 1868, when mass public hangings outside the gates were stopped. Today, the courts are open to the public when in session.

DRINK

Merchant House
Hidden away down an alley, this basement bar and lounge serves up exceptional cocktails, which evoke the Empire. The Brig, a private bar inside seating up to 4 people, can also be booked.

🚇 M5 🏛 13 Well Court, off Bow Lane EC4 🕐 Sun 🌐 merchanthouse.bar

Elegant wrought-iron and glass vaulting at Leadenhall Market

⑰ (🍴) (🖥) (🛍)

Leadenhall Market

📍N5 **🚉Gracechurch St EC3** **🚇Bank, Monument** **🕐24 hours; business times vary** **🌐leadenhallmarket.co.uk**

There has been a food market here, on the site of a Roman forum, since the Middle Ages.

Today's ornate Victorian covered shopping arcade was designed in 1881 by Sir Horace Jones and Leadenhall is now home to boutique wine shops, cheesemongers, florists and fine food shops, along with several traditional pubs and wine bars. At Christmas the decorated stores are an attractive sight.

---

⑱ (🛍)

Guildhall

📍M4 **🚉Guildhall Yard EC2** **🚇St Paul's** **🕐Great Hall: 10am–5pm Mon–Sat, noon–4pm Sun** **🕐1 Jan, 25 & 26 Dec, occasionally for events** **🌐guildhall.cityoflondon.gov.uk**

Guildhall has been the administrative centre of the City for at least 800 years. For centuries its Great Hall was used for trials, and many people were condemned to death here, including Henry Garnet, one of the Gunpowder Plot conspirators.

Overlooking the Great Hall at one end are the figures of legendary giants Gog and Magog, the guardians of the City, while statues of notable figures such as Churchill and Nelson line its 46-m- (150-ft-) long sides. Each year, a few days after the Lord Mayor's parade, the prime minister addresses a banquet here.

On the south side of Guildhall Yard is a Wren-designed church, St Lawrence Jewry, while on the east side is the **Guildhall Art Gallery**. It houses the studio collection of 20th-century artist Sir Matthew Smith, portraits from the 16th century to the present day, 18th-century works including John Singleton Copley's *Defeat of the Floating Batteries at Gibraltar*, and numerous Victorian works.

In 1988, the foundations of a Roman amphitheatre were discovered beneath the gallery. Built in AD 70 and with a capacity of about 6,000 spectators, the arena would have hosted animal hunts, executions and gladiatorial combat. Public access to the atmospheric ruins is through the art gallery.

Guildhall Art Gallery

🕐10am–5pm Mon–Sat, noon–4pm Sun **🕐1 Jan, 24–26 Dec**

---

⑲ (🍴) (🖥) (🛍)

St Katharine Docks

📍O6 **🚉E1** **🚇Tower Hill** **🌐skdocks.co.uk**

This most central of all London's docks was designed by Thomas Telford and opened in 1828 on the site of St Katharine's Hospital. Commodities as diverse as tea, marble and live turtles (turtle soup was a Victorian delicacy) were unloaded here.

During the 19th and early 20th centuries, the docks flourished, but by the mid-20th century, cargo ships were delivering their wares in massive containers. The old docks became too small and closed in 1968.

The redevelopment of St Katharine's has been one

of the City's most successful – the old warehouse buildings have shops and restaurants on their ground floors, and offices above. In front is a marina, and there are other entertainment facilities.

The dock is well worth wandering through after visiting the Tower (p180) or Tower Bridge (p188). A weekly street food market is held here on Saturdays from 11am to 3pm.

20

St Katharine Cree

N5 **86 Leadenhall St EC3** **Aldgate, Tower Hill** **11am-3pm Tue** **Aug** **stkatherinecree.com**

A rare pre-Wren 17th-century church with a medieval tower, this was one of only eight in the City to survive the fire of 1666. Some of the elaborate plasterwork on and beneath the high ceiling of the nave portrays the coats of arms of the guilds, with which the church has special links. The rose window is said to be modelled on that of old St Paul's Cathedral, destroyed in the Great Fire. The 17th-century organ, supported by carved columns, has been played by Purcell and Handel.

21

Charterhouse

L3 **Charterhouse Sq EC1** **Barbican** **Museum: 11am-5:20pm Tue-Sat** **1 Jan, 24-26 Dec** **thecharterhouse.org**

The Tudor gateway on the north side of Charterhouse square leads to the site of a former Carthusian monastery, which was dissolved under Henry VIII. In 1611, the buildings were converted into a hospital for poor pensioners, and a charity school – called Charterhouse – whose pupils included Methodism founder John Wesley, writer William Thackeray and Robert Baden-Powell, founder of the Boy Scouts.

In 1872, the school relocated to Godalming in Surrey. Part of the original site was subsequently taken over by St Bartholomew's Hospital medical school. Some of the old buildings remain, including the chapel and part of the cloisters. Today Charterhouse is still home to more than 40 pensioners supported by the charitable foundation. There is a small museum open to all, but access to the rest of the site is by guided tour only, conducted every day except Sunday and Monday; book online.

EAT

José Pizarro

Classic Spanish tapas and inventive dishes.

N4 **36 Broadgate Circle EC2** **Sat & Sun** **josepizarro.com**

£££

The Jugged Hare

Gastropub serving excellent game dishes.

M3 **49 Chiswell St EC1** **thejugged hare.com**

£££

22

Museum of the Order of St John

L3 **St John's Lane EC1** **Farringdon** **10am-5pm Mon-Sat (Jul-Sep: daily)** **3 weeks over Christmas/Jan** **museumstjohn.org.uk**

The Tudor gatehouse and parts of the 12th-century church are all that remain of the priory of the Knights of St John, which flourished here for 400 years and was the precursor of the St John Ambulance. Over the years, the priory buildings have had many uses, such as offices for Elizabeth I's Master of the Revels and a coffee shop run by the artist William Hogarth's father.

The museum contains hundreds of treasures from the order's history, including illuminated manuscripts and a bronze cannon donated by Henry VIII. The rest of the building, including the priory church with its 12th-century crypt, can be seen on free guided tours at 11am and 2:30pm on Tuesdays, Fridays and Saturdays, and on Sundays at 2pm from July to September.

St Katharine Docks, a working quay turned marina

A SHORT WALK
THE CITY

Distance 1.5 km (1 mile) **Time** 25 minutes
Nearest Tube St Paul's

This route through the business centre of London unsurprisingly takes in vast institutions, such as the the Bank of England and Bloomberg's European headquarters. Alongside these 20th- and 21st-century buildings stand the majestic architectural visions of Christopher Wren, England's most sublime and probably most prolific architect *(p176)*. Marvel at his genius as you pass some of his churches.

Did You Know?

Watling Street is a section of a Roman road that once extended from the Kent coast to Shrewsbury in Shropshire.

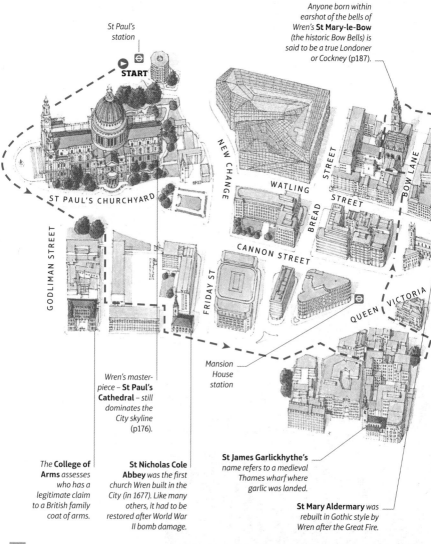

St Paul's station

START

Anyone born within earshot of the bells of Wren's **St Mary-le-Bow** *(the historic Bow Bells) is said to be a true Londoner or Cockney (p187).*

NEW CHANGE

WATLING STREET

BREAD STREET

BOW LANE

ST PAUL'S CHURCHYARD

GODLIMAN STREET

CANNON STREET

FRIDAY ST

QUEEN VICTORIA

Mansion House station

Wren's master-piece – **St Paul's Cathedral** *– still dominates the City skyline (p176).*

The **College of Arms** *assesses who has a legitimate claim to a British family coat of arms.*

St Nicholas Cole Abbey *was the first church Wren built in the City (in 1677). Like many others, it had to be restored after World War II bomb damage.*

St James Garlickhythe's *name refers to a medieval Thames wharf where garlic was landed.*

St Mary Aldermary *was rebuilt in Gothic style by Wren after the Great Fire.*

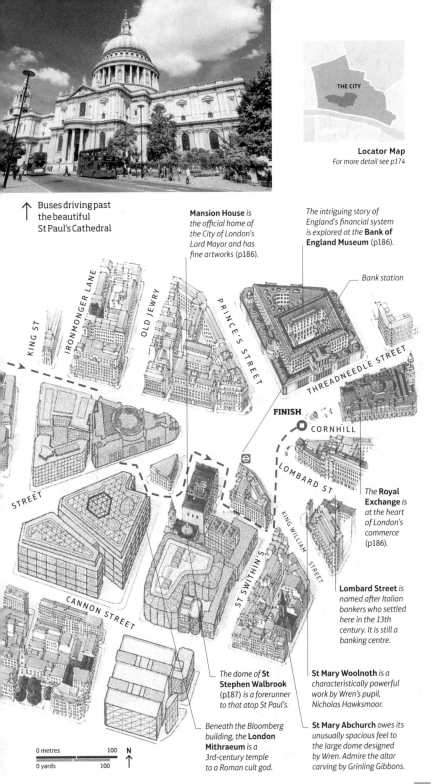

THE CITY

↑ Buses driving past the beautiful St Paul's Cathedral

Mansion House *is the official home of the City of London's Lord Mayor and has fine artworks (p186).*

The intriguing story of England's financial system is explored at the **Bank of England Museum** *(p186).*

Bank station

IRONMONGER LANE

KING ST

OLD JEWRY

PRINCE'S STREET

THREADNEEDLE STREET

FINISH

⊖ CORNHILL

LOMBARD ST

KING WILLIAM STREET

STREET

The **Royal Exchange** *is at the heart of London's commerce (p186).*

CANNON STREET

ST SWITHIN'S

Lombard Street *is named after Italian bankers who settled here in the 13th century. It is still a banking centre.*

The dome of **St Stephen Walbrook** *(p187) is a forerunner to that atop St Paul's.*

St Mary Woolnoth *is a characteristically powerful work by Wren's pupil, Nicholas Hawksmoor.*

Beneath the Bloomberg building, the **London Mithraeum** *is a 3rd-century temple to a Roman cult god.*

St Mary Abchurch *owes its unusually spacious feel to the large dome designed by Wren. Admire the altar carving by Grinling Gibbons.*

0 metres 100
0 yards 100
N ↑

Trendy street food complex in Shoreditch

SHOREDITCH AND SPITALFIELDS

Just outside the boundaries of the City, Spitalfields has long revolved around its market, which first emerged in the late 17th century after traders had begun operating outside the city gates. As the market expanded people began to settle in its vicinity, notably Huguenots fleeing religious persecution in France. The Huguenots also moved to nearby Shoreditch and their skilled weavers soon dominated the textile industry in the area. Waves of Irish, then Jewish and most recently Bangladeshi immigrants followed. The market survived, was given its own building in the late 19th century and flourished for decades as a wholesale market. It was saved from destruction in the early years of this century and reborn as a market for vintage clothing, antiques, arts and crafts, in keeping with the recent gentrification of the area, extending across Shoreditch and beyond.

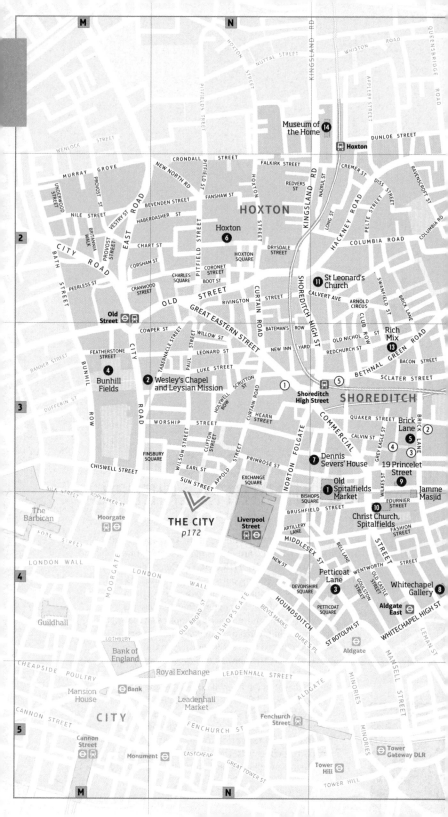

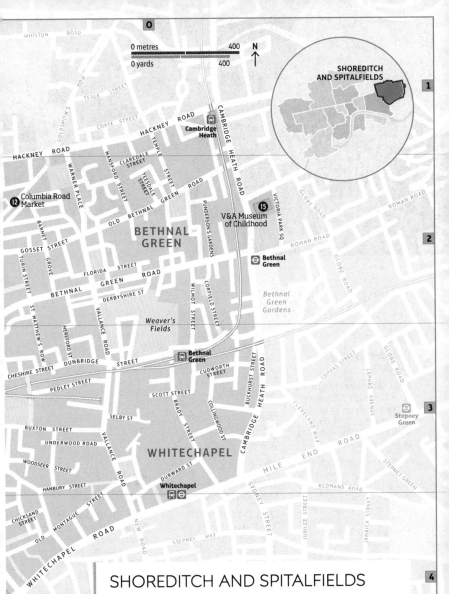

SHOREDITCH AND SPITALFIELDS

Experience

1. Old Spitalfields Market
2. Wesley's Chapel and Leysian Mission
3. Petticoat Lane
4. Bunhill Fields
5. Brick Lane
6. Hoxton
7. Dennis Severs' House
8. Whitechapel Gallery
9. 19 Princelet Street
10. Christ Church, Spitalfields
11. St Leonard's Church
12. Columbia Road Market
13. Rich Mix
14. Museum of the Home
15. V&A Museum of Childhood

Eat

1. Dinerama
2. The Brick Lane Food Hall
3. Sunday Upmarket
4. Ely's Yard

Shop

5. Boxpark

↑ Independent traders with their wares on display at Old Spitalfields Market

EXPERIENCE

① 🍴 📺 🛍
Old Spitalfields Market

📍 O3 🏠 16 Horner Sq E1
🚇 Liverpool St, Aldgate
🕐 Market stalls: 10am–6pm daily (to 5pm Sun), 8am–6pm Thu 🌐 oldspitalfields market.com

Produce has been traded at Spitalfields Market since 1682, though the original covered market buildings date to 1887. The vegetable market finally moved out in 1991, after which today's version of the market – known for antiques, fashion, bric-a-brac and crafts stalls – started to take shape. Today the market space is a mix of restaurants, shops and traditional market stalls. It is open every day; Thursdays are good for antiques and collectables, and every other Friday for vinyl records, but it is on Sundays that the crowds really arrive, in search of vintage clothing and unique

items. This is also a major foodie destination, with superb street food from top names, both global and local – from Pacific pokè and Burmese tea leaf salad to East Anglian oysters and the unrivalled Reuben sandwich from the iconic Monty's Deli.

---

②
Wesley's Chapel and Leysian Mission

📍 M3 🏠 49 City Rd EC1
🚇 Old Street, Moorgate
🕐 10am–4pm Mon–Sat
🌐 wesleyschapel.org.uk

John Wesley, the founder of the Methodist Church, laid this chapel's foundation stone in 1777. He preached here until his death in 1791 and is buried behind the chapel. Next door is the house where he lived, in which some of his furniture, books and other possessions can be seen. The chapel is more ornate than in Wesley's day, with stained-glass windows

and French jasper pillars, which replaced the original ones made from ships' masts. Beneath the chapel is a museum devoted to the history of Methodism; within this voluminous collection are portraits, furniture, books and ceramics. There are free lunch-time recitals most Tuesdays.

---

③
Petticoat Lane

📍 O4 🏠 Middlesex St E1
🚇 Aldgate East, Aldgate, Liverpool St 🕐 9am–3pm Sun (main market); 8am–4pm Mon–Fri (smaller market on Wentworth St)

During the prudish Victorian era, the name of this street, long famous for its market, was changed to the more respectable but colourless Middlesex Street. That is still its official designation, but the old name, derived from the petticoats and lace sold here by the Huguenots who came from France, has stuck, and is now applied to the market held every Sunday morning in this and the surrounding streets. Though the street is not particularly attractive, the

> **Thursdays are good for antiques and collectables, and every other Friday for vinyl records, but it is on Sundays that the crowds really arrive, in search of vintage clothing and unique items.**

lively market creates plenty of atmosphere. A great variety of goods are sold, but there is still a bias towards clothing, especially leather coats. It's a noisy and cheerful scene, with Cockney stallholders making use of their wit to attract custom. There are street-food vendors for pitstops.

↑ Upmarket stalls at the Old Truman Brewery estate on Brick Lane

4 (Ⓜ)

Bunhill Fields

📍 M3 🚌 38, City Rd EC1 🚇 Old Street 🕐 8am-7pm or dusk Mon-Fri, 9:30am-7pm or dusk Sat, Sun & public hols 🔒 1 Jan, 25 & 26 Dec 🌐 cityoflondon.gov.uk

Situated on the edge of the city, and shaded by large plane trees, this burial ground was first designated a cemetery after the Great Plague of 1665, when it was enclosed by a brick wall and gates. Twenty years later it was allocated to Nonconformists, who were banned from being buried in churchyards because of their refusal to use the Church of England prayer book.

It's now the final resting place of writers Daniel Defoe, John Bunyan and William Blake, clergyman and hymn writer Isaac Watts, as well as members of the Cromwell family. John Milton wrote his epic poem *Paradise Lost* while he lived in Bunhill Row, located on the west side of the cemetery. In summertime (Apr–Oct), there are guided walks of the cemetery on Wednesdays at 12:30pm.

NEAR BY LIE THE REMAINS OF THE POET-PAINTER WILLIAM BLAKE 1757 — 1827 AND OF HIS WIFE CATHERINE SOPHIA 1762 — 1831

5 (🍴) (🥤) (🛍)

Brick Lane

📍 O3 🚌 E1 🚇 Liverpool St, Aldgate East 🚆 Shoreditch High St 🕐 Market: 10am-5pm Sun 🌐 visitbrick lane.org

Once a lane running through brickfields, Brick Lane has long been synonymous with the area's British-Bangladeshi community. Now their curry houses sit next to hip galleries and quirky boutiques. Shops and houses, some dating from the 18th century, have seen immigrants of many nationalities, and ethnic foods, spices, silks and saris are all on sale here. In the 19th century this was mainly a Jewish quarter, and some Jewish shops remain, most famously a 24-hour bagel shop at No 159. On Sundays, a large market is held here and in the surrounding streets. Towards the northern end of Brick Lane is the Old Truman Brewery, home to a mix of bars, shops and stalls: separate markets at weekends sell food, vintage clothes and new fashion.

←

A monument to William Blake and his wife in Bunhill Fields

EAT

Dinerama
Best spot for street food after dark, this old truck depot offers craft beer and cocktails.

📍 N3 🚌 19 Great Eastern St EC2 🕐 Thu-Sat 🌐 streetfeast.com

£ £ £

The Brick Lane Food Hall
Treats from Poland, Ethiopia, Japan, Korea and more inside a red-brick warehouse.

📍 O3 🚌 Old Truman Brewery, Brick Lane E1 🕐 Sat & Sun

£ £ £

Sunday Upmarket
International street food is found among artsy stalls.

📍 O3 🚌 Old Truman Brewery, Brick Lane E1 🕐 Sun

£ £ £

Ely's Yard
The food trucks and stalls are here all week.

📍 O3 🚌 Old Truman Brewery, Dray Walk, E1

£ £ £

6 🍴 🖥 🛍

Hoxton

📍N2 🚇N1, E2
🚇Old St

Hoxton, at the heart of hipster London, is a loosely defined district that revolves around its two main streets: Old Street and Kingsland Road. This once-gritty landscape of Victorian warehouses and postwar estates is now home to trendy places to eat, increasingly pricey clothes stores and a significant percentage of the city's newer street art. The converted warehouses house some of the city's most rambunctious nightlife, with clubs and bars radiating out from the Shoreditch High Street and Old Street junction, some of them on neatly proportioned Hoxton Square, just behind Old Street.

---

7 🎨 🏛

Dennis Severs' House

📍O3 🚇18 Folgate St E1
🚇Liverpool St 🕐Noon-
2pm & 5-9pm Mon, 5-9pm
Wed & Fri, noon-4pm Sun
🌐dennissevershouse.co.uk

At No 18 Folgate Street, built in 1724, the late designer and performer Dennis Severs re-created a historical interior that takes you on a journey from the 17th to the 19th centuries. It offers what he called "an adventure of the imagination… a visit to a time-mode rather than… merely a look at a house".

The rooms are like a series of *tableaux vivants*, as if the occupants had simply left for a moment. There is bread on the plates, wine in the glasses, fruit in the bowl; the candles flicker and horses' hooves are heard clattering on the cobbles outside.

This highly theatrical experience is far removed from the usual museum re-creations, and the house is particularly atmospheric during the "Silent Night" evening sessions and at Christmas. Praised by many, including artist David

↑ The immaculately re-created interior of Dennis Severs' House

Hockney, it is truly unique. The house's motto is "You either see it or you don't."

Around the corner on Elder Street are two of London's earliest surviving terraces, where several Georgian red-brick houses have been carefully restored.

---

8 🖥 🛍

Whitechapel Gallery

📍O4 🚇77-82 Whitechapel
High St E1 🚇Aldgate East,
Aldgate 🕐11am-6pm Tue-
Sun (to 9pm Thu) 🗓1 Jan,
24-26 Dec 🌐whitechapel
gallery.org

A striking Art Nouveau façade by C Harrison Townsend

→ Industrial chic in the gentrified Hoxton district

fronts this light, airy gallery, founded in 1901 and later expanded in the 1980s and again in 2007–9. Situated close to Brick Lane and the area's burgeoning art scene, this independent gallery was founded with the aim of bringing great art to the people of east London. Today it enjoys an international reputation for high-quality shows of major contemporary artists and for events, talks, live performances, films and art-themed evenings (especially on the first Thursday of each month, when many galleries in the area open late).

In the 1950s and 1960s, the likes of Jackson Pollock, Anthony Caro, Mark Rothko, Robert Rauschenberg and John Hoyland all displayed their work in the gallery. In 1970 David Hockney's first exhibition was held here.

The gallery has a well-stocked arts bookshop and a relaxed café which on Thursday evenings becomes a popular wine bar. There is an entry charge for some special exhibitions.

9 19 Princelet Street

⌖ 03 **⌂** 19 Princelet St E1 **⊖** Liverpool St **⌚** For group tours only **ⓦ** 19princelet street.org.uk

This 1719 Huguenot silk merchant's house, with a Victorian synagogue hidden within, epitomizes the area's multicultural history as a refuge for the dispossessed. Now it exists as a museum of immigration, with exhibitions celebrating the people who have arrived and settled in London's East End. It is hoped that, with funding, this historic gem can be further developed into a permanent centre. For now, it is only open for one-off group visits (booked in advance via the website), but there are occasional open days and special events.

↑ Standing proudly over the streets of Spitalfields, the iconic Christ Church

10 Christ Church, Spitalfields

⌖ 04 **⌂** Commercial St E1 **⊖** Liverpool St **⌚** 10am-4pm Mon-Fri (unless in use as venue), 1-4pm Sun **ⓦ** ccspits.org

Christopher Wren's pupil Nicholas Hawksmoor built six London churches, and this is his finest. Christ Church was commissioned by parliament in the Fifty New Churches Act of 1711, which was aimed at combating the threat of Nonconformism and intended to make a powerful statement in an area fast becoming a Huguenot stronghold.

Completed in 1729, the building was mauled by alterations in the 1850s. And by 1960 it had become derelict, narrowly escaping demolition. After a lengthy programme of restoration promoted by the Friends of Christ Church Spitalfields, the church was returned to its former glory by 2004. The superb organ was restored to full working order in 2015, and the renovated crypt revealed much of the original walls. The impression of size and strength created by its portico and spire is continued inside by such features as the high ceiling and the gallery. Tours are for groups, and should be booked at least two weeks ahead.

HUGUENOTS IN LONDON

Among the first really significant waves of immigration into east London was the influx of tens of thousands of Huguenots from France in the late 17th century. These were Protestant refugees, fleeing persecution in their home country, and their numbers were highest in Spitalfields. Many were weavers by trade and they came to dominate the silk and textile industry that already existed in this part of the city. Spitalfields became known as "Weaver Town".

Beautiful blooms at the Columbia Road flower market ↑

⑪ St Leonard's Church

🚩 O2 🏠 119 Shoreditch High St E1 ⊖ Old St 🚆 Shoreditch High St ⏰ Jul-Oct: noon-5pm Fri-Sun; services on Sun year-round 🌐 shoreditchchurch.org.uk

Standing as it does on the spot where several major Roman roads converged, this has been a site of worship for millennia. The Norman-era St Leonard's was the original "Actors' Church" (p129) and many famous names of Tudor theatre are buried in the crypt, including Richard Burbage, who played the first Hamlet, Macbeth and Romeo, and his brother Cuthbert, founder of the Globe Theatre.

Erected in 1736–40, the current Palladian-style church is the oldest building in Shoreditch. Its fine acoustics make it still popular today as a performance space for actors and musicians. Sunday service is at 10:30am.

⑫ Columbia Road Market

🚩 O2 🏠 Columbia Rd E2 🚆 Hoxton ⏰ 8am-3pm Sun 🌐 columbiaroad.info

A visit to this flower and plant market is one of the most delightful things to do on a Sunday morning in London, whether you want to take advantage of the exotic species on offer or not – though it's hard to resist, as prices are competitive and the range impressive. Set in a well-preserved street of small Victorian shops, it is a lively, sweet-smelling and colourful affair. Apart from the stalls, there are several shops selling, among other things, home-made bread, vintage apparel, antiques and interesting objects, many flower related. There are also cafés, a tapas bar and pubs to refuel at along the street. Visit early to miss the crowds.

⑬ Rich Mix

🚩 O3 🏠 35-47 Bethnal Green Rd E1 ⊖ Shoreditch High St ⏰ 9am-late Mon-Fri, 10am-late Sat & Sun 🌐 richmix.org.uk

This hip independent cultural centre spread over five floors offers a diverse programme of live music, theatre, dance,

SHOP

Boxpark
Independent clothing brands, accessories, cosmetics, homewares and kooky gifts are traded from repurposed shipping containers in this fun, pop-up-style retail park.

🚩 O3 🏠 2-10 Bethnal Green Rd E1 🌐 boxpark.co.uk

spoken word, comedy and film. There's an emphasis on multiculturalism, feminism and breaking down stereotypes reflected in the eclectic mix of film festivals for which its three-screen cinema has become a major venue. The building is a converted leather factory with an unusual mishmash of performance and exhibition spaces giving off an industrial vibe. There are three bars within its straight-edged interior, and an Indian street-food café faces the street.

---

14 (Ⓜ) (▱) (🛍)

Museum of the Home

📍01 📮136 Kingsland Rd E2 🚇Hoxton 🕐Times vary, check website 🌐museum ofthehome.org.uk

Formerly known as the Geffrye Museum, this delightful collection reopened in 2020 following a major redevelopment. The museum is housed in a set of restored almshouses that were built in 1715 on land bequeathed by Sir Robert Geffrye, a 17th-century Lord Mayor of London. Inside, you take a trip through historical room settings, each providing an insight into the domestic interiors of the urban middle classes from 1630 to the 1990s, reflecting changes in society, behaviour, style and taste. Each room contains superb examples of British furniture of the period and showcases personal stories. Running the length of the main almshouse, the Home Gallery explores everyday experiences of home-making over the past 400 years in a wider context. In another restored almshouse, regular tours tell the story of how the poor and elderly lived in previous times. Outside, period garden "rooms" show designs and planting schemes popular in urban gardens, including a herb garden and a 21st-century green roof.

The museum runs temporary exhibitions and there are often events in the green space in front of the buildings, such as an outdoor cinema.

---

15 (▱) (🛍)

V&A Museum of Childhood

📍O2 📮Cambridge Heath Rd E2 🚇Bethnal Green 🕐10am–5:45pm daily 🌐vam.ac.uk/moc

With an amazing array of toys, games, puzzles, lavish dolls' houses, model train sets, furniture and costumes, dating from the 16th century up to the present day, this museum has the largest collection of childhood-related objects in the UK.

There are plenty of activities to keep children amused, including storytelling, arts and crafts workshops, and fun trails.

↑ The V&A Museum of Childhood, home to toys and games through the ages, including (inset) puppets

French
CHARCUTE...

A MAGNIFIQUE
Range of
SAUCISSONS

...ed ham · Pork belly
...ied beef · Smoked Ham
...sette   etc.

...handpick the best quality
...oducts from our
...ions best artisans

...ur friendly staff are happy
...swer all your questions
...esday to Saturday

...hefrenchcomte.co.uk
@thefrenchcomte

this week's
offer!!
SMOKED
HAM
-%.20 off
£ 20
/kg

QUALITY FRENCH CHARCUT...
· It is traditionally hand made by small passionate artisan...
· It is made with meat that comes from happy local animals
  are free range and fed a natural diet.
· The pork meat we use has the PGI label which
  standards are respected when...
· Most of...

Charcuterie and cheese at The French Comté in Borough Market

SOUTHWARK AND BANKSIDE

Southwark and its stretch of riverbank, known as Bankside, once offered an escape from the City, a place to indulge in the many forms of entertainment that were banned across the river. Among the illicit pleasures that thrived here from the late 16th century were brothels, theatres, and bear and cock pits. Even today, the streets leading off Borough High Street are lined with a remarkable number of pubs, and the George survives as the only galleried inn in London. Shakespeare's company was famously based at the Globe Theatre, which has been reconstructed close to its original site. Docks, wharves and warehouses were built along Bankside in the 18th and 19th centuries as the area industrialized, but a century later, bomb damage during World War II, and the decline in river trade that followed, ushered in a period of decline. Southwark's riverside renaissance as one of the capital's top visitor destinations began in the 1990s and since the turn of the millennium, Tate Modern, the Millennium Bridge and the Shard have all opened, accompanied by a sweeping regeneration of the whole area.

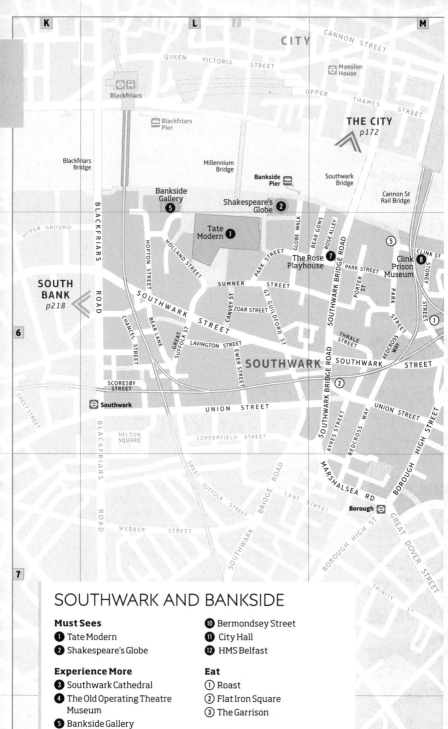

SOUTHWARK AND BANKSIDE

Must Sees
1. Tate Modern
2. Shakespeare's Globe

Experience More
3. Southwark Cathedral
4. The Old Operating Theatre Museum
5. Bankside Gallery
6. Borough Market
7. The Rose Playhouse
8. Clink Prison Museum
9. The Shard

10. Bermondsey Street
11. City Hall
12. HMS Belfast

Eat
1. Roast
2. Flat Iron Square
3. The Garrison

Drink
4. The George
5. The Anchor

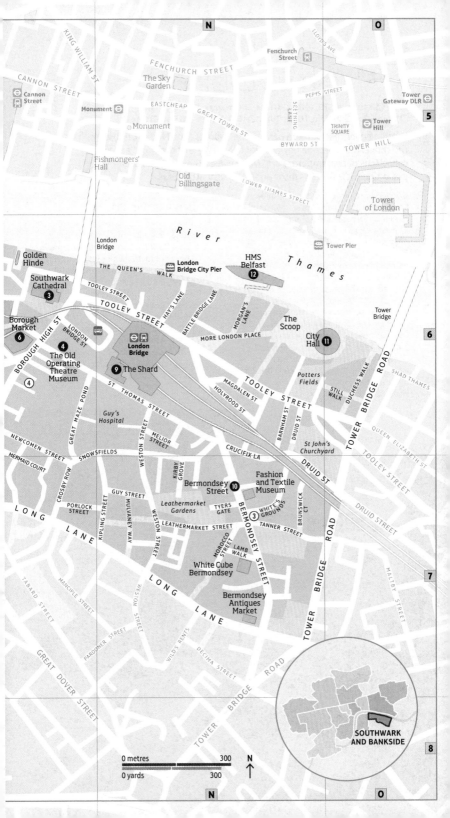

① ⑤ ⑪ ⑫ ⑬

TATE MODERN

Q L6 **A** Bankside SE1 **⊖** Blackfriars, Southwark **⊜** Blackfriars
Ⓒ 10am-6pm Sun-Thu, 10am-10pm Fri & Sat **Ⓒ** 24-26 Dec **W** tate.org.uk

Looming over the southern bank of the Thames, Tate Modern, housed in
the converted Bankside power station, holds one of the world's premier
collections of contemporary art. With an ever-changing roster of
exhibitions, it is Britain's most popular visitor attraction.

Opened to coincide with the new millennium,
this Goliath of a gallery boasts a vast collection
of modern artworks, featuring paintings and
sculptures by some of the most significant
artists of the 20th and 21st centuries, Pablo
Picasso, Salvador Dalí, Mark Rothko and
Francis Bacon among them. Lesser-known
artists and less mainstream art forms also
abound, with pieces composed of bottle
tops or, most famously, a porcelain urinal,
in the guise of Marcel Duchamp's notorious
Fountain. The focal point of the building is
the awesome Turbine Hall, which is often
filled by a specially commissioned work.
Other exhibition spaces, including the
galleries of the towering Blavatnik Building,
feature collections on a single theme or
hugely popular temporary shows.

INTERACTIVE ART

Tate Modern has created a series of
interactive activities and experiences
under its Bloomberg Connects umbrella.
These products, including the Timeline
of Modern Art, the TateShots digital
gallery and the digital Drawing Bar, in
which you can immerse yourself in the
studios and cities of artists, enable members of the public to actively connect
with art, artists and other visitors. The
award-winning handheld multimedia
guides present audio commentary
alongside images, film clips and games.

One Two Three Swing!
by SUPERFLEX, an
installation in the Turbine Hall ↓

4.2 million

The number of bricks
used to build the
original Bankside
power station.

1 The striking 99-m- (325-ft-) high chimney of Tate Modern reveals the building's former role as a power station.

2 The Tate Modern has an excellent and extensive permanent collection displayed across the site, spanning photographs, paintings, sculptures and video art.

3 The cool interior of the Blavatnik Building extension has added a large number of galleries and performance spaces to the Tate.

GREAT VIEW
Top of the Tower

On Level 10, the top floor of the fantastic Blavatnik Building extension, the 360-degree viewing terrace gives spectacular views of London. You can also enjoy more or less the same views, taking in St Paul's Cathedral, the rest of the City and beyond, from the restaurant on Level 9.

② 🔶 🎭 🍴 🖥 🛍

SHAKESPEARE'S GLOBE

⊙ L5 **⌂ 21 New Globe Walk SE1** **⊜ Blackfriars, London Bridge, Mansion House** **⊙ Tours every 30 min 9:30am-12:30pm; book online** **🕐 24 & 25 Dec** **Ⓦ shakespearesglobe.com**

To see a Shakespeare play at the reconstructed Globe is a magical experience. Time-travel to the 1600s and watch Romeo woo Juliet, Beatrice and Benedick squabble, and Hamlet seek revenge.

Built along the south bank of the Thames, Shakespeare's Globe is a fine reconstruction of the Elizabethan theatre where many of the famous playwright's works were first performed. The circular wooden structure is open in the middle, leaving some of the audience exposed to the elements. Those holding seated tickets enjoy a roof over their heads. Performances (staged from mid-April until mid-October) are thrilling, with first-rate acting. A second theatre, the Sam Wanamaker Playhouse, is a splendidly atmospheric, candlelit reproduction of a Jacobean indoor theatre, with performances year-round. Lively tours take you into the theatre itself, telling the story of the original 1599 theatre, its 1614 replacement and Wanamaker's bold reconstruction in the 1990s. Tours of the Sam Wanamaker Playhouse are also sporadically run; check the website for details.

↑ The theatre, built with green oak beams and lime plaster to replicate the 1599 original

💬 INSIDER TIP
Wrap Up

Got tickets? Dress warmly: plays tend to run for several hours and even during the summer months London evenings can be very cool.

① A performance at the Globe is always a lively experience.

② The ornate and intimate Sam Wanamaker Playhouse is indoors.

③ The roof of the Globe is made of water reed thatch. There has been a law banning the use of thatch in the city since the Great Fire of London in 1666, so the theatre had to line the roof with fire-retardant material in order to gain special permission to use it.

Did You Know?

The original Globe Theatre burned down in 1613, when stage cannon fire ignited the roof during a performance.

EXPERIENCE MORE

3

Southwark Cathedral

📍 M6 🏠 Montague Close
SE1 🚇 London Bridge
🕐 8:30am–6pm Mon–Sat,
8:30am–5pm Sun
🌐 cathedral.southwark.
anglican.org

This church did not become
a cathedral until 1905 – yet
some parts of it date back to
the 12th century, when the
building was attached to
a priory, and many of its
medieval features remain.
The memorials are quite
fascinating and include a late-
13th-century wooden effigy
of a knight. John Harvard, the
first benefactor of Harvard
University, was baptized here
in 1607 and there is a chapel
named after him.

In the south aisle there's a
memorial to Shakespeare –
who worshipped here – and
above it is a stained-glass
window depicting characters
from his plays. The churchyard
has been landscaped to
create a herb garden, with the
attractive Millennium Courtyard
leading to the riverside.

4

The Old Operating Theatre Museum

📍 M6 🏠 9a St Thomas St
SE1 🚇 London Bridge
🕐 2–5pm Mon, 10:30am–
5pm Tue–Fri & public hols,
noon–4pm Sat & Sun
🌐 oldoperatingtheatre.com

St Thomas' Hospital, one of
the oldest in Britain, stood
here from its foundation in
the 12th century until it was
moved west in 1862. At this
time, nearly all of its buildings
were demolished in order to
make way for the railways. The
women's operating theatre
survived only because it had

↑ Surgical items forming
a *memento mori* at The
Old Operating Theatre

been constructed in a garret
over the hospital church. The
UK's oldest operating theatre,
dating from 1822, it remained
forgotten until the 1950s. It
has now been fitted out just
as it would have been in the
early 19th century, before the
discovery of either antiseptics
or anaesthetics. Another
section of the garret, which
was once used by the hospital
apothecary to store herbs, has
a collection of traditional herbs
and remedies, plus displays of
antiquated medicines.

5

Bankside Gallery

📍 L5 🏠 48 Hopton St SE1
🚇 Blackfriars, Southwark
🕐 11am–6pm daily during
exhibitions 🔒 1 Jan, 24–26
Dec 🌐 banksidegallery.com

This modern riverside gallery
is the headquarters of two
historic British societies: the
Royal Watercolour Society and
the Royal Society of Painter-
Printmakers. The members of

← The tower and east end of
Southwark Cathedral, built in
golden sandstone and flint

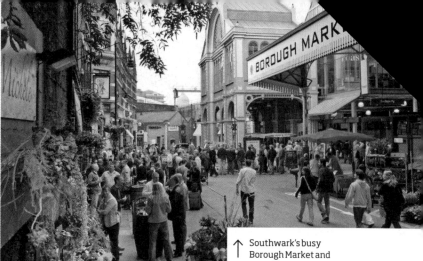

↑ Southwark's busy Borough Market and surrounding area

these societies are elected by their peers in a tradition that dates back over 200 years. The exhibitions held here feature the work of both societies and many of the pieces on display are for sale. There is also a superb specialist art shop that sells both books and materials.

There is an unparalleled view of St Paul's Cathedral from the nearby pub, the Founders' Arms – built on the site of the foundry where the cathedral's bells were cast.

6 Borough Market

M6 **8 Southwark St SE1** **London Bridge** **10am–5pm Mon–Thu, 10am–6pm Fri, 8am–5pm Sat (Dec: also 10am–4pm Sun)** **Some stalls Mon & Tue** **boroughmarket.org.uk**

Borough Market has existed in some form or another for over a thousand years. It moved to its current position in 1756 and became one of Britain's biggest fruit and vegetable markets after the arrival of the railways in the 19th century. Today, it's an extremely popular fine-food market (beware: the crowds can be huge, especially on Fridays and Saturdays), known for gourmet goods, as well as quality fruit and vegetables, and organic meat, fish and dairy produce. A number of hot-food stalls, selling a tempting array of dishes from around the world, also share the space. Food demonstrations take place in the glass atrium on Borough High Street on Thursdays and Fridays. The specialist food shops and pubs on the streets around the market are also well worth checking out.

7 The Rose Playhouse

M6 **56 Park St SE1** **London Bridge** **Noon–4pm Sat** **rosetheatre.org.uk**

In 1989 the remains of the Rose theatre, dating from Elizabethan times, were discovered during excavations ahead of building work for a new office block. The Rose, built in 1587, was the first of the Bankside theatres, and it staged plays by Shakespeare and Christopher Marlowe. The site of the original Globe theatre was just over the road on Park Street (a plaque marks the spot). Preserved in a specially designed space, with a modern building overhead, the archaeological remains are submerged in water, with lights indicating the shape of the theatre. A small volunteer-run exhibition tells the story of the excavation. The atmospheric space is also sometimes used as a small theatre – check the website for details.

DRINK

The George

The only remaining galleried coaching inn in London. Enjoy a pint of ale in the courtyard seating area.

M6 **75–77 Borough High St SE1** **greene king-pubs.co.uk**

The Anchor

Ales have been quaffed here for centuries. Originally dating from 1615, the present 18th-century premises has a fine canopied terrace from which to admire the river views.

M6 **34 Park St SE1** **greeneking-pubs.co.uk**

Scary skeletons
spooking visitors at the
Clink Prison Museum ↑

EAT

Roast

Traditional British food
at its best in a smart
dining room overlooking
Borough Market.

📍M6 🏠The Floral Hall,
Stoney St SE1 🌐roast-
restaurant.com

£££

Flat Iron Square

A sociable hub for street
food and quality
independent fast-food
restaurants in the
railway arches near
Borough Market.

📍M6 🏠68 Union St SE1
🌐flatironsquare.co.uk

£££

The Garrison

The seasonal British
menu served here is
a mixture of the
creatively modern and
the satisfyingly
traditional.

📍N7 🏠99–101
Bermondsey St SE1
🌐thegarrison.co.uk

£££

8

Clink Prison Museum

📍M6 🏠1 Clink St SE1
🚇London Bridge ⏰Jul–Sep:
10am–7:30pm Mon–Fri,
10am–9pm Sat & Sun; Oct–
Jun: 10am–6pm Mon–Fri,
10am–7:30pm Sat & Sun
🌐clink.co.uk

The prison that was once
located here was founded
in the 12th century. It was
owned by successive Bishops
of Winchester, who lived in
the adjoining palace, of which
little remains now aside from
the lovely rose window on
Clink Street. During the 15th
century, the prison became
known as the "Clink", and this
has become a British slang
term for any prison or jail cell.
It closed down in 1780.

The museum alongside the
remains of the palace illustrates
the history of the prison. Tales
are told of the inmates incarce-
rated here, including prostitutes, debtors, and religious
dissenters who sailed on the
Mayflower. Visitors can handle
instruments of torture that
leave little to the imagination –
not for the faint-hearted.

9

The Shard

📍N6 🏠London Bridge St
🚇London Bridge ⏰The
View from the Shard:
10am–10pm daily (last
adm: 9pm; sometimes
closes earlier for events)
🗓25 Dec 🌐theviewfrom
theshard.com

Designed by Renzo Piano, the
Shard is the tallest building
in Western Europe. At 310 m
(1,016 ft) high with a crystalline
façade, the 95-storey tower
houses offices, restaurants –
several with incredible views –
a five-star hotel, exclusive
apartments and the country's
highest observation gallery,
the View from the Shard.

→

The Shard, rising up
behind the visor-
shaped City Hall

Take a high-speed lift from the entrance on Joiner Street to the top of the building for spectacular, unobstructed views of the capital. There are two viewing floors, the higher of which is right among the "shards" with the breeze blowing overhead.

10

Bermondsey Street

📍N7 🏠SE1 🚇London Bridge, Borough

Bermondsey's winding streets still hold traces of its past in the form of medieval, 18th-century and Victorian buildings. Today, Bermondsey Street is home to galleries, coffee shops and a few great restaurants. The area is also famous for its antiques market, held in Bermondsey Square at the bottom end of the street. Each Friday morning from 6am, seriously committed antiques dealers trade their latest acquisitions, and the best bargains tend to go before most people are even awake.

The **Fashion and Textile Museum** at No 83 puts on a programme of exhibitions covering all aspects of fashion and design, and also runs an education programme. Further along the street,

White Cube Bermondsey is a major space for international contemporary art.

Fashion and Textile Museum

⊕🏠🕐11am-6pm Tue-Sat (to 8pm Thu), 11am-5pm Sun 🌐ftmlondon.org

---

11 🖥

City Hall

📍O6 🏠The Queen's Walk SE1 🚇London Bridge 🕐8:30am-6pm Mon-Thu, 8:30am-5:30pm Fri 🌐london.gov.uk/about-us

The Norman Foster-designed domed glass building just by Tower Bridge is the head-quarters for London's mayor and the Greater London Authority. Anyone can visit the building and head up the walkway to the second floor to look in on the assembly chamber, or sit in on Mayor's Question Time, when assembly members interrogate the mayor on London issues; this takes place ten times a year on Thursday mornings (check website for dates). On the lower ground floor are temporary exhibitions and a café. Outside, the stone amphi-theatre known as

the Scoop hosts free events in summer, including plays, music and screenings.

12

HMS Belfast

📍N6 🏠The Queen's Walk SE1 🚇London Bridge, Tower Hill 🕐10am-6pm daily (last adm: 5pm) 🚫24-26 Dec 🌐iwm.org. uk/visits/hms-belfast

Launched in 1938 to serve in World War II, HMS *Belfast* was instrumental in the destruction of the German battle cruiser *Scharnhorst* in the Battle of North Cape, and also played a role in the Normandy landings.

After the war, the battle cruiser was sent to work for UN naval forces during the Korean War, and remained in service with the Royal Navy until 1965. The only surviving World War II cruiser, it has been used as a floating naval museum since 1971.

Visitors can climb down ladders to the engine room 4.5 m (15 ft) below sea level, and experience what it was like in the gun turrets during a battle. Interactive exhibits explore the ship's 80-year history with stories from some of its veterans. Due to reno-vation work it is not expected to open until late 2021.

A SHORT WALK
SOUTHWARK

Distance 2 km (1.5 miles) **Time** 25 minutes
Nearest Tube Blackfriars

Out of the jurisdiction of the City authorities, Southwark was the place for illicit pleasures from medieval times until the 18th century. The 18th and 19th centuries brought new business, and docks, warehouses and factories

were built to meet the demand. Today, a riverside walk here provides spectacular views of St Paul's and the Shard, and takes in the Tate Modern, a regenerated Borough Market and the re-creation of Shakespeare's Globe Theatre.

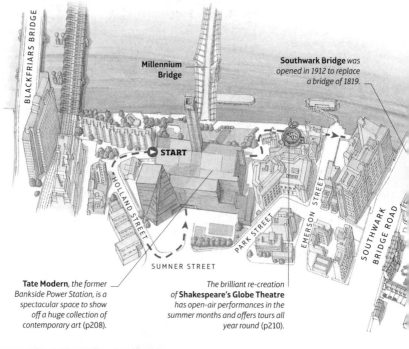

BLACKFRIARS BRIDGE

Millennium Bridge

Southwark Bridge *was opened in 1912 to replace a bridge of 1819.*

▶ **START**

HOLLAND STREET

PARK STREET

EMERSON STREET

SOUTHWARK BRIDGE ROAD

SUMNER STREET

Tate Modern, *the former Bankside Power Station, is a spectacular space to show off a huge collection of contemporary art (p208).*

The brilliant re-creation of **Shakespeare's Globe Theatre** *has open-air performances in the summer months and offers tours all year round (p210).*

0 metres 100
0 yards 100
N ↑

←
One Two Three Swing! by SUPERFLEX at the Tate Modern

The historic Anchor pub, a popular drinking establishment since the time of Shakespeare

SOUTHWARK AND BANKSIDE

Locator Map
For more detail see p206

Clink Prison Museum, *on the site of the notorious old prison, looks back at Southwark's colourful past (p214).*

The riverside **Anchor** *pub has been a firm favourite for centuries (p213).*

14th-century rose window

The **Golden Hinde II** *is a replica of Sir Francis Drake's galleon built in the 1970s; it sailed the globe for several decades before docking here.*

London Bridge, *in its various forms, was the only river crossing in London from Roman times until 1750. The present bridge, completed in 1972, replaced the one of 1831.*

BANK END

PARK STREET

CLINK STREET

STREET

MONTAGUE CLOSE

CATHEDRAL STREET

LONDON BRIDGE

Despite major alterations, **Southwark Cathedral** *still contains medieval elements (p212).*

There has been a market on or near the site of **Borough Market** *since around 1014 (p213).*

SOUTHWARK STREET

BOROUGH HIGH STREET

ST THOMAS STREET

FINISH

The **Hop Exchange** *was where hops from Kent for brewing were traded; its pediment features carved scenes of the hop harvest.*

The **War Memorial**, *commemorating soldiers who fell in World War I, was erected in 1924 on Borough High Street.*

The **George** *is London's only surviving traditional galleried inn (p213).*

SOUTH BANK

It was not until the 18th century that the stretch of marshy land over the river from Westminster, opposite what would later become the Victoria Embankment, was drained and developed, and referred to as the South Bank. Pleasure gardens gave way to industrialization, and by the late 1830s the riverfront was dominated by the Lion Brewery, which stood here until it was demolished in 1949, by which time it had already been abandoned. After World War II the land lay bomb-damaged and derelict until London County Council decided to develop it for the 1951 Festival of Britain. Conceived as a much-needed tonic for a war-worn population, a large exhibition site full of cultural and leisure venues and installations was created for the festival. The only permanent construction was the Royal Festival Hall, and the Southbank Centre, which now dominates the site, grew up around that building. It was in the spirit of the Festival of Britain that the new millennium was marked on the South Bank with the raising of the London Eye, a gigantic ferris wheel.

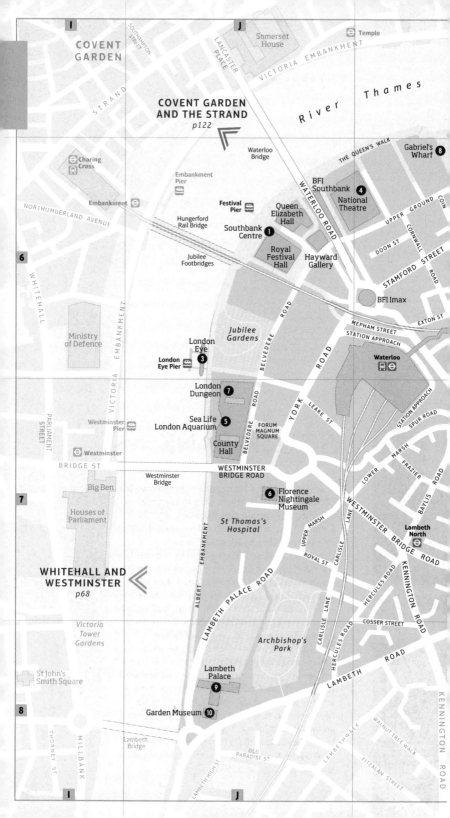

COVENT
GARDEN

I

J

SOUTHAMPTON STREET

LANCASTER PLACE

Somerset
House

Temple

VICTORIA EMBANKMENT

River   Thames

**COVENT GARDEN
AND THE STRAND**
p122

Waterloo
Bridge

THE QUEEN'S WALK

Gabriel's
Wharf 8

Charing
Cross

Embankment
Pier

BFI
Southbank 4

UPPER GROUND

COIN STREET

NORTHUMBERLAND AVENUE

Embankment

Hungerford
Rail Bridge

**Festival
Pier**

Queen
Elizabeth
Hall

National
Theatre

CORNWALL STREET

DOON ST

STAMFORD STREET

WATERLOO ROAD

Jubilee
Footbridges

**Southbank
Centre** 1

Royal
Festival
Hall

Hayward
Gallery

6

WHITEHALL

VICTORIA EMBANKMENT

BFI Imax

MEPHAM STREET

STATION APPROACH

EXTON ST

Ministry
of Defence

*Jubilee
Gardens*

BELVEDERE ROAD

Waterloo

London
Eye

**London
Eye Pier** 3

London
Dungeon 7

YORK ROAD

LEAKE ST

STATION APPROACH

SPUR ROAD

PARLIAMENT STREET

Westminster
Pier

VICTORIA EMBANKMENT

Sea Life
London Aquarium 5

BELVEDERE ROAD

FORUM
MAGNUM
SQUARE

MARSH

FRAZIER ROAD

Westminster

County
Hall

**WESTMINSTER
BRIDGE ROAD**

LOWER MARSH

BAYLIS ROAD

BRIDGE ST

Westminster
Bridge

7

Big Ben

Houses of
Parliament

Florence
Nightingale
Museum 6

*St Thomas's
Hospital*

UPPER MARSH

CARLISLE LANE

WESTMINSTER BRIDGE ROAD

Lambeth
North

ROYAL ST

**WHITEHALL AND
WESTMINSTER**
p68

ALBERT EMBANKMENT

LAMBETH PALACE ROAD

CARLISLE LANE

HERCULES ROAD

KENNINGTON ROAD

*Victoria
Tower
Gardens*

*Archbishop's
Park*

COSSER STREET

HERCULES ROAD

THORNEY ST

St John's
Smith Square

Lambeth
Palace 9

LAMBETH ROAD

8

MILLBANK

Garden Museum 10

Lambeth
Bridge

LAMBETH HIGH ST

OLD
PARADISE ST

LAMBETH WALK

WALNUT TREE WALK

FITZALAN STREET

KENNINGTON ROAD

I

J

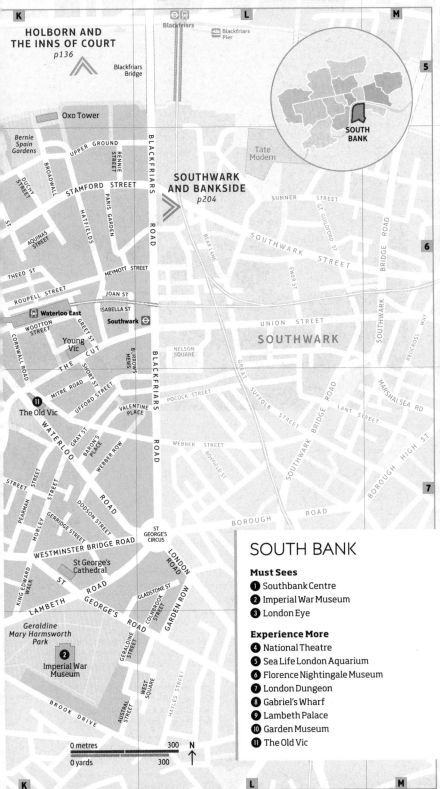

HOLBORN AND
THE INNS OF COURT
p136

Blackfriars

Blackfriars
Pier

Blackfriars
Bridge

SOUTH
BANK

Oxo Tower

*Bernie
Spain
Gardens*

UPPER GROUND

RENNIE STREET

BLACKFRIARS

Tate
Modern

DUCHY STREET

BROADWALL

STAMFORD STREET

PARIS GARDEN

HATFIELDS

ROAD

SOUTHWARK
AND BANKSIDE
p204

SUMNER   STREET

GT GUILDFORD ST

BRIDGE   ROAD

6

ST

AQUINAS STREET

THEED ST

MEYMOTT STREET

BEAR LANE

SOUTHWARK

STREET

EWER ST

ROUPELL STREET

JOAN ST

ISABELLA ST

UNION   STREET

Waterloo East

Southwark

SOUTHWARK

SOUTHWARK WAY

WOOTTON
STREET

GREEN ST

THE CUT

Young
Vic

SHORT ST

BURROWS MEWS

NELSON
SQUARE

CORNWALL ROAD

MITRE ROAD

UFFORD STREET

POCOCK STREET

GREAT

REDCROSS WAY

The Old Vic

GRAY ST

BARONS PLACE

VALENTINE
PLACE

WEBBER   STREET

SUFFOLK

STREET

BRIDGE

ROAD

LANT STREET

MARSHALSEA RD

7

WATERLOO

WEBBER ROW

BOYFIELD ST

SOUTHWARK

BOROUGH HIGH ST

STREET

PEARMAN STREET

MORLEY STREET

GERRIDGE STREET

DODSON STREET

ROAD

WESTMINSTER BRIDGE ROAD

ST
GEORGE'S
CIRCUS

LONDON

BOROUGH   ROAD

St George's
Cathedral

GLADSTONE ST

KING EDWARD WALK

LAMBETH

ST

GEORGE'S

ROAD

ROAD

COLNBROOK STREET

GARDEN ROW

*Geraldine
Mary Harmsworth
Park*

GERALDINE STREET

Imperial War
Museum

WEST
SQUARE

HAYLES STREET

BROOK   DRIVE

AUSTRAL STREET

0 metres ———— 300

0 yards ———— 300

N ↑

SOUTH BANK

Must Sees

❶ Southbank Centre

❷ Imperial War Museum

❸ London Eye

Experience More

❹ National Theatre

❺ Sea Life London Aquarium

❻ Florence Nightingale Museum

❼ London Dungeon

❽ Gabriel's Wharf

❾ Lambeth Palace

❿ Garden Museum

⓫ The Old Vic

Did You Know?

The foundation stone of the Royal Festival Hall was laid in 1949 by Prime Minister Clement Attlee.

SOUTHBANK CENTRE

J6 **Belvedere Rd, South Bank SE1** **Waterloo, Embankment** **Waterloo, Waterloo East, Charing Cross** **Festival Pier, London Eye Pier** **southbankcentre.co.uk**

With a major art gallery and three world-class auditoriums for music, dance and other events lined up along the river, the Southbank Centre is one of London's pre-eminent cultural and performance venues.

London's high-profile, much-respected and visited multi-dimensional arts centre takes centre stage among the other great arts institutions on the South Bank: the National Theatre and the British Film Institute. The Southbank Centre itself comprises four main venues: the Royal Festival Hall, the Hayward Gallery, the Queen Elizabeth Hall and the Purcell Room. The centre's always buzzing, with bustling bars and restaurants slotted into and between the terraces, platforms, walkways and rooftops of this concrete complex. There are always innumerable visitors making their way to performances, primarily of classical music but also of opera, folk, world music and all kinds of contemporary leftfield genres. Comedy, talks and dance all feature too, while there is a multitude of regular festivals, seasons and weekends staged here, including the London Jazz Festival, Women of the World (WOW) Festival, the London Literature Festival and Meltdown.

Crowds enjoying the
sun outside the Queen
Elizabeth Hall

Strolling along the riverfront past
the Southbank Centre, towards the
monumental London Eye

1951 FESTIVAL OF BRITAIN

The 1951 Festival of Britain was timed
to mark the centenary of the Great
Exhibition but also to provide some
optimism and cultural celebration in
the aftermath of war. The wharves and
factories that once stood on this site
suffered considerable bomb damage
during World War II, so the area was
cleared for the event and a set of weird
and wonderful temporary structures
were erected in their place, forming a
kind of cultural theme park. The one
permanent structure was the Royal
Festival Hall.

The South Bank

Hugging the curve of the River Thames, the Southbank Centre is a sprawling complex with the Royal Festival Hall at its heart. Just a little further along the bank are the enormous London Eye and County Hall, home to other top attractions – the London Dungeon and the London Aquarium. There is plenty to entertain here, making it perfect for a gentle afternoon.

EAT

Southbank Centre Food Market

This excellent little food market is located to the rear of the Royal Festival Hall. A wide range of street eats is available, from pizzas and curries to Korean BBQ and Ethiopian vegan food, as well as treats to take home, like wine, cheese and jam.

◨ Noon–8pm Fri, 11am–8pm Sat, noon–6pm Sun & public hols

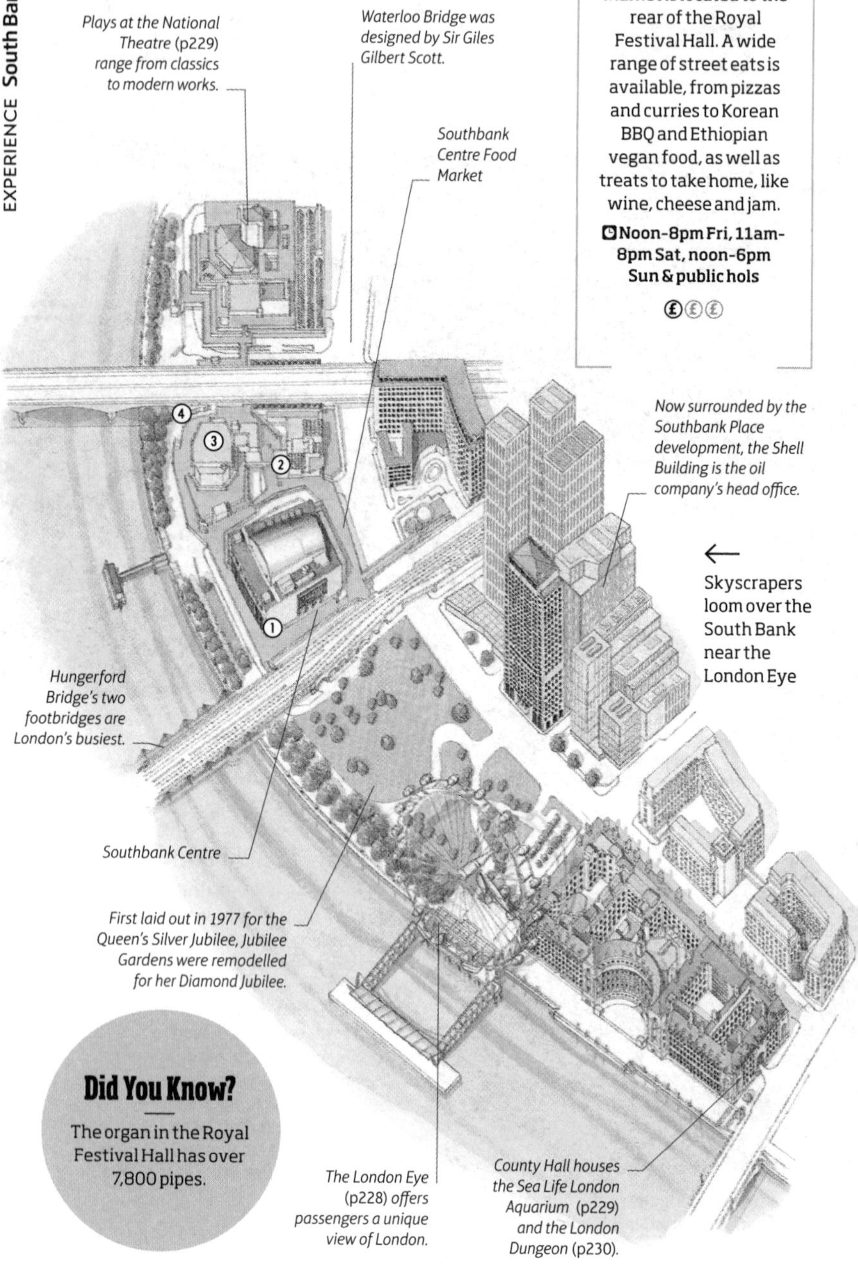

ⓕⓔⓕ

Plays at the National Theatre (p229) range from classics to modern works.

Waterloo Bridge was designed by Sir Giles Gilbert Scott.

Southbank Centre Food Market

Now surrounded by the Southbank Place development, the Shell Building is the oil company's head office.

← Skyscrapers loom over the South Bank near the London Eye

Hungerford Bridge's two footbridges are London's busiest.

Southbank Centre

First laid out in 1977 for the Queen's Silver Jubilee, Jubilee Gardens were remodelled for her Diamond Jubilee.

Did You Know?

The organ in the Royal Festival Hall has over 7,800 pipes.

The London Eye (p228) offers passengers a unique view of London.

County Hall houses the Sea Life London Aquarium (p229) and the London Dungeon (p230).

1 The Southbank Centre Food Market takes place on Fridays, Saturdays and Sundays, in the square behind the Royal Festival Hall.

2 The concrete exterior of the Hayward Gallery is well suited to the modern works that it displays within. The building's stark design is a landmark of Brutalist architecture.

3 BFI Southbank, previously the National Film Theatre, was originally established to show historic films; today it offers an eclectic programme of films from around the world.

① 🍴 🖥 🏛
Royal Festival Hall

📍 J6 🕐 10am–11pm daily

With its 2,500-seat auditorium, this modernist building is the Southbank Centre's largest concert hall and one of the city's best classical music venues. The airy halls outside the auditorium house the free-access Clore Ballroom, where concerts are frequently staged in sight of the casual bar. The foyer is also used for exhibitions and contains a café, while the Skylon restaurant sits on the third floor. In summer, pop-up venues and bars are installed and DJ-led parties take place on the riverside terrace.

② 🎨 🖥 🏛
Hayward Gallery

📍 J6 🕐 11am–7pm Wed–Mon (to 9pm Thu)

Reopened in 2018 after a lengthy refurbishment, the Hayward Gallery, an icon of 1960s Brutalist architecture with its slabby grey concrete exterior and distinctive pyramidal glass roof panels, is one of London's foremost venues for large, often provocative, contemporary art exhibitions. The gallery exhibits paintings, drawings, photography, sculpture, installation art and more, by interesting, innovative and internationally renowned artists from around the world. Paul Klee, Andreas Gursky, Bridget Riley and Anthony Caro are among the artists who have had exhibitions here.

③ 🖥
Queen Elizabeth Hall and Purcell Room

📍 J6 🕐 10am–11pm daily

Inaugurated in 1967, the Queen Elizabeth Hall reopened in 2018 after extensive reno-vations. Smaller orchestral performances, genre-bending music and dance, stand-up comedy, spoken word poetry and literary events are all staged in this relatively intimate, comfortable concert venue. The Purcell Room, in the same building, is smaller still and also hosts readings, while its music events tend to be small ensembles, piano recitals, chamber music and the like. The foyer is also regularly used as a performance venue, hosting free events as well as occasional club nights.

④ 🍴 🖥 🏛
BFI Southbank

📍 J6 🌐 bfi.org.uk

BFI Southbank, previously the National Film Theatre, was established in 1953, and though adjacent to the Southbank Centre it's not actually part of it. It has four cinema screens and offers a huge and diverse selection of films, both British and international. It also holds regular screenings of rare and restored films and television programmes and has a free Mediatheque where the BFI's archives can be browsed.

Did You Know?

During the "Blitz" in World War II, bombs fell on London for 76 consecutive nights.

WH725

↑ Military aircraft on display in the main atrium at the Imperial War Museum

2 Ⓜ 🍴 🖥 🛍

IMPERIAL WAR MUSEUM

📍K8 🚇Lambeth Rd SE1 ⊜Waterloo, Lambeth North, Elephant & Castle
🚆Waterloo, Elephant & Castle 🕐10am–6pm daily (last adm to the
Holocaust Gallery: 5:30pm) 🚫24–26 Dec 🖥iwm.org.uk

With great creativity and sensitivity, the immersive exhibitions at
the terrific Imperial War Museum provide a fascinating insight into
the history of war and themes of conflict.

Inevitably the two World Wars feature heavily at the Imperial
War Museum, but they are covered in innovative ways. In the
First World War Galleries a re-created trench vividly evokes
the experience of fighting at the front. The museum's main
galleries covering World War II, including the particularly
poignant exhibition dedicated to the Holocaust, are under-
going major expansion programmes, reappraising these
pivotal events in light of the latest research and archive
releases, and expected to be completed in 2021. Other highly
original permanent displays include Curiosities of War, which
is full of unexpected items such as a sofa made by troops in
Afghanistan out of HESCO bastion fencing. More conventionally,
there are tanks, artillery and aircraft, including a Mark 1 Spitfire
and a Harrier jet, on show in the main atrium.

> 💬 INSIDER TIP
> **Get a Guide**
>
> There is a guide book
> to the museum aimed
> specifically at children
> aged 7 and above. There
> are also daily 40-minute
> tours (£10, children £5;
> check website for times)
> that introduce the
> collections. Tickets can
> be bought in person.

① The museum is housed in
what used to be the Bethlem
Royal Hospital for the Insane
(commonly known as "Bedlam"),
built in 1811.

② Military hardware on display
includes a T-34 World War II
Soviet tank captured in
1973 by Israeli forces.

③ Hanging in the atrium is the
famous Battle of Britain fighter
plane, the Spitfire, from 1940.

80 spokes
made from
6 km (3.7 miles)
of tensioned
cable support
the wheel.

The wheel
rim was
floated down
the Thames
in sections.

The glass
capsules are
mounted on
the outside of
the rim.

The Eye turns slowly
enough that the
capsules are boarded
while they are moving.

↑ Illustration of
the London Eye,
on the South Bank

③ 🗺️

THE LONDON EYE

📍J6 🚇Jubilee Gardens SE1 🚉Waterloo, Westminster ⏰From 10am daily; closing times between 6pm and 9:30pm, check website for details 🔧Two weeks in Jan for maintenance 🌐londoneye.com

Stunning views of London's historic skyline can be had from the glass capsules of the city's famous ferris wheel, the London Eye. Situated right beside the River Thames, it gives visitors a 360-degree view of the city.

The London Eye is a 135-m- (443-ft-) high observation wheel. Opened in 2000 as part of London's millennium celebrations, it immediately became one of the city's most recognizable landmarks, notable not only for its size, but for its circularity amid the block-shaped buildings flanking it. Thirty-two capsules, each holding up to 25 people, take a gentle 30-minute round trip. On a clear day, the Eye affords a 40-km (25-mile) view over the capital in all directions and out to the countryside beyond.

BOOKING TICKETS

Queues for the London Eye can be long, so make sure to pre-book your tickets online to secure a timed slot and to make the most of online offers. For those who plan to visit more sites around the city, multi-attraction tickets, combining a trip on the Eye with various other London attractions, carry heavy discounts.

↑ A capsule mid-tour with unimpeded views of the city

↑ Taking a selfie against the London skyline

↑ The London Eye peering over the River Thames

EXPERIENCE MORE

④ ⓂⓎ🍴🖼🏛

National Theatre

📍K6 🚪South Bank SE1 🚇Waterloo 🕐9:30am–11pm Mon–Sat (Sherling Walkway closes 7:30pm) 📅24 & 25 Dec 🌐national theatre.org.uk

Even if you don't want to see a play, this complex is worth a visit, especially for a backstage tour. These are offered Monday to Saturday, and should be booked in advance. You can also get a glimpse of the backstage area from the Sherling High-Level Walkway (entrance near the Dorfman Theatre), which runs above the prop-building areas.

Sir Denys Lasdun's building opened in 1976 after 200 years of debate: should there be a national theatre and, if so, where? The theatre company was formed in 1963, under Laurence (later Lord) Olivier. The largest of the three theatres is named after him; the others are the Dorfman and the Lyttleton. Prestigious productions are streamed live to theatres and cinemas all over the UK, and occasionally the world, via the National Theatre Live initiative, as well as taken on tours.

⑤ 🐟Ⓜ🖼🏛

Sea Life London Aquarium

📍J7 🚪County Hall, Westminster Bridge Rd SE1 🚇Waterloo 🕐10am–6pm Mon–Fri, 9:30am–7pm Sat, Sun & summer hols (last adm: 6pm) 🌐visitsealife.com/london

Once the home of London's elected government, County Hall now houses the Sea Life London Aquarium and London Dungeon (p230), alongside two hotels and other themed attractions.

The aquarium is home to myriad aquatic species, such as stingrays, turtles, jellyfish, starfish and penguins. There's a 25-m (82-ft) glass tunnel walkway through a tropical ocean environment, and a large tank housing numerous shark species, which you can view from several levels. Book ahead for discounts and to skip large queues.

↑ The controversial Brutalist architecture of the National Theatre

↑ A bust of Florence Nightingale in nursing cape and bonnet

6 Florence Nightingale Museum

J7 ⏷ 2 Lambeth Palace Rd SE1 ⏷ Waterloo, Westminster ⏷ 10am-5pm daily ⏷ 1 Jan, 21-27 & 31 Dec ⏷ florence-nightingale. co.uk

This determined woman captured the nation's imagination as the "Lady of the Lamp" who nursed the wounded soldiers of the Crimean War (1853–6). She founded the country's first school of nursing at old St Thomas' Hospital in 1860, and revolutionized modern nursing. She was also an advocate for women in the workplace.

Sited near the entrance to St Thomas' Hospital, this museum gives an account of Nightingale's career through displays of original documents and personal memorabilia. They illustrate her life and the developments she pioneered in health care, until her death in 1910 at the age of 90. Tours are daily at 3:30pm, plus at 11:30am on weekends.

→ Riverside shopping and refreshment at Gabriel's Wharf

7 London Dungeon

J7 ⏷ County Hall, Westminster Bridge Rd SE1 ⏷ Waterloo ⏷ 10am-5pm Sun-Fri (from 11am Thu), 10am-6pm Sat; extended hours in school holidays ⏷ 25 Dec ⏷ thedungeons.com

This scary attraction is a great hit with older children. Illustrating the most bloodthirsty events in British history with live actors and special effects, the dungeon plays strictly for terror, and screams abound during the 90-minute tour. Gory scenes recount tales of such characters as Guy Fawkes and Jack the Ripper. Don't miss the Tyrant Boat Ride along a black River Thames to find out what happened to Tudor queen Anne Boleyn and her co-conspirators.

8 Gabriel's Wharf

K6 ⏷ 56 Upper Ground SE1 ⏷ Waterloo

This pleasant enclave of boutiques, craft shops and cafés was the product of a long and stormy debate over the future of what was once an industrial riverside area. Residents of Waterloo strongly opposed various schemes for office developments before a community association was able to acquire the site in 1984 and build cooperative housing.

Adjoining the market area is a small public garden with grass to sit on and a river pier with fine views of the City. The Oxo Tower to the east was adapted from an older power station in 1928 to surreptitiously advertise a well-known meat extract by means of its window shapes. It now houses galleries and design shops on the lower floors and a bar, restaurant and brasserie on the top floor (p51).

GREAT VIEW
Waterloo Bridge

Making any Londoner's list of favourite views is this one from a busy bridge spanning the Thames. Whether you look up or down river, the scene in front of you is a reminder of the beauty of Britain's capital city.

↑ The centuries-old Lambeth Palace and its grounds

9

Lambeth Palace

📍 J8 🏠 SE1 🚇 Lambeth North, Westminster, Waterloo, Vauxhall 🕐 For tours only 🌐 archbishopof canterbury.org

This Grade I-listed palace has housed Archbishops of Canterbury since the 13th century and today remains the archbishop's official London residence. The chapel and its undercroft contain elements from the 13th century, but a large part of the rest of the building is far more recent. It has been frequently restored, including by Edward Blore in 1828. The Tudor gatehouse dates from 1485 and is one of the city's most familiar riverside landmarks.

The garden, planted with many mature trees, is open on the first Friday of the month in summer, while you can visit the palace year-round by pre-booking a place on a guided tour (check website).

Until the first Westminster Bridge was built, the horse ferry that operated between here and Millbank was a principal river crossing. The revenues from this ferry went to the archbishop.

10

Garden Museum

📍 J8 🏠 5 Lambeth Palace Rd SE1 🚇 Waterloo, Lambeth North, Westminster 🕐 10:30am–5pm daily 🚫 1st Mon of month; 25 Dec–5 Jan 🌐 garden museum.org.uk

The world's first museum of garden history is housed in the restored church of St Mary of Lambeth Palace, where it is set around a central knot garden. In the grounds are the tombs of John Tradescant, father and son, who, as well as being gardeners to Charles I and Charles II, were adventurous plant hunters. The tomb of William Bligh of HMS *Bounty*, the ship set adrift in the Pacific Ocean after the fateful mutiny, can also be seen here. Coincidentally, his vessel had been on a plant-collecting voyage.

The museum presents a history of gardening in Britain, including objects collected by the Tradescants, and an archive of garden design. It also runs a programme of exhibitions and events, and has an excellent shop and café. During renovations in 2017, which created a new garden and opened up the church tower for the first time, a vault was discovered containing 30 lead coffins.

11 🅼 💻

The Old Vic

📍 K7 🏠 Waterloo Rd SE1 🚇 Waterloo 🕐 For performances and tours 🌐 oldvictheatre.com

Established as the Royal Coburg Theatre in 1818, this splendid building changed its name to the Royal Victoria in 1833 in honour of the future queen. The theatre became a centre for music hall, the immensely popular Victorian entertainment. In 1912, Lillian Baylis became manager and from 1914 to 1923 staged all of Shakespeare's plays here.

In 2003 the Old Vic Theatre Company was set up as the resident company, and although tickets can be pricey, there are cheap seats for younger people. Fascinating theatre tours take place around once a month, and are full of backstage snippets and anecdotes.

Did You Know?

Despite the fact that it was named in her honour, Queen Victoria only visited the Old Vic once, aged 14.

CHELSEA AND BATTERSEA

Chelsea was last in vogue in the 1960s when showy young shoppers, including the Rolling Stones, paraded along the King's Road. Formerly a riverside village, it first became fashionable in Tudor times, with Henry VIII liking it so much that he had a small palace (long vanished) built here. In the 18th century it featured renowned riverside pleasure gardens, painted by Canaletto. Later artists, including Turner, Whistler and Rossetti, were attracted by the river views from Cheyne Walk over to Battersea. From the mid-19th century those views featured picturesque Battersea Park, whose landscaping was enhanced in 1951 when it too was laid out as pleasure gardens for the Festival of Britain. In graceless but impressive contrast, just east of Chelsea Bridge, the colossal chimneys of Battersea Power Station clouded the skies with smoke between its opening in 1933 and its decommissioning in 1983. Decades of failed bids to make use of the vast site – including turning it into a theme park and football stadium – ensued until a Malaysian consortium bought it for £400 million in 2012. It is now part of London's largest area of urban regeneration, stretching down to Vauxhall, featuring apartment blocks, shops and restaurants.

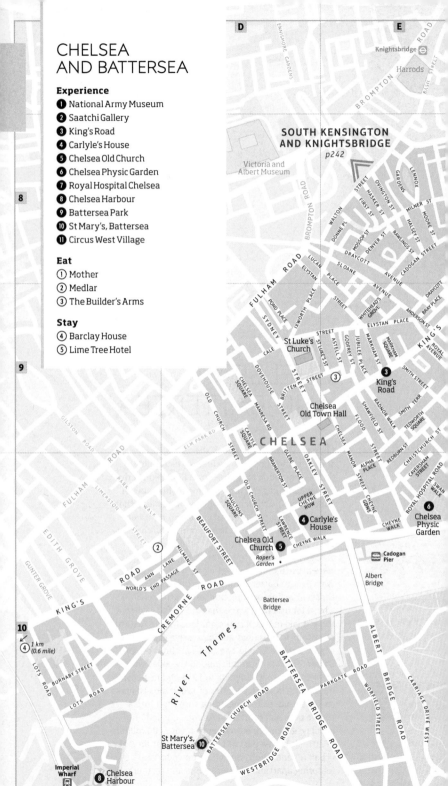

CHELSEA
AND BATTERSEA

Experience
1. National Army Museum
2. Saatchi Gallery
3. King's Road
4. Carlyle's House
5. Chelsea Old Church
6. Chelsea Physic Garden
7. Royal Hospital Chelsea
8. Chelsea Harbour
9. Battersea Park
10. St Mary's, Battersea
11. Circus West Village

Eat
1. Mother
2. Medlar
3. The Builder's Arms

Stay
4. Barclay House
5. Lime Tree Hotel

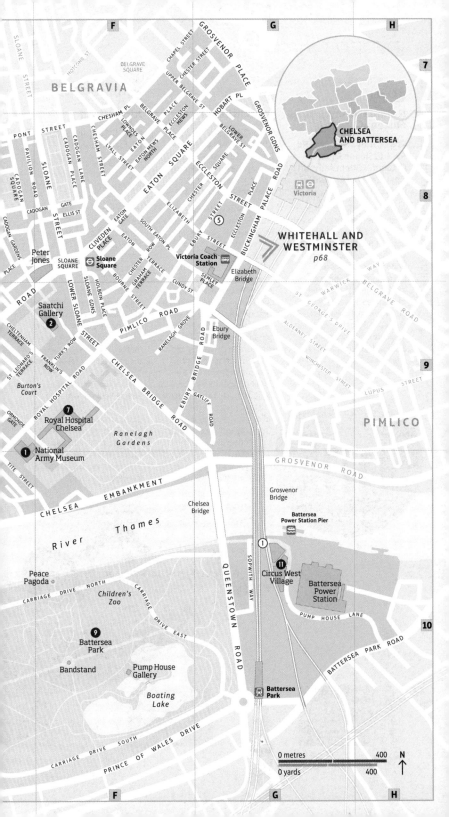

EXPERIENCE

❶
National Army Museum

📍 E9 ⛔ Royal Hospital Rd SW3 ⊜ Sloane Square ⏰ 10am–5.30pm daily, till 8pm first Wed of month 🌐 nam.ac.uk

Adjoining the Royal Hospital Chelsea is the official museum of the British Army, with a collection that spans its 600-year history, including many uniforms, paintings and portraits. Its five galleries explore the role of the armed forces in society. As well as displays of militaria there are some thought-provoking audiovisual presentations and loads of great interactive stuff for kids.

❷
Saatchi Gallery

📍 F9 ⛔ Duke of York's HQ, King's Rd SW3 ⊜ Sloane Square ⏰ 10am–6pm daily (last adm: 5:30pm) 📞 For private events 🌐 saatchigallery.com

Set up by advertising mogul Charles Saatchi in order to showcase his impressive contemporary art acquisitions, the Saatchi Gallery has moved location several times in London. Now, however, it is firmly established in Chelsea at the Duke of York's Headquarters building, which dates from 1801. Saatchi is perhaps best known for his espousal, in the 1980s and 1990s, of the Young British Artists movement led by Damien Hirst. Today, the exhibitions of contemporary art staged here (some of which attract a fee) are wide-ranging and international in scope, covering every-thing from new Chinese artists to Pop Art and rave culture.

❸
King's Road

📍 E9 ⛔ SW3 and SW10 ⊜ Sloane Square

This is Chelsea's central artery, with a wealth of upmarket high-street shops and smaller boutiques. The miniskirt revolution of the 1960s – the birth of so-called "Swinging London" – began here, with Mary Quant's first shop, Bazaar, and so have many subsequent style trends, perhaps the most famous of them being punk.

Look out for the Pheasantry at No 152, with its columns and statuary; built in 1881 as the shopfront of a furniture-maker's premises, it now conceals a pizza restaurant.

At the top of King's Road is attractive 18th-century Sloane Square, named after Sir Hans Sloane, the wealthy physician and collector who bought the manor of Chelsea in 1712. On the east side is the Royal Court Theatre, which for over 130 years has fostered new drama.

STAY

Barclay House

A classy B&B in an exquisite Victorian property, with an impressive attention to detail in the three luxurious guest rooms, from the underfloor heating to the rainforest showers.

C10 **21 Barclay Rd SW6** **barclayhouse london.com**

£ £ £

Lime Tree Hotel

Comfy, spotlessly maintained rooms, each individually decorated and homely, make this large boutique B&B a cut above the rest.

G8 **135 Ebury St SW1** **limetree hotel.co.uk**

£ £ £

4

Carlyle's House

D10 **24 Cheyne Row SW3** **Sloane Square, South Kensington** **Mar-Oct: 11am–5pm Wed-Sun** **nationaltrust.org.uk**

The historian Thomas Carlyle moved into this modest 18th-century house in 1834, and wrote many of his best-known books here, notably *The French Revolution*. His presence at this address made Chelsea more fashionable and the house became a mecca for literary figures, including novelists Charles Dickens and William Thackeray, poet Alfred Lord Tennyson and naturalist Charles Darwin. The house has been restored and looks as it would have done during Carlyle's lifetime.

5

Chelsea Old Church

D10 **64 Cheyne Walk SW3** **Sloane Square, South Kensington** **2–4pm Tue-Thu** **chelseaoldchurch.org.uk**

Rebuilt after World War II, this square-towered building is a careful replica of the medieval church here that was largely destroyed in World War II.

←

The installation Golden Lotus (Inverted) *by Conrad Shawcross, at the Saatchi Gallery (inset)*

↑ Statue of Thomas More located outside Chelsea Old Church

The glory of this church is its Tudor monuments. One to Sir Thomas More, who built a chapel here in 1528, contains an inscription he wrote (in Latin) asking to be buried next to his wife. Among other monuments is a 17th-century memorial to Lady Jane Cheyne, after whose husband Cheyne Walk was named. Outside the church is a statue in memory of More, "statesman, scholar, saint", gazing piously across the river.

6

Chelsea Physic Garden

E10 **66 Royal Hospital Rd SW3** **Sloane Square** **Mar-Oct: 11am–5:30pm Sun-Fri; Nov-Feb: 11am–4pm Mon-Fri** **Five weeks mid-Dec-Jan** **chelsea physicgarden.co.uk**

Established by the Society of Apothecaries in 1673 to study plants for medicinal use, this garden was saved from closure in 1722 by a gift from Sir Hans Sloane, whose statue adorns it. New varieties nurtured in its glasshouses have included cotton sent to the plantations of the southern United States. Visitors to London's oldest botanic garden can see ancient trees and one of Britain's first rock gardens, installed in 1772.

 7 Ⓜ 🖥 🏛

Royal Hospital Chelsea

📍F9 🏠Royal Hospital Rd SW3 🚇Sloane Square
🕐Great Hall: 10am–noon, 2–4pm daily; chapel: 10am–4pm Mon–Sat; museum: 10am–4pm Mon–Fri
🚫2 weeks over Christmas, public hols, for functions
🌐chelsea-pensioners.co.uk

This graceful complex was commissioned by Charles II from Christopher Wren in 1682 as a retirement home for old or wounded soldiers, who have been known as Chelsea Pensioners ever since. The hospital opened ten years later and is still home to about 300 retired soldiers, whose distinctive uniform of scarlet coat and tricorn hat dates from the 17th century. The Pensioners lead guided tours of the hospital on selected days each month (see website).

Flanking the northern entrance are Wren's two main public rooms: the chapel, notable for its wonderful simplicity, and the panelled Great Hall. A small museum covers the history of the Chelsea Pensioners.

A statue of Charles II by Grinling Gibbons is to be found on the terrace outside,

from where there is a fine view of Battersea Power Station across the river.

8 🍴 🖥 🏛

Chelsea Harbour

📍C10 🏠SW10 🚇Fulham Broadway 🚆Imperial Wharf

This is an impressive development of modern apartments, shops, offices, restaurants, a hotel and a marina. It is near the site of Cremorne Pleasure Gardens, which closed in 1877 after more than 40 years as a venue for dances and circuses. The centrepiece of the harbour is the Belvedere, a 20-storey apartment tower with an external glass lift and a pyramid roof, topped with a golden ball on a rod that rises and falls with the tide.

9 🖥

Battersea Park

📍F10 🏠Albert Bridge Rd SW11 🚇Sloane Square then bus 137 🚆Battersea Park 🕐6:30am–10:30pm daily 🌐wandsworth.gov.uk/batterseapark

This was the second public park created to relieve the growing urban stresses of

EAT

Mother

The hip Copenhagen pizza joint has a London outpost under the hangar-like railway arch in Circus West Village.

📍G10 🏠Circus West Village SW11 🌐mother restaurant.co.uk

💷💷💷

Medlar

Refined French cuisine in a romantic, low-key environment. Good fixed-price menus.

📍C10 🏠438 King's Rd SW10 🌐medlar restaurant.co.uk

💷💷💷

The Builder's Arms

Smart neighbourhood pub serving traditional British food. It's a congenial place to drink too.

📍E9 🏠13 Britten St SW3 🌐thebuildersarms chelsea.co.uk

💷💷💷

The Great Hall at the Royal Hospital Chelsea, laid out for the Pensioners' lunch

Victorian Londoners – the first was Victoria Park (*p322*) in the East End. It opened in 1858 on the former Battersea Fields, a swampy area notorious for vice centred on the Old Red House, a disreputable pub.

The new park was immediately popular, especially for its man-made boating lake, with its romantic rocks, gardens and waterfalls. In 1985, the Peace Pagoda was unveiled – a 35-m- (100-ft-) high monument built by Japanese Buddhist nuns and monks and presented to the park as a gift. There is also an excellent children's zoo (entry fee), a playground, sports activities and an art gallery, the Pump House.

10

St Mary's, Battersea

📍D10 🏠Battersea Church Rd SW11 🚇Sloane Sq then bus 19 or 319 🕐For services & by arrangement 🌐stmarysbattersea.org.uk

There has been a church here since at least the 10th century. The present brick building dates from 1775, but the

17th-century stained glass, commemorating Tudor monarchs, comes from the former church. In 1782, the poet and artist William Blake was married in the church. Later, J M W Turner painted views of the Thames from the church tower. Benedict Arnold, who served George Washington in the American War of Independence but defected to the British side, is buried here in the crypt.

Battersea Park's Peace Pagoda, which looks out ↓ over the river

BATTERSEA POWER STATION

This is one of the London landmarks least known to visitors but best known to locals - and, of course, to Pink Floyd fans: the monstrous industrial building with its four towering smoke stacks graces the cover of their album *Animals*. After it was decommissioned in 1983, numerous proposals for its redevelopment came and went. Now, finally, the colossal Grade II-listed structure is coming back into use. A new riverside park, an extension to the Thames Path, a new Tube station and a myriad of restaurants, shops and pricey housing all form part of the new district now beginning to come to life.

11 🍴 🖥 👜

Circus West Village

📍G10 🏠Battersea Power Station 🚇Sloane Sq then bus 452 or 137 🚆Battersea Power Station 🌐battersea powerstation.co.uk

Most easily reached by boat, Circus West is the first stage of the gargantuan redevelopment of Battersea Power Station, part of the regeneration of riverside land stretching between Battersea Park and Vauxhall in between the towering power station and the train lines heading into Victoria Station. Its ongoing development, though certainly commercially driven, just about bridges the gap between the independent and corporate business worlds.

An interesting mix of restaurants, bars and shops have been installed inside the railway arches and by the new-builds gathering around the site, including a brewpub, three-screen cinema and the Turbine Theatre.

A LONG WALK
CHELSEA AND BATTERSEA

Distance 6.5 km (4 miles) **Time** 90 minutes
Nearest Tube Sloane Square

This delightful circular walk ambles through the impressive grounds of the Royal Hospital Chelsea and across the river to Battersea Park, which features tidy Victorian landscaping. It then returns to the narrow village streets of Chelsea, winding past quaint town-houses and beautiful, historic churches. The route ends on King's Road, a shopping hub lined with stylish boutiques and pleasant eateries.

Chelsea and Battersea

CHELSEA AND BATTERSEA

Locator Map
For more detail see p234

Leave the market on Sydney Street and cross into the garden of **St Luke's Church**, where Charles Dickens was married in 1836.

The **Pheasantry** was a dance and painters' studio then a music venue in the 1960s and 70s.

Cross King's Road to reach **Chelsea Farmers Market**, an enclave of cafés and craft shops.

Charming **Glebe Place** has retained much of its original character, with some Grade II listed houses.

There are two early Georgian houses on **Justice Walk** – Duke's House and Monmouth House.

Previous residents of the medieval **Crosby Hall** include Richard III and Sir Walter Raleigh.

Walk past the sought-after residences on **Cheyne Walk**, an area renowned for intellectual gatherings.

Return to Chelsea via the Albert Bridge and pause at David Wynne's sculpture **Boy with a Dolphin**.

Boy with a Dolphin

Cadogan Pier

Albert Bridge

Blossom blooming as spring comes to Battersea Park

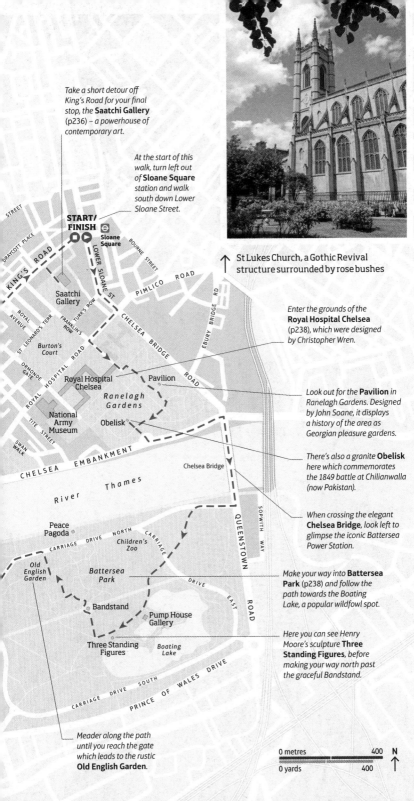

Take a short detour off King's Road for your final stop, the **Saatchi Gallery** (p236) – a powerhouse of contemporary art.

At the start of this walk, turn left out of **Sloane Square** station and walk south down Lower Sloane Street.

START/FINISH Sloane Square

↑ St Lukes Church, a Gothic Revival structure surrounded by rose bushes

Enter the grounds of the **Royal Hospital Chelsea** (p238), which were designed by Christopher Wren.

Look out for the **Pavilion** in Ranelagh Gardens. Designed by John Soane, it displays a history of the area as Georgian pleasure gardens.

There's also a granite **Obelisk** here which commemorates the 1849 battle at Chilianwalla (now Pakistan).

When crossing the elegant **Chelsea Bridge**, look left to glimpse the iconic Battersea Power Station.

Make your way into **Battersea Park** (p238) and follow the path towards the Boating Lake, a popular wildfowl spot.

Here you can see Henry Moore's sculpture **Three Standing Figures**, before making your way north past the graceful Bandstand.

Meander along the path until you reach the gate which leads to the rustic **Old English Garden**.

STREET
DRAYCOTT PLACE
KING'S ROAD
ROYAL AVENUE
ST LEONARD'S TERR
Saatchi Gallery
LOWER SLOANE ST
TURK'S ROW
FRANKLIN'S ROW
BOURNE STREET
PIMLICO ROAD
CHELSEA BRIDGE ROAD
EBURY BRIDGE RD
Burton's Court
ORMONDE GATE
ROYAL HOSPITAL ROAD
Royal Hospital Chelsea
Pavilion
Ranelagh Gardens
TITE STREET
National Army Museum
Obelisk
SWAN WALK
CHELSEA EMBANKMENT
River Thames
Chelsea Bridge
SOPWITH WAY
QUEENSTOWN ROAD
Peace Pagoda
CARRIAGE DRIVE NORTH
Children's Zoo
CARRIAGE DRIVE EAST
Old English Garden
Battersea Park
DRIVE
Bandstand
Pump House Gallery
Three Standing Figures
Boating Lake
CARRIAGE DRIVE SOUTH
PRINCE OF WALES DRIVE

| 0 metres | 400 |
| 0 yards | 400 |

N ↑

SOUTH KENSINGTON AND KNIGHTSBRIDGE

The tone was set for Kensington from the late 17th century when William III and Mary II bought Kensington Palace. With the arrival of the royal court it soon became a highly desirable residential area, as it still is today, attracting the wealthy as well as those who sought to sell them goods. It remained largely rural until the late 18th century when a period of urban expansion slowly began, with Knightsbridge among the first spots to be developed. It was in the 1850s that the pace of transformation really exploded, the fuse lit by the Great Exhibition of 1851. Held in Hyde Park, the exhibition was the brainchild of Queen Victoria's husband, Prince Albert, who sought to demonstrate and promote British industry and invention. It was a huge success and the profits were ploughed into the creation of a permanent showcase for the arts and sciences in South Kensington. The great museums, the Royal Albert Hall and the Royal Colleges of Art and Music are all part of that legacy.

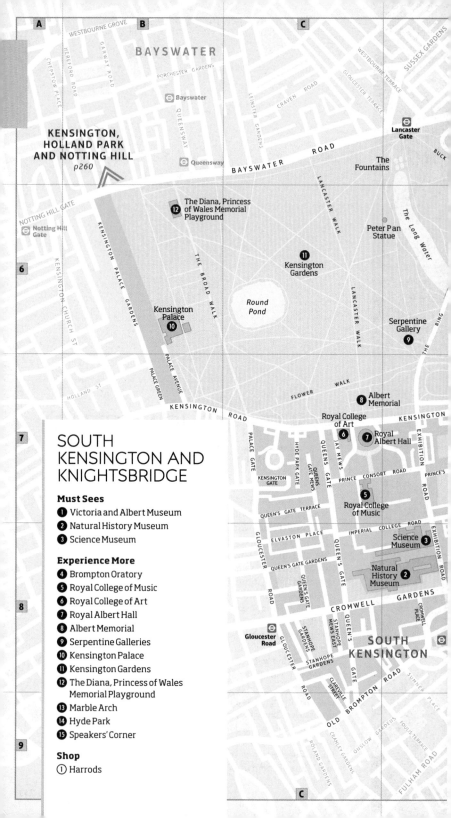

A **Bayswater**
B **BAYSWATER**

WESTBOURNE GROVE
HEREFORD ROAD
GARWAY ROAD
CHEPSTOW PLACE
PORCHESTER GARDENS
QUEENSWAY
LEINSTER GARDENS
CRAVEN ROAD
GLOUCESTER TERRACE
WESTBOURNE TERRACE
SUSSEX GARDENS

KENSINGTON, HOLLAND PARK AND NOTTING HILL
p260

Bayswater
Queensway
BAYSWATER ROAD
Lancaster Gate
The Fountains
BUCK

NOTTING HILL GATE
Notting Hill Gate
KENSINGTON CHURCH ST
KENSINGTON PALACE GARDENS

12 The Diana, Princess of Wales Memorial Playground

THE BROAD WALK

11 Kensington Gardens

Round Pond

Peter Pan Statue
The Long Water
LANCASTER WALK

10 Kensington Palace

PALACE AVENUE
PALACE GREEN
HOLLAND ST
KENSINGTON ROAD

FLOWER WALK

9 Serpentine Gallery
THE RING

8 Albert Memorial
Royal College of Art **6**
7 Royal Albert Hall

KENSINGTON

PALACE GATE
KENSINGTON GATE
HYDE PARK GATE
QUEEN'S GATE
QUEEN'S GATE MEWS
JAY MEWS
PRINCE CONSORT ROAD
EXHIBITION ROAD
PRINCE'S ROAD

5 Royal College of Music

QUEEN'S GATE TERRACE
ELVASTON PLACE
IMPERIAL COLLEGE ROAD
QUEEN'S GATE
GLOUCESTER ROAD
QUEEN'S GATE GARDENS

3 Science Museum

2 Natural History Museum

GARDENS
CROMWELL PLACE

Gloucester Road
STANHOPE GARDENS
STANHOPE MEWS EAST
STANHOPE GARDENS
QUEEN'S GATE
CROMWELL ROAD
SOUTH KENSINGTON
SUMNER PLACE

GLOUCESTER ROAD
CLAREVILLE STREET
OLD BROMPTON ROAD
FOULIS TERRACE
ROLAND GARDENS
CRANLEY GARDENS
ONSLOW GARDENS
FULHAM ROAD

SOUTH KENSINGTON AND KNIGHTSBRIDGE

Must Sees

1 Victoria and Albert Museum
2 Natural History Museum
3 Science Museum

Experience More

4 Brompton Oratory
5 Royal College of Music
6 Royal College of Art
7 Royal Albert Hall
8 Albert Memorial
9 Serpentine Galleries
10 Kensington Palace
11 Kensington Gardens
12 The Diana, Princess of Wales Memorial Playground
13 Marble Arch
14 Hyde Park
15 Speakers' Corner

Shop

① Harrods

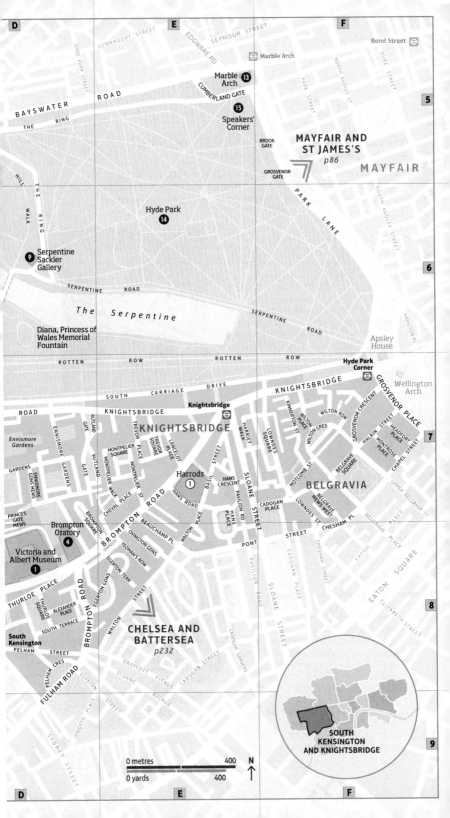

1 🏃 🍴 🍵 🖥 🛍

VICTORIA AND ALBERT MUSEUM

📍 D8 🏛 Cromwell Rd SW7 🚇 South Kensington 🕐 10am–5:45pm daily (to 10pm Fri) 🗓 24–26 Dec 🌐 vam.ac.uk

Housed in Victorian splendour, as well as modern state-of-the-art galleries, the V&A is the world's leading museum of art and design, with its collection spanning 5,000 years of furniture, glass, textiles, fashion, ceramics and jewellery.

The Victoria and Albert Museum (V&A) contains one of the world's broadest collections of art and design, with exhibits ranging from early Christian devotional objects to cutting-edge furniture. Originally founded in 1852 to inspire design students as the Museum of Manufactures, it was renamed by Queen Victoria in 1899 in memory of Prince Albert. The museum has undergone extensive renovation since the early 2000s, including the opening in 2017 of a new quarter on Exhibition Road, encompassing the Sackler Courtyard and an expanded Photography Centre in 2018. More projects are in the pipeline.

↑ The grand Cromwell Road entrance to the V&A

←

The welcoming neon information desk at the museum

GALLERY GUIDE

The V&A has six levels numbered from -1 to 4. Level 0 houses the China, Japan and South Asia galleries, the Fashion Gallery and the Cast Courts. The British Galleries are on Levels 1 and 3. Level 2 has the 20th Century galleries and silver, ironwork, paintings and photography. The glass display is on Level 3. The Ceramics Galleries and Furniture are on Level 4. The fantastic European galleries from 300 to 1815 span levels -1 and 1.

↑ The reading room of the National Art Library in the V&A

↑ Large-scale works, that were
once part of buildings, in the
Medieval & Renaissance gallery

British Galleries

A sequence of grand rooms starting on Level 1 and continuing on Level 3 are devoted to British design and decorative arts from 1500 to 1900. The luxurious galleries chart Britain's rise from obscure island to "workshop of the world".

The galleries present the evolution of British design and the numerous influences, whether technological or aesthetic, that it has absorbed from all over the world. Beautiful textiles, furniture, costumes and household objects illustrate the tastes and lifestyles of the country's ruling classes. Among the highlights are the opulent State Bed from Melville House, and a number of carefully preserved period rooms, including the stunning Rococo Norfolk House Music Room. Discovery Areas give visitors a chance to delve even deeper into the past by trying on a hoop and petticoat or viewing 3D images through a Victorian stereoscope.

Asia: Middle East, South Asia, China and Japan

The Jameel Gallery of Islamic Art in Room 42 houses a collection of objects from the early days of the Caliphs in the 7th century through to the years preceding World

Vibrant examples of stained glass in the Sacred Silver and Stained Glass galleries ↑

War I. Beautifully crafted ceramics, textiles, metalwork and glass from Iran, Egypt and Turkey show the Islamic influence on fine and decorative arts. The vast sixteenth-century Ardabil Carpet, one of the largest, oldest and most intricate in the world, is the key exhibit. Next door, the famous Tipu's Tiger automaton from Mysore and Ranjit Singh's sheet-gold-decorated throne are the highlights of the extensive South Asia collection, which ranges across 400 years from the Mughal emperors to the Raj. The China collection encompasses rare jade and ceramics pieces and a fine collection of Buddhas, dating back to the 6th century, while Japanese art is concentrated in the gallery in Room 45,

and is particularly notable for lacquerware, Samurai armour and woodblock prints.

Architecture Gallery

The Architecture Gallery features drawings, models, photographs and architectural fragments from the V&A and the Royal Institute of British Architects (RIBA) in both permanent displays and temporary exhibitions.

A superb collection of artifacts and illustrations from around the world explores key themes, such as construction techniques and the role of public buildings. Don't miss the detailed architectural scale models, including a traditional Japanese house, Modernist constructions from Ernö Goldfinger and others, and Charles Barry's Gothic plans for the Palace of Westminster, though models are often out on loan.

Europe

Ten galleries, occupying an entire wing of the museum, house some of the world's greatest treasures of medieval and Renaissance Europe. Among the many remarkable exhibits are the notebooks of Leonardo da Vinci; sculptures by Italian masters such as Donatello and Giambologna, some set in a Renaissance courtyard garden setting; the fine enamel Becket Casket (c 1180);

↑ Ancient kimonos on display in the Toshiba Gallery of Japanese Art

and the reconstructed Santa Chiara Chapel, the only one of its kind outside Italy, on Level 1.

The Europe collection continues in the Level -1 galleries of the opposite wing, which cover the period 1600 to 1815, and include several re-created period rooms. Room 48a on the ground floor is dedicated to the famous Raphael Cartoons – huge designs for tapestries planned for the Sistine Chapel, given a refurbished gallery for their 500th anniversary in 2020.

Another of the most famous sights at the V&A are the extraordinary Cast Courts, which have been part of the museum since its founding. They house large plaster casts of major European sculptures, such as Rome's Trajan's Column and a 5-m- (16-ft-) tall reproduction of Michaelangelo's *David*, deemed so shocking by Queen Victoria that a fig leaf was created to cover his modesty.

Fashion and Textiles

The popular Fashion Gallery displays items from the largest and most comprehensive collection of dress in the world. Around 100 exhibits spanning more than 250 years are arranged chronologically. They feature a magnificent mantua from the 1750s, an 1850s wedding dress with veil and shoes, a Schiaparelli evening coat embroidered with a design

→ Enamelled casket depicting the murder of Thomas Becket

by Jean Cocteau, elegant ballgowns from the 1950s; and stunning dresses from Alexander McQueen. Textiles are also found throughout the museum's collections; the Japanese gallery in particular has some exquisite kimonos and other traditional textiles.

Materials and Techniques

This group of galleries is located on Level 2. In the Silver Galleries, 3,500 pieces from 1400 to the present day are displayed in the beautifully refurbished Victorian Rooms 65 to 69. The Gilbert Collection of gold, silver and micromosaics is in Rooms 70–73.

English landscapes feature among the works in the Paintings galleries (Rooms 81, 82, 87 and 88), including scenes by Turner. The Sacred Silver and Stained Glass galleries situated in Rooms 83 and 84 display devotional treasures. The highlight of the Ironwork galleries (Rooms 113 to 114e), is the Hereford Screen, a choir screen designed by Sir George Gilbert Scott in 1862. The dazzling screen became the V&A's largest-ever conservation project.

In the Photography Centre (Rooms 99–101), there are changing displays drawn from the museum's 800,000- strong collection, and you can handle antique cameras such as a 1920s Kodak Brownie.

Glass and Ceramics

The museum has the most comprehensive collection of glass and ceramics in the world. Examples of glass covering 2,000 years are largely housed in Room 131, which has a stunning glass balustrade on the staircase and mezzanine by artist Danny Lane. Displays of international contemporary glass are on display in this room and in Room 129.

The ceramics collection has an introductory gallery presenting the history and development of ceramics across the world. All of the major British pottery factories are represented.

Alexander McQueen's animal print dress Plato's Atlantis, from 2010 ↑

NATURAL HISTORY MUSEUM

📍D8 🏠Cromwell Rd SW7 🚇South Kensington 🕐10am–5:50pm daily (till 10pm last Fri of month), last admission 5:30pm 🚫24–26 Dec 🌐nhm.ac.uk

A paradise for budding botanists, explorers and geologists, the superlative Natural History Museum, with its specimens, skeletons and simulators, is quite simply a national treasure and an absolute must for any visitor to the capital.

Using interactive techniques and traditional displays, life on earth and the earth itself are vividly explained at this awe-inspiring museum. And the building that houses the vast collection is a masterpiece in itself. Founded as just one of several of the Victorian temples to learning, it opened in 1881 and was designed by Alfred Waterhouse using revolutionary building techniques. It is built on an iron and steel framework concealed behind arches and columns, richly decorated with sculptures of plants and animals.

The museum is divided into four zones, plus the Hintze Hall, the grand centrepiece of the building dominated by a huge skeleton of a blue whale. In the Blue Zone discover Human Biology, Mammals, Dinosaurs and Images of Nature. The Green Zone has Creepy Crawlies, Fossils, Treasures and the Vault. The giant escalator in the Earth Hall leads through a stunning globe to Red Zone highlights Restless Surface and Earth's Treasury. The Orange Zone includes the Darwin Centre's Cocoon and, outside, the Wildlife Garden.

① The elegant museum is set in grounds that include a peaceful wildlife garden.

② One of the museum's impressively lifelike animatronic models, a *T. rex* lurches and roars in this popular gallery. Exhibits of fossilised skeletons and eggs are also on display.

③ Life-size models are a major attraction in the vast Mammals gallery.

2   3

TOP 5 **UNMISSIBLE EXHIBITS**

Triceratops Skull
The gigantic skull of a plant-eating three-horned dinosaur.

Guy the Gorilla
London Zoo's most famous denizen in his time now graces the Treasures gallery.

Archaeopteryx
This valuable fossil of a feathered dinosaur provided the link between birds and dinosaurs.

Earthquake Simulator
Experience the effects of an earthquake in this simulation.

Wildlife Photography
Annual exhibition of the world's best nature images (Oct–May).

↑ The 25.5-m- (84-ft-) long skeleton of "Hope", the blue whale hanging over Hintze Hall

③ Ⓜ Ⓨ ▱ 🛍

SCIENCE MUSEUM

📍D8 🏛Exhibition Rd SW7 Ⓢ South Kensington 🕙10am–6pm daily (last adm: 5:15pm; closes later in school hols) 🚫24–26 Dec 🌐sciencemuseum.org.uk

Centuries of continuing scientific and technological innovation lie at the heart of the Science Museum's huge collection. Discover the science fact behind science fiction and explore humanity's achievements so far – and where we might be heading next.

From steam engines to aeroengines, space-craft to robotics, this museum has a vast range of scientific objects. Equally important is the social context of science – what discoveries and inventions mean for day-to-day life – and the process of discovery itself. The high-tech Wellcome Wing, at the western end of the museum, has hands-on displays, an IMAX cinema, a 3D theatre and galleries devoted to scientific advancements.

The Science Museum's exhibits are spread over five floors, with two major new spaces unveiled in 2019. Displaying over 3,000 artifacts spanning five centuries, the spectacular Wellcome Galleries on the first floor form the largest space devoted to the history of medicine and health in the world, while Science City 1550–1800 explores London's inexorable rise to become the hub of global science.

↑ The unassuming exterior of the fascinating Science Museum

💬 INSIDER TIP
Get Some Air

Though there are several places to eat in the museum, pack a picnic and walk five minutes to Hyde Park – a perfect place for kids to let off some steam.

↑ Early flying machines and fighter planes suspended over the Flight and Fly Zone galleries on the third floor

---

TOP 5 UNMISSABLE EXHIBITS

Apollo 10
US astronauts orbited the moon in May 1969 in the Apollo 10 capsule.

Who Am I?
Explore how your genetics and your upbringing make you who you are.

Fly 360°
Adrenaline-pumping flight simulator, with barrel rolls and loop-the-loops.

Space Descent VR
A virtual reality 400-km (250-mile) journey from space back to earth.

Wonderlab
Hands-on science gallery for kids and adults alike.

→ A child enjoying the hands-on exhibits in the immersive and imaginative Wonderlab, which has over 50 mind-boggling exhibits, shows and demonstrations

↑ Discovering more about the earth's climate in the Atmosphere gallery

←

The soaring interior of the Brompton Oratory, rich in Italianate decoration

6 Royal College of Art

📍 C7 🚇 Kensington Gore SW7 🚉 High St Kensington, South Kensington ⏰ For exhibitions, lectures, film screenings 🌐 rca.ac.uk

Sir Hugh Casson's mainly glass-fronted building (1962) is in stark contrast to the Victoriana around it. The college was founded in 1837 to teach design and practical art for the manufacturing industries. It became noted for modern art in the 1950s and 1960s, when David Hockney, Peter Blake and Eduardo Paolozzi attended.

7 Royal Albert Hall

📍 C7 🚇 Kensington Gore SW7 🚉 High St Kensington, South Kensington ⏰ For tours & performances daily 🌐 royalalberthall.com

Completed in 1871, this huge concert hall was modelled on

EXPERIENCE MORE

4 Brompton Oratory

📍 D8 🚇 Brompton Rd SW7 🚉 South Kensington, Knightsbridge ⏰ 6:30am-8pm daily 🌐 brompton oratory.co.uk

Famous for its splendid musical tradition, the Italianate Oratory is a rich (some think a little too rich) monument to the English Catholic revival of the late 19th century, established by John Henry Newman (later Cardinal Newman).

The church was opened in 1884; its façade and dome were added in the 1890s, and the interior has been progressively enriched ever since. Inside, all the most eye-catching treasures predate the church – many of them were brought here from Italian churches. Giuseppe Mazzuoli carved the huge marble figures of the 12 apostles for Siena Cathedral in the late 17th century. The beautiful Lady Altar was originally created in 1693 for the

Dominican church in Brescia, and the 18th-century altar in St Wilfrid's Chapel came from a church in Rochefort, Belgium.

5 Royal College of Music

📍 C7 🚇 Prince Consort Rd SW7 ⏰ Times vary, check website 🚉 South Kensington 🌐 rcm.ac.uk

Sir Arthur Blomfield designed the turreted Gothic palace, with Bavarian overtones, that has housed this distinguished institution since 1894. Pupils have included the composers Benjamin Britten and Samuel Coleridge-Taylor. The RCM's museum has over 15,000 musical treasures, including a 15th-century clavicytherium – the world's earliest stringed keyboard instrument – and a choirbook that belonged to Anne Boleyn. Student-led tours of the campus take place each Wednesday during term time.

SHOP

Harrods

The department store that could supply anything from a packet of pins to an elephant - not quite true today, but Harrods still remains as grand as ever.

📍 E7 🚇 87-135 Brompton Rd, Knightsbridge SW1 🌐 harrods.com

Roman amphitheatres. On the elegant red-brick exterior the only ostentation is a frieze symbolizing the triumph of arts and science. Originally planned as the Hall of Arts and Science, Queen Victoria renamed it in memory of her husband when she laid the foundation stone in 1868.

The hall is best known for hosting the "Proms", but it also stages rock concerts, comedy shows and even sports events. In preparation for its 150th anniversary in 2021, the hall's exterior has undergone cleaning and renovation, with a special series of events planned in celebration.

8
Albert Memorial

Q C7 **A** South Carriage Drive, Kensington Gdns SW7 **⊖** High St Kensington, South Kensington **W** royalparks.org.uk

This grand Gothic Revival memorial to Prince Albert,

Queen Victoria's beloved consort, was completed in 1872, 11 years after his death. Fittingly, it is near the site of the 1851 Exhibition, which Albert co-organized. The statue, by John Foley, shows him with an exhibition catalogue on his knee.

The Queen chose Sir George Gilbert Scott to design the monument, which stands 55 m (175 ft) high. It is loosely based on a medieval market cross – although considerably more elaborate, with a black and gilded spire, multi-coloured marble canopy, stones, mosaics, enamels and wrought iron. The Frieze of Parnassus around the base of the memorial depicts almost

Did You Know?
There are 169 carvings of notable figures from the arts in the frieze around the Albert Memorial.

200 notable figures from the arts, including painters, poets, architects and musicians.

9
Serpentine Galleries

Q D6 **A** Kensington Gdns W2 **⊖** Lancaster Gate, South Kensington **Ⓒ** 10am-6pm Tue-Sun, public hols **Ⓒ** 24-26 Dec and between exhibitions **W** serpentinegalleries.org

The Serpentine Gallery houses temporary exhibitions of major and rising contemporary artists' and architects' work, excitingly transforming its space to suit the exhibits. Every summer, a temporary pavilion is commissioned from a major architect. A second building, the Serpentine Sackler Gallery, in a former gunpowder store a five-minute walk away, displays similarly ambitious exhibits. An extension, designed by the late Zaha Hadid, houses the Chucs café, and there is also an art bookshop.

↑ The Royal Albert Hall, home to musical events across a wide variety of genres

10

Kensington Palace

📍 B6 🏛 Kensington Palace Gardens W8 🚇 High St Kensington, Queensway, Notting Hill Gate ⏱ Mar–Oct: 10am–6pm daily; Nov–Feb: 10am–4pm daily (last adm: 1 hr before closing) 🌐 hrp.org.uk

Half of this spacious palace is used as royal apartments; the other half, which includes the 18th-century state rooms, is open to the public. When William of Orange and his wife Mary came to the throne in 1689, they bought a mansion, dating from 1605, and commissioned Christopher Wren to convert it into a royal palace.

The palace has seen some important royal events: in 1714, Queen Anne died here from apoplexy brought on by overeating and, on 20 June 1837, Princess Victoria of Kent was woken at 5am to be told that her uncle William IV had died and she was now queen – the start of her 64-year reign. After the death in 1997 of Diana, Princess of Wales, the gold gates to the south were deluged with bouquets in their thousands.

Visitors can explore inside the King's and Queen's state apartments, the latter little changed since it was designed for Mary in the 17th century. The palace also often displays clothes worn by many of the royals, including the Queen and Princess Diana.

11

Kensington Gardens

📍 C6 🏛 W8 🚇 Bayswater, High St Kensington, Queensway, Lancaster Gate ⏱ 6am–dusk daily 🌐 royalparks.org.uk

The former grounds of Kensington Palace became a public park in 1841. The gardens are full of charm, starting with Sir George Frampton's statue (1912) of J M Barrie's fictional Peter Pan, playing his pipes for the bronze fairies and animals that cling to the column below. Just north of here are many lovely ornamental fountains and statues, while to the south is George Frederick Watts' muscular horse and rider, *Physical Energy*.

Close by is a summer house designed by William Kent in 1735. The Round Pond, built in 1728, is often packed with model boats navigated by enthusiasts young and old.

In the north, near Lancaster Gate, is a dogs' cemetery, created in 1880 by the then Duke of Cambridge.

→
Passing the time aboard a rowing boat on Hyde Park's Serpentine

12

The Diana, Princess of Wales Memorial Playground

📍 B6 🏛 Kensington Gardens 🚇 Bayswater, Queensway ⏱ From 10am daily; closing times vary, from 3:45pm Nov–Jan to 7:45pm May–Aug 🌐 royalparks.org.uk

The newest of Kensington Gardens' three playgrounds, on the site of an earlier playground funded by J M Barrie, takes the boy who didn't want to grow up as its theme and includes a beach cove with a 15-m (50-ft) pirates' galleon, a treehouse and a mermaid's fountain with a slumbering crocodile. Though all children under 13 must be accompanied by an adult, staff are on hand too. Many features of the playground are accessible to children with specific needs.

←
The sunken garden with reflecting pool adjoining Kensington Palace

INSIDER TIP
On the Water

Rent a pedalo or rowing boat from the Boathouse (Apr–Oct) and enjoy a tranquil tour of Hyde Park's Serpentine lake. The brave can dive in for a refreshing swim at the lido in summer (weekends in May; daily Jun–early Sep).

13

Marble Arch

E5 **Park Lane W1** **Marble Arch**

John Nash designed the arch in 1827 as the main entrance to Buckingham Palace, though it proved too narrow for the grandest coaches and in 1851 was moved here. Historically, only senior members of the royal family and one of the royal artillery regiments are allowed to pass under it.

The arch stands near the site of the old Tyburn gallows, where until 1783 the city's most notorious criminals were hanged in front of crowds of bloodthirsty spectators.

14

Hyde Park

E6 **W2** **Hyde Park Corner, Knightsbridge, Lancaster Gate, Marble Arch** **5am–midnight daily** **royalparks.org.uk**

The ancient manor of Hyde was part of the lands of Westminster Abbey seized by Henry VIII on the Dissolution of the Monasteries in 1536. It has remained a royal park ever since. Henry used it for hunting, but James I opened it to the public in the early 17th century. The Serpentine, an artificial lake used for boating and bathing, was created when Caroline, George II's queen, dammed the flow of the Westbourne River in 1730. The Princess Diana Memorial Fountain is to the south of the Serpentine.

In its time, the park has been a venue for duelling, horse racing, demonstrations and musical performances. The 1851 Great Exhibition was held here in a vast glass palace. Come Christmas time, the festive Winter Wonderland takes over, with markets, an ice rink and a funfair.

↑ The *Serenity*, a bronze sculpture of an ibis, overlooks the Serpentine in Hyde Park

15

Speakers' Corner

E5 **Hyde Park W2** **Marble Arch**

An 1872 law made it legal for anyone to assemble an audience and address them on whatever topic they chose. Since then, this corner of Hyde Park has become the established venue for budding public orators and a fair number of eccentrics. On Sunday mornings, speakers from fringe groups and one-member political parties reveal their plans for the betterment of humanity (or otherwise) while assembled onlookers heckle them.

A SHORT WALK
SOUTH KENSINGTON

Distance 1.5 km (1 mile) **Time** 30 minutes
Nearest Tube South Kensington

This area is characterized by its world-renowned museums, which are housed in grandiose buildings celebrating Victorian self-confidence. Take a stroll from the Albert Memorial in Kensington Gardens, past the Royal Albert Hall, to the Victoria and Albert Museum and admire the monuments to the royal couple that made London a world capital of industry and knowledge.

David Hockney and Peter Blake are among the great artists who trained at the **Royal College of Art** *(p254).*

The former **Royal College of Organists** *was decorated by F W Moody in 1876.*

Opened in 1871, the **Royal Albert Hall** *has a beautiful curved exterior (p254).*

Historic musical instruments are exhibited at the **Royal College of Music** *(p254).*

PRINCE

CONSOR

IMPERIAL COLLEGE ROAD

EXHIBITION

Did You Know?

The Royal Albert Hall was partly funded by selling seats on a 999-year lease.

The **Natural History Museum** *houses everything from dinosaurs to moon rocks (p250).*

CROMWELL ROAD

Visitors can experiment with interactive displays at the **Science Museum** *(p252).*

FINISH

CROMWELL

| 0 metres | 100 |
| 0 yards | 100 |

N

START

The **Albert Memorial** was built to commemorate Queen Victoria's consort (p255).

The **Albert Hall Mansions**, built by Norman Shaw in 1879, started a fashion for red brick.

The **Royal Geographical Society** was founded in 1830. Scottish missionary and explorer David Livingstone (1813–73) was a member.

SOUTH KENSINGTON AND KNIGHTSBRIDGE

Locator Map
For more detail see p244

KENSINGTON GORE

ALBERT COURT

ROAD

ROAD

PRINCE'S GARDENS

Imperial College is one of the country's leading scientific institutions.

A wealth of objects from around the globe illustrate a rich history of design and decoration at the **Victoria and Albert Museum** (p246).

Holy Trinity church dates from the 19th century and is located among cottages in a calm backwater.

↑ The gilded Albert Memorial gleams in the sunshine

The **Brompton Oratory** was built during the 19th-century Catholic revival (p254).

Brompton Square, begun in 1821, established this as a fashionable residential area.

GARDENS

259

Brightly painted shops and houses on Portobello Road

KENSINGTON, HOLLAND PARK AND NOTTING HILL

Kensington remained a country village of market gardens and mansions until the 1830s. Outstanding among these mansions was Holland House, part of whose grounds are now Holland Park. The area grew up rapidly in the mid-19th century and most of its buildings date from then – mainly expensive apartments, mansion flats and fashionable shops. It was during that century that a slew of famous artists and writers settled in the area, notable among them Henry James, William Thackeray, Edward Linley Sambourne and Lord Leighton, the striking homes of the latter two, 18 Stafford Terrace and Leighton House, now open to the public. It was also during the 19th century that Notting Hill emerged as a suburb, initially attracting well-to-do residents in much the same vein as elsewhere in Kensington. By the end of World War II, however, many of the stuccoed terraced houses had been converted to multiple-occupancy tenements. They became homes, during the 1950s, to West Indian immigrant families who began arriving in the area in large numbers – their presence spawned the first Notting Hill Carnival, in 1966.

KENSINGTON, HOLLAND PARK AND NOTTING HILL

Must See
1. Design Museum

Experience More
2. Portobello Road
3. Holland Park
4. 18 Stafford Terrace
5. Leighton House
6. High Street Kensington
7. Little Venice
8. Notting Hill
9. Museum of Brands, Packaging and Advertising
10. St Sophia's Cathedral
11. Kensington Square

Eat
1. Montparnasse Café
2. Café Tarte
3. Holland Park Café
4. Candella
5. The Muffin Man Tea Shop

Stay
6. The Main House

1 🍴 🖥 🛍

DESIGN MUSEUM

📍 A7 🏠 224–8 Kensington High St W8 Ⓔ Kensington High St, Holland Park 🕐 10am–6pm daily (to 8pm on first Fri of every month; last adm: 1 hour before closing) 🚫 24–26 Dec 🌐 designmuseum.org

The Design Museum, housed in a truly unique building, is dedicated to every element of contemporary design, including architecture, transport, graphics, furniture and fashion. Its imaginatively curated temporary exhibitions usually outshine its rather small but nevertheless engaging permanent display.

The museum is housed in what was once the Commonwealth Institute, built in the 1960s and famed for its dramatically cascading roof – a hyperbolic parabola made with 25 tonnes of Zimbabwean copper. The institute closed in 2002 and the interior was completely refashioned as the museum's new home in 2016, with a huge atrium of sweeping, geometric spaces. There is room enough for four galleries – three of them for the superlative programme of temporary exhibitions and one to house the excellent and occasionally interactive permanent collection, called Designer Maker User, which is free to explore. The exhibition covers design disciplines from architecture and the digital world to fashion and graphics.

The building also houses a lecture theatre, café and two appealing shops. The beautiful green woodland of Holland Park is located right next door.

SHOP

Designer Shopping

The Design Museum shop is one of the best museum shops in London for the originality and diversity of its carefully selected stock. Items include clothing, stylish stationery, models and miniatures, prints, kitchenware and more.

Exhibits displayed beneath the museum's remarkable roof ↓

GALLERY GUIDE

The permanent exhibition, called Designer Maker User, examines some of the most iconic product designs of the modern world. It also shows a cross-section of recent innovations from the three perspectives of its title.

1 Attractive displays of innovative design feature in the permanent collection.

2 The Grade II-listed building has an unusual sweeping roof design.

3 The Design Museum is housed in the former Commonwealth Institute building, which was originally opened in 1962.

EXPERIENCE MORE

2 🍴 ☕ 🛍️

Portobello Road

📍 A5 🚇 W11 🚉 Notting Hill Gate, Ladbroke Grove ⏰ Main market: 9am-7pm Fri & Sat; general market, bric-a-brac: 9am-6pm Mon-Wed, 9am-1pm Thu 🌐 portobelloroad.co.uk

There has been a market here since 1837. Today the southern end of the road consists mostly of stalls that sell antiques, jewellery, souvenirs and other collectables. The market is extremely popular and tends to be quite lively, but it is well worth visiting, if only to experience its bustling, cheerful atmosphere. The busiest day is Saturday, when the antiques arcades are open. If you are looking for bargains, be warned – the stallholders have a sound idea of the value of what they are selling. Other markets run along the rest of the street on different days, with vintage and new clothes featured around Portobello Green, under Westway near Ladbroke Grove Tube (Fri–Sun).

3 🍴 ☕

Holland Park

📍 A7 🚇 Ilchester Place, W8 🚉 Holland Park, High Street Kensington, Notting Hill Gate ⏰ 7:30am-dusk daily 🌐 rbkc.gov.uk

This small but delightful park, more wooded and intimate than the large royal parks to its east, Hyde Park (*p257*) and Kensington Gardens (*p256*), was opened in 1952 on what remained of the grounds of the Jacobean Holland House. The rest had been sold off in the late 19th century for the construction of new, large houses. During its heyday in the 19th century, the mansion was a noted centre of social and political intrigue. The 3rd Baron Holland, nephew of the statesman Charles James Fox, hosted parties for the likes of the poet Lord Byron, who met Lady Caroline Lamb here.

The house suffered heavy bomb damage during World War II, but surviving parts and outbuildings have been put to various uses: the orangery is presently used as a wedding venue while the old Garden Ballroom is now a restaurant. The former front terrace of the house is often used as a backdrop for summer musical events and open-air film screenings, and theatre, opera and dance performances.

The park still contains some of the formal gardens laid out in the early 19th century. Surprisingly, there is also a Japanese garden, created for the 1991 London Festival of Japan. Look out for koi carp in the pond beneath the waterfall. Colourful peacocks roam the grounds here, and there is a well-equipped playground perfect for kids to while away an afternoon in.

Did You Know?

Lord Leighton held Britain's shortest peerage: made a baron on 24 January 1896 – he died the next day.

4 🎨 🖼️ 🛍️

18 Stafford Terrace

📍 A7 🚇 W8 🚉 High St Kensington ⏰ 2-5:30pm Wed, Sat & Sun 🌐 rbkc.gov. uk/subsites/museums.aspx

The former home of Linley Sambourne, built in about 1870, remains much as Sambourne furnished it – in the Victorian manner, with Oriental ornaments and heavy velvet curtains. Some rooms have William Morris wallpaper. Sambourne was a cartoonist for the satirical magazine *Punch*; drawings cram the walls of the house. Tours take place at 11am on Wednesday and Sunday (booking required).

Exquisite tilework in Eastern style in Leighton House's Arab Hall

5

Leighton House

A7 12 Holland Park Rd W14 High St Kensington 10am-5:30pm Wed-Mon rbkc.gov.uk/subsites/museums.aspx

Lord Leighton was one of the most respected Victorian painters – his work *Flaming June* is regarded by many as the apotheosis of the Pre-Raphaelite movement. His house, built in 1864–9, has been preserved with its opulent decoration as an extraordinary monument to the Victorian aesthetics Leighton embodied. The highlight is the Arab Hall, added in 1879 to house Leighton's collection of Islamic tiles, some inscribed with text from the Koran.

There are paintings and drawings displayed, including some by Edward Burne-Jones, John Millais, G F Watts and many works by Leighton himself. There are free guided tours of the house at 3pm on Wednesday and Sunday and free walking tours of other houses in the area built by Leighton and his contemporaries on Thursday and Saturday at 11am (booking required).

6

High Street Kensington

B7 W8 High St Kensington

One of west London's main shopping areas, High Street Kensington reflects the tastes of this affluent neighbourhood, with lots of rather conservative clothing stores and various British and international high-street names.

At nos 101–111, Japan House is an exquisite Japanese cultural centre, with a gallery staging excellent temporary exhibitions, a restaurant and a shop selling beautifully crafted stationery, homeware and lots more.

← Stylized Japanese elegance in the Kyoto Garden, Holland Park

7 Ⓨ ▢ 🛍

Little Venice

📍C4 🚇W2 🚇Warwick Avenue, Edgware Road

This is a charming corner of London where the western end of the Regent's Canal, the eastern end of the Grand Union Canal and the short waterway to the Paddington Basin converge. Three bridges frame a small triangle of water populated with floating cafés and even a puppet theatre – there are plenty of delightful pubs and restaurants in the nearby terraced streets too. Towpath walks will take you for miles in either direction along the canals, and narrowboats sail up to Camden Lock (p170).

8 Ⓨ ▢ 🛍

Notting Hill

📍A6 🚇W11 🚇Notting Hill Gate

Now the home of Europe's biggest street carnival, most of this area was farmland until the 19th century. In the 1950s and 60s, it became a centre for the Caribbean community, many of whom lived here when they first arrived in Britain. The riotous carnival started in 1966 and takes over the area every August bank holiday weekend, when costumed parades meander through the streets.

9 ⬡ ▢ 🛍

Museum of Brands, Packaging and Advertising

📍A5 🏠111–117 Lancaster Rd W11 🚇Ladbroke Grove 🕐10am–6pm Tue–Sat, 11am–5pm Sun & public hols 🌐museumofbrands.com

This out-of-the-ordinary museum is at once a permanent exhibition for the history of product packaging in the UK, a study of the changing tastes and fashions since the Victorian period and a gleeful trip down memory lane. The sheer volume of items on display is dizzying: tins, bottles, boxes, magazines, toys, games, household appliances and much more besides. In the main exhibition space, the twisty Time Tunnel, familiar products appear multiple times, their packaging updated as the years pass. Displays reflect past trends, like the Egyptomania of the 1920s and the militarization of marketing during the two World Wars. There's a section for every decade of the 20th and 21st centuries and an intriguing 19th-century section, including teapots, gift sets and guides from the Great Exhibition of 1851.

NOTTING HILL CARNIVAL

The centrepiece in Europe's largest street carnival is a procession of flamboyant floats accompanied by steel bands, costumed dancers and mobile sound systems, transforming the area around Notting Hill, Ladbroke Grove and Westbourne Park into a celebration of Caribbean culture. Along the parade route are static sound systems, stages and food stalls. Born out of the British West Indian experience in London, the carnival has expanded exponentially, and today over 2.5 million people attend.

↑ Houseboats packed along the moorings at Little Venice

⑩ St Sophia's Cathedral

⑨ B5 **⌂** Moscow Rd W2 **Ⓔ** Queensway **Ⓒ** 10am–2pm daily **Ⓦ** stsophia.org.uk

The richly decorated interior of this Greek Orthodox cathedral is a riot of coloured marble and gilded mosaics. After the service on the second Sunday of each month it's possible to visit the treasury down in the crypt. The services feature a superb polyphonic choir.

⑪ Kensington Square

⑨ B7 **⌂** W8 **Ⓔ** High St Kensington

One of London's oldest squares, it was laid out in the 1680s, and a few early 18th-century houses still remain (Nos 11 and 12 are the oldest). The renowned philosopher John Stuart Mill lived at No 18, and the Pre-Raphaelite painter and illustrator Edward Burne-Jones at No 41.

↑ Houses on Kensington Square; some with blue plaques *(inset)* commemorating notable residents

ENGLISH HERITAGE
SIR EDWARD BURNE-JONES
1833–1898
Artist
lived here
1865–1867

EAT

Montparnasse Café
Homely French café and pâtisserie offering simple breakfasts, lunches and pastries.

⑨ B7 **⌂** 22 Thackeray St W8

Ⓔ Ⓔ Ⓔ

Café Tarte
Nicely prepared light lunches at this friendly café – the irresistible cakes steal the show.

⑨ A7 **⌂** 270 Kensington High St W8 **Ⓦ** cafetarte.co.uk

Ⓔ Ⓔ Ⓔ

Holland Park Café
Great location, on the edge of the picturesque park. Enjoy soups, sandwiches and cakes.

⑨ A7 **⌂** Holland Park, W8 **Ⓦ** cooksandpartners.co.uk

Ⓔ Ⓔ Ⓔ

Candella
Teas on vintage china, dainty sandwiches and light meals.

⑨ B7 **⌂** 34 Kensington Church St W8 **Ⓦ** candellatearoom.com

Ⓔ Ⓔ Ⓔ

The Muffin Man Tea Shop
Archetypally quaint, traditional tea shop with a hint of English village about it.

⑨ B7 **⌂** 12 Wrights Lane W8 **Ⓦ** themuffinmanteashop.co.uk.

Ⓔ Ⓔ Ⓔ

A SHORT WALK
KENSINGTON AND HOLLAND PARK

Distance 3 km (2 miles) **Time** 45 minutes
Nearest Tube High Street Kensington

Although now part of central London, as recently as the 1830s this was a country village of market gardens and mansions. Outstanding among these was Holland House; part of its grounds are now Holland Park. A walk through the area takes you past many of its attractive mid-19th century buildings, including expensive apartments, mansion flats and fashionable shops.

Did You Know?

Holland Park was once notorious as a location for highway robbers.

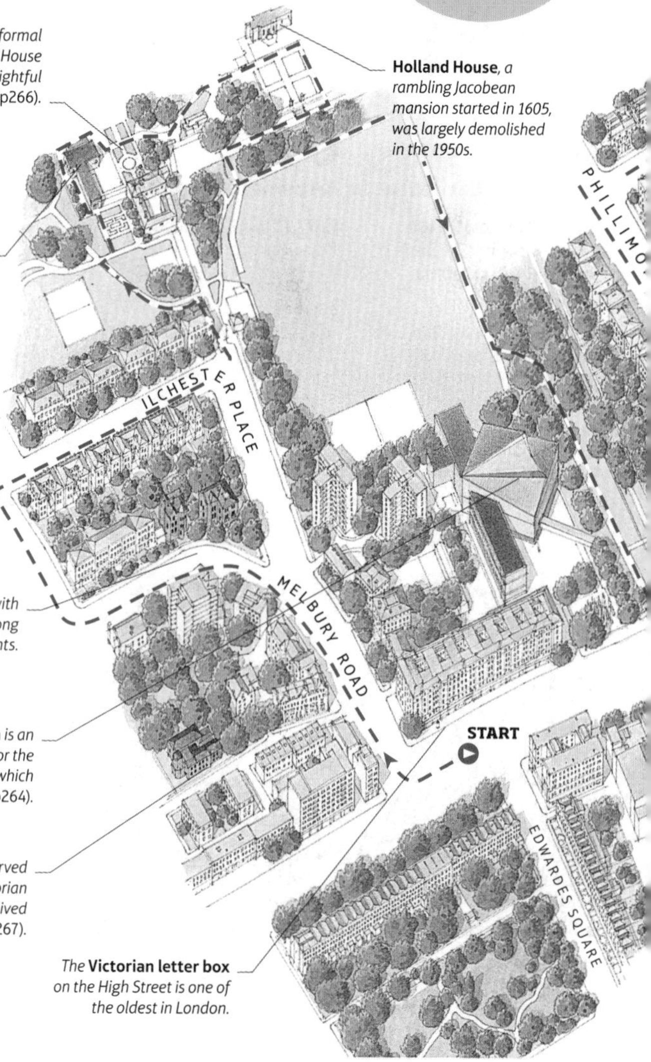

Parts of the old formal gardens of Holland House feature in the delightful **Holland Park** *(p266).*

Holland House, *a rambling Jacobean mansion started in 1605, was largely demolished in the 1950s.*

The **Summer Ballroom**, *now an upmarket restaurant, has parts that date from the 1630s.*

Melbury Road *is lined with large Victorian houses, long home to celebrity residents.*

The **Design Museum** *is an international showcase for the many design skills at which Britain excels (p264).*

Leighton House *is preserved as it was when the Victorian painter Lord Leighton lived here (p267).*

The **Victorian letter box** *on the High Street is one of the oldest in London.*

ILCHESTER PLACE

MELBURY ROAD

PHILLIMO

EDWARDES SQUARE

START

KENSINGTON, HOLLAND PARK AND NOTTING HILL

Drayson Mews *is one of the quaint alleys that were built behind large town houses for stables. Today most have been converted into small houses.*

Locator Map
For more detail see p262

Kensington Civic Centre, *an assertive modern building by Sir Basil Spence, was completed in 1976.*

No 16 Phillimore Place *was home to Kenneth Grahame, author of the children's classic* The Wind in the Willows, *from 1901 to 1908.*

PHILLIMORE PLACE

ESSEX VILLAS

GARDENS

STAFFORD TERRACE

ARGYLE ROAD

CAMPDEN HILL ROAD

HORNTON STREET

DRAYSON MEWS

HORNTON PLACE

FINISH ⊖

PHILLIMORE WALK

KENSINGTON HIGH STREET

Kensington High Street station

18 Stafford Terrace *has a carefully preserved late Victorian interior, complete with original furnishings and draperies (p266).*

Sticky Fingers, *a lively café on the corner of Phillimore Gardens, is owned by Bill Wyman, former bassist of the Rolling Stones.*

0 metres   100   N
0 yards   100   ↑

→
A statue in the grounds of Holland Park

Marylebone High Street at dusk

REGENT'S PARK AND MARYLEBONE

The name Marylebone is a derivation of "St Mary by the Bourne", the church that once stood next to the River Tyburn (also called Tybourne), long since buried underground. Many of the street names around Marylebone, including Wigmore Street and Portland Place, are taken from ancestral connections to the Howard de Walden family whose estate still occupies more or less the entire district. The estate dates from the early 18th century but before this time the land had been in royal hands. Henry VIII established hunting grounds to the north of Marylebone, some of which became Regent's Park when it was formally laid out from 1812 by John Nash, the architect responsible for the design of much of Regency London. Along the northern perimeter of the park runs the Regent's Canal, also laid out by Nash in the early 19th century. Not long after its completion, the recently founded Zoological Society of London opened their Zoological Gardens in five acres of the park – the beginnings of London Zoo.

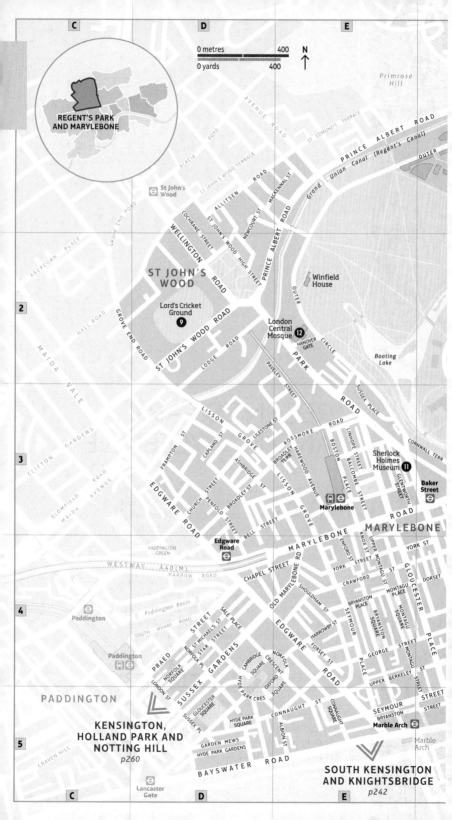

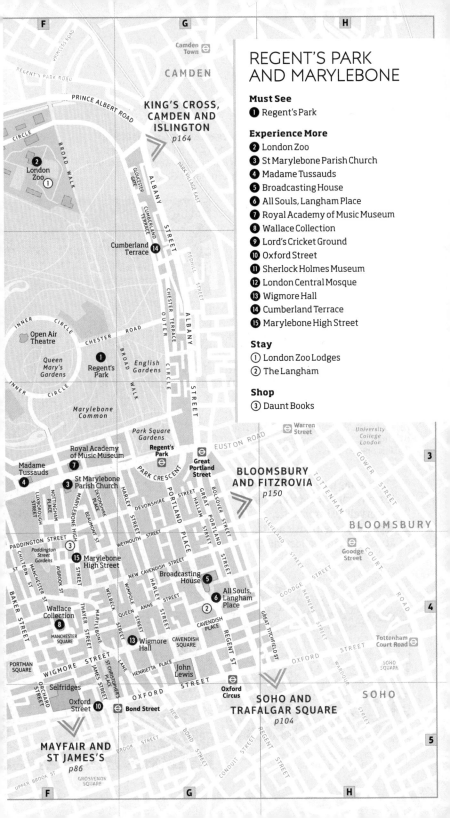

REGENT'S PARK AND MARYLEBONE

Must See
❶ Regent's Park

Experience More
❷ London Zoo
❸ St Marylebone Parish Church
❹ Madame Tussauds
❺ Broadcasting House
❻ All Souls, Langham Place
❼ Royal Academy of Music Museum
❽ Wallace Collection
❾ Lord's Cricket Ground
❿ Oxford Street
⓫ Sherlock Holmes Museum
⓬ London Central Mosque
⓭ Wigmore Hall
⓮ Cumberland Terrace
⓯ Marylebone High Street

Stay
① London Zoo Lodges
② The Langham

Shop
③ Daunt Books

REGENT'S PARK

F2 **NW1** **Regent's Park, Baker St, Great Portland St** **5am–dusk daily**
royalparks.org.uk

One of the city's largest green spaces, Regent's Park has something for everyone. Its attractions include London Zoo, an open-air theatre and a boating lake, as well as a vast network of pathways that take you to sights such as Regent's Canal and Queen Mary's Gardens.

This area of land became enclosed as a park in 1812. John Nash designed the scheme and originally envisaged a kind of garden suburb, dotted with 56 villas in a variety of Classical styles, and a pleasure palace for the Prince Regent. In the event only eight villas – but no palace – were built inside the park (three survive round the edge of the Inner Circle).

The boating lake, which is home to many water birds, is marvellously romantic, especially when music drifts across from the bandstand. Queen Mary's Gardens are a mass of wonderful sights and smells in summer, when visitors can also enjoy a full programme of outdoor theatre, including Shakespeare, musicals and children's plays, at the Open Air Theatre nearby. The park is also renowned for its excellent sports facilities.

Nash's master plan for the park continues just beyond its northeastern edge in Park Village East and West. These elegant stucco buildings date from 1828, the same year in which London Zoo first opened.

> **Did You Know?**
>
> There are more than 12,000 roses in Queen Mary's Gardens – London's largest collection.

> **The boating lake, which is home to many varieties of water birds, is marvellously romantic, especially when music drifts across from the bandstand.**

↑ Enjoying the view of swans swimming in the lake at Regent's Park

EXPERIENCE MORE

2

London Zoo

Q F1 **⌂** Regent's Park NW1 **Ⓔ** Camden Town, Regent's Park **⏱** From 10am daily; closing times vary, check website (last adm: 1 hr before closing) **✕** 25 Dec **🌐** zsl.org

By international standards, London Zoo is relatively small but it packs a lot in, including a Sumatran tiger, Western lowland gorillas, spider monkeys, giraffes, iguanas, pythons and bird-eating tarantulas. In total, the zoo has more than 650 animal species and over 1,000 mammals, amphibians, birds and reptiles.

Despite its dense population, many of the larger animals here enjoy relatively spacious and interesting enclosures, especially since the zoo embarked on an extensive series of imaginative rede-velopments in the early 2000s. Since then, new enclosures have included Penguin Beach, Gorilla Kingdom, Rainforest Life, Tiger Territory and In with the Lemurs, with the Snowdon Aviary set to reopen as a colobus monkey walk-through following a Foster + Partners reboot in 2021.

The largest enclosure is the Land of the Lions, where Asiatic lions prowl around the zoo's rendering of the Gir Forest in western India. Visitors look on from walk-ways and an imagining of a Gujarat village, complete with train station, high street and temple ruins.

The zoo emphasizes its important international role in conservation and research work and is run by, as well as home to, the Zoological Society of London.

↑ Watching penguins swim underwater at Penguin Beach

STAY

London Zoo Lodges
Wake up to the roaring of lions after spending the night at a lodge in the Land of the Lions, a set of comfortable, charming cabins inside the zoo. Also included are two full days at the zoo, tours at sunset, after dark and in the morning, as well as breakfast and dinner.

Q F1 **🌐** zsl.org/zsl-london-zoo/london-zoo-lodge

£££

The Langham
The Palm Court at this grand hotel is suppos-edly the original home of the afternoon tea. Elegant restaurants, bars and rooms.

Q G4 **⌂** 1c Portland Place W1B 1JA **🌐** langhamhotels.com

£££

↑ Meticulously-designed flowerbeds and trees as seen from above

3 🖵

St Marylebone Parish Church

📍F3 🚇Marylebone Rd NW1 🚉Regent's Park 🕐9am–5pm Mon–Fri, 8am–4pm Sat & Sun 🌐stmarylebone.org

Noted poets Robert Browning and Elizabeth Barrett were married here in 1846 after eloping from her strict family home on nearby Wimpole Street. The large, stately church by Thomas Hardwick was built in 1817 after the former church, where Admiral Lord Nelson worshipped and where Lord Byron was christened in 1778, had become too small. Hardwick was determined that the same should not happen to his new church – so everything is on a grand scale.

4 🖌 🖵 🛍

Madame Tussauds

📍F3 🚇Marylebone Rd NW1 🚉Baker St 🕐Usually 9/10am–4/5pm daily; times vary, check website 🌐madametussauds.com

Madame Tussaud began her wax-modelling career rather morbidly, making death masks of well-known victims of the French Revolution. Today, traditional wax-modelling techniques are still used to re-create politicians, royals, actors, rock stars and sporting heroes, the displays changing fairly regularly to keep up with who's in and who's out.

Visitors can step onto the palace balcony with Her Majesty or "attend" a celebrity bash. In "Spirit of London" you can travel in stylized London taxi-cabs through momentous events in the city's history, such as the Great Fire of 1666 and 1960s Swinging London. There are also sections dedicated to franchises such as Marvel and Star Wars, with detailed walk-in sets and a 4D Marvel film experience.

Ticket prices are fairly steep, but cheaper if you buy online in advance. Opting for timed tickets can help reduce queuing times.

5

Broadcasting House

📍G4 🚇Portland Place W1 🚉Oxford Circus 🌐bbc.co.uk

The first radio broadcast was made from here in 1932, two months before the Art Deco building was officially opened. Redevelopment has now turned it into a state-of-the-art digital centre for BBC Radio, TV and BBC News and

↑ The spacious interior of St Marylebone Parish Church

online services. The only way to get a look inside is to apply for a place, via the website, on one of the BBC's television or radio shows as a studio audience member.

6

All Souls, Langham Place

📍G4 🚇Langham Place W1 🚉Oxford Circus 🕐10am–5pm Mon–Fri, 9am–2pm & 5–7:30pm Sun 🌐allsouls.org

Designed by John Nash in 1824, this church's quirky round frontage is best seen from Regent Street. When it was first built, the spire was ridiculed as it appeared too slender and flimsy, and the church itself was described as "one of the most miserable structures in the metropolis".

The only Nash church in London, it had close links with the BBC, based across the street at Broadcasting House; the daily service, a stalwart of the radio schedule, was

> Noted poets Robert Browning and Elizabeth Barrett were married at St Marylebone Parish Church in 1846 after eloping from her strict family home on nearby Wimpole Street.

broadcast from here for many years. It maintains this broadcasting tradition with a "sermon streaming" resource on its website.

7

Royal Academy of Music Museum

📍F3 🚇Marylebone Rd NW1 🚇Baker Street, Regent's Park 🕐11:30am–5:30pm Mon–Fri, noon–4pm Sat 🚫Dec 🌐ram.ac.uk

This simple museum in one of the country's finest music schools showcases the Royal Academy's collection of historical instruments. The three small rooms, staffed by student volunteers, are dispersed across three floors. On the ground floor you can find out about the history of the institution; in the Strings Gallery and the Piano Gallery upstairs are a prized Stradivari violin and viola and a 17th-century harpsichord. There's a restaurant and frequent free concerts in the revamped performance spaces.

8

Wallace Collection

📍F4 🚇Hertford House, Manchester Sq W1 🚇Bond St, Baker St 🕐10am–5pm daily 🌐wallacecollection.org

This is one of the world's finest private collections of art. Bequeathed to the government in 1897 with the stipulation that it go on public display with nothing added or removed, it remained intact until 2020 when loans were permitted for the first time. The product of passionate

→ The late-Victorian pavilion at Lord's Cricket Ground

↑ Eighteenth-century European art in the Wallace Collection

collecting of four generations of the Hertford family, it is a must for anyone with even a passing interest in the progress of European art up to the late 19th century.

Among the 70 masterworks are Frans Hals's *The Laughing Cavalier*, Velázquez's *The Lady with a Fan*, Titian's *Perseus and Andromeda*, Rembrandt's *Titus* and Canaletto's two paintings of Venice. There are several superb portraits by Reynolds, Romney and Gainsborough. Other highlights include Sèvres porcelain and sculpture by Houdon and Roubiliac. The fine European and Oriental

armour collection is the second largest in the UK.

There are regular tours and talks daily; details are on the website.

9

Lord's Cricket Ground

📍D2 🚇NW8 🚇St John's Wood 🕐For guided tours: Apr–Oct 10am–3pm; Nov–Mar 10am–2pm 🚫21 Dec–1 Jan 🌐lords.org

Set up in 1814 by professional cricketer Thomas Lord, the ground can be visited on guided tours that take in the Long Room, the dressing rooms and the Marylebone Cricket Club Museum, which is full of memorabilia from cricketing history, including a stuffed sparrow killed by a cricket ball and the Ashes urn. This tiny urn contains, supposedly, the burned remains of a cricket bail signifying "the death of English cricket" after a notable defeat by Australia. It is still the object of ferocious competition between the two national teams. The museum explains the history of the game, and mementos of notable cricketers make it a place of pilgrimage for devotees of the sport. Tours are hourly and it is essential to book ahead; there are no tours on major match days, but ticket holders do get free access to the museum.

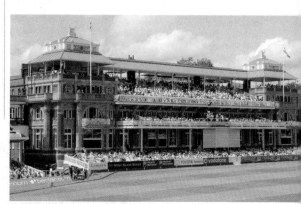

← Another case for the great detective unfolding in the Sherlock Holmes Museum

and is furnished exactly as described in the books. Visitors are greeted by Holmes's "housekeeper" and shown to his re-created rooms on the first floor. The shop sells souvenirs including short stories and deerstalker hats.

Did You Know?

There have been more films starring Sherlock Holmes than any other (human) character.

such as Nike, UNIQLO and Gap plus British favourites such as Marks & Spencer and Topshop.

11

Sherlock Holmes Museum

📍 E3 🏠 221b Baker St NW1 🚇 Baker St 🕐 9:30am–6pm daily 🌐 sherlock-holmes.co.uk

Sir Arthur Conan Doyle's fictional detective lived at 221b Baker Street, an address that did not exist at the time, because Baker Street was then much shorter. This building, dating from 1815, is on what Conan Doyle would have known as Upper Baker Street, above Marylebone Road. It has been converted to resemble Holmes's flat,

12

London Central Mosque

📍 E2 🏠 146 Park Rd NW8 🚇 Marylebone, St John's Wood, Baker St 🕐 10am–last prayer 🌐 iccuk.org

Surrounded by trees on the edge of Regent's Park, this large, golden-domed mosque was designed by Sir Frederick Gibberd and completed in 1978. Built to cater for the increasing number of Muslim residents in and visitors to London, the mosque is capable of holding 1,800 worshippers. The main hall of worship is a plain square chamber with a domed roof and a magnificent carpet. Visitors must remove their shoes before entering the mosque, and women should remember to cover their head.

10

Oxford Street

📍 F5 🏠 W1 🚇 Marble Arch, Bond St, Oxford Circus, Tottenham Court Rd 🌐 oxfordstreet.co.uk

This is London's biggest and busiest shopping street, running from Marble Arch at the western end right along Marylebone's southern border and then beyond, dividing Soho and Fitzrovia and ending at the Centre Point tower block. The western half of the street is home to several department stores, most notably Selfridges, the largest and most famous (don't miss its magnificent Food Hall), although John Lewis, opened in 1864, predates it by half a century. Along the street's length and its shopper-clogged pavements are the UK flagship stores of brands

→ Immaculate Cumberland Terrace, among London's most desirable addresses

Welcoming pubs and bars offering refreshment on Marylebone High Street ↑

13 🍽

Wigmore Hall

📍 G4 🏠 36 Wigmore St W1
🚇 Bond St, Oxford Circus
🌐 wigmore-hall.org.uk

This appealing little concert hall for chamber music was designed by T E Collcutt, architect of the Savoy hotel, in 1900. At first it was called Bechstein Hall because it was attached to the Bechstein piano showroom; the area used to be the heart of London's piano trade. Opposite is the Art Nouveau emporium built in

1907 as Debenham and Freebody's department store – now known as Debenhams.

14

Cumberland Terrace

📍 G2 🏠 NW1 🚇 Great Portland St, Regent's Park, Camden Town

Architect James Thomson is credited with the detailed design of this, the longest and most elaborate of the Neo-Classical terraces created by John Nash that border Regent's Park. Completed in 1828, it was designed to be visible from a palace Nash planned for the Prince Regent (later George IV). The palace was never built because the prince was too busy with his plans for Buckingham Palace (p90).

---

15 🍽 🖥 🛍

Marylebone High Street

📍 F4 🏠 NW1 🚇 Baker St, Regent's Park, Bond St
🌐 marylebonevillage.com

This boutique-heavy high street, the most villagey part

of central London, is often overlooked by visitors. Inside smart red-and-yellow brick townhouses are organic food shops, independent fashion stores and refined, often high-end restaurants, frequented by a well-dressed set of local shoppers. Must-sees are iconic design depot the Conran Shop and the incomparable Daunt Books. Nearby, St Vincent and Aybrook streets host the Marylebone Farmers' Market every Sunday (10am–2pm), one of the largest and most upmarket in London.

SHOP

Daunt Books

The most wonderful feature of this original Edwardian bookshop is its long oak galleries. Shelves carry travel guides and literature on each country.

📍 F4 🏠 83 Marylebone High St W1
🌐 dauntbooks.co.uk

A SHORT WALK
MARYLEBONE

Distance 2.5 km (1.5 miles) **Time** 30 minutes
Nearest Tube Regent's Park

Just south of Regent's Park lies the medieval village of Marylebone (originally Maryburne, the stream by St Mary's church). Until the 18th century it was surrounded by fields, but these were built over as fashionable London drifted west. The area has maintained its elegance, and your walk will take you past the spacious houses that professionals, especially doctors, used in the mid-19th century to receive wealthy clients. The route also takes in Marylebone High Street, full of interesting, high-quality food and clothes shops, bookshops and cafés.

↑ The splendid Edwardian interior of Daunt Books, built in 1910

John Nash laid out **Regent's Park** (p276), one of the city's royal parks, in 1812 as a setting for classically designed villas and terraces.

FINISH

The **Royal Academy of Music** (p279), England's first music academy, was founded in 1822. The present brick building, with its own concert hall, is from 1911.

Poets Robert Browning and Elizabeth Barrett were married in 1846 in **St Marylebone Parish Church** (p278).

The **Madame Tussauds** waxworks museum (p278) has been in business since 1835 and remains one of London's most popular attractions.

Baker Street station

Marylebone High Street (p281) is lined with attractive shops. At No 83 is Daunt Books with its galleried interior. On the corner of Marylebone Lane, V V Rouleaux is a colourful haberdashery shop.

YORK BRIDGE

CIRCLE

YORK TERRACE EAST

OUTER

YORK TERRACE WEST

YORK GATE

MARYLEBONE ROAD

ALLSOP PLACE

NOTTINGHAM PLACE

MARYLEBONE HIGH STREET

LUXBOROUGH STREET

NOTTINGHAM STREET

Locator Map
For more detail see p274

Park Crescent's *breathtaking façades by Nash have been preserved, although the interiors were rebuilt as offices in the 1960s. The crescent seals the north end of Nash's ceremonial route from St James's to Regent's Park via Regent Street and Portland Place.*

Regent's Park station

START

Consulting rooms of eminent medical specialists have been located at **Harley Street** *for more than a century.*

In the centre of broad **Portland Place** *is a statue of Field Marshal Sir George Stuart White, who won the Victoria Cross for gallantry in the Afghan War of 1879.*

PARK SQUARE WEST

HARLEY ST

PARK CRESCENT

PORTLAND PLACE

HARLEY STREET

DEVONSHIRE STREET

The **Royal Institute of British Architects** *is housed in a striking Art Deco building designed by George Grey Wornum in 1934.*

UPPER WIMPOLE ST

BEAUMONT STREET

→ Enjoying café life along the pleasant Marylebone High Street

A LONG WALK
ALONG THE REGENT'S CANAL

Distance 5 km (3 miles) **Time** 70 minutes
Nearest Tube Warwick Avenue

Master builder John Nash wanted the Regent's Canal to pass through Regent's Park, but instead it circles the northern border of the park. Opened in 1820, it is long defunct as a commercial waterway but is now popular with cyclists and walkers. This long walk starts in Little Venice, an area known for its peaceful canals, then diverts to take in the spectacular cityscape view from Primrose Hill. The route ends in the cool and quirky streets of Camden, where you can browse the colourful shops or grab a bite to eat.

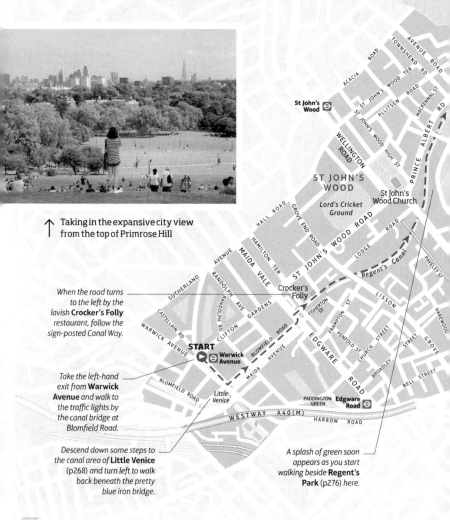

↑ Taking in the expansive city view from the top of Primrose Hill

When the road turns to the left by the lavish **Crocker's Folly** restaurant, follow the sign-posted Canal Way.

Take the left-hand exit from **Warwick Avenue** and walk to the traffic lights by the canal bridge at Blomfield Road.

Descend down some steps to the canal area of **Little Venice** (p268) and turn left to walk back beneath the pretty blue iron bridge.

A splash of green soon appears as you start walking beside **Regent's Park** (p276) here.

START Warwick Avenue

Little Venice

St John's Wood

ST JOHN'S WOOD

Lord's Cricket Ground

St John's Wood Church

Crocker's Folly

Regent's Canal

PADDINGTON GREEN   Edgware Road

WESTWAY   A40(M)   HARROW   ROAD

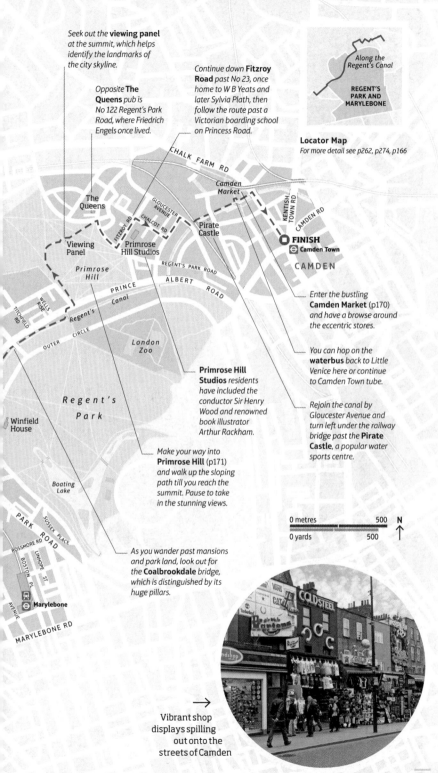

Seek out the **viewing panel** at the summit, which helps identify the landmarks of the city skyline.

Opposite **The Queens** pub is No 122 Regent's Park Road, where Friedrich Engels once lived.

Continue down **Fitzroy Road** past No 23, once home to W B Yeats and later Sylvia Plath, then follow the route past a Victorian boarding school on Princess Road.

Locator Map
For more detail see p262, p274, p166

Along the
Regent's Canal

REGENT'S PARK AND MARYLEBONE

CHALK FARM RD

Camden Market

KENTISH TOWN RD

CAMDEN RD

The Queens

GLOUCESTER AVENUE

FITZROY RD

CHALCOT RD

Pirate Castle

FINISH
Camden Town

Viewing Panel

Primrose Hill Studios

Primrose Hill

REGENT'S PARK ROAD

CAMDEN

WELLS RISE

PRINCE

ALBERT ROAD

Canal

TICHFIELD RD

Regent's

CIRCLE

OUTER

London Zoo

Enter the bustling **Camden Market** (p170) and have a browse around the eccentric stores.

You can hop on the **waterbus** back to Little Venice here or continue to Camden Town tube.

Rejoin the canal by Gloucester Avenue and turn left under the railway bridge past the **Pirate Castle**, a popular water sports centre.

Regent's Park

Winfield House

Primrose Hill Studios residents have included the conductor Sir Henry Wood and renowned book illustrator Arthur Rackham.

Make your way into **Primrose Hill** (p171) and walk up the sloping path till you reach the summit. Pause to take in the stunning views.

Boating Lake

PARK

SUSSEX PLACE

ROSSMORE RD

LINHOPE ST

BOSTON PL

ROAD

PLACE

0 metres 500
0 yards 500

N ↑

As you wander past mansions and park land, look out for the **Coalbrookdale** bridge, which is distinguished by its huge pillars.

AVENUE

Marylebone

MARYLEBONE RD

→ Vibrant shop displays spilling out onto the streets of Camden

Cycling through the woodland on Hampstead Heath

HAMPSTEAD AND HIGHGATE

These rather exclusive north London neighbourhoods, perched on either side of the vast, bucolic Hampstead Heath, were distinct villages centuries before they were swallowed up by the metropolis, a quality still tangible to this day. There has been a settlement in Highgate since at least the early Middle Ages, when an important staging post on the Great North Road from London was established, with a gate to control access. Hampstead is known to have existed as far back as the 10th century. From around the 17th century both became fashionable retreats from the capital, an allure only partially dampened in the 19th century by their own urban expansion, the arrival of the railway and the encroachment of the city. They also share illustrious literary and artistic connections, though Hampstead's arguably have the edge, with the likes of John Keats having set up home there. Though they may have lived in Hampstead, many of the city's intellectuals are buried in Highgate's cemetery – among them political theorist Karl Marx.

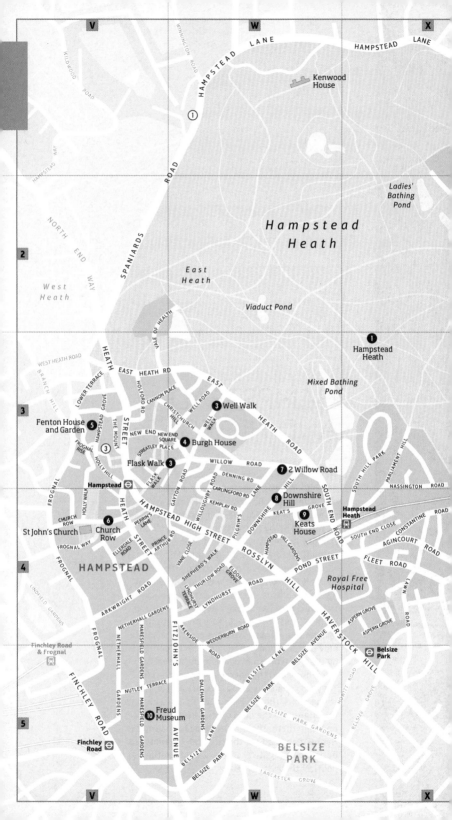

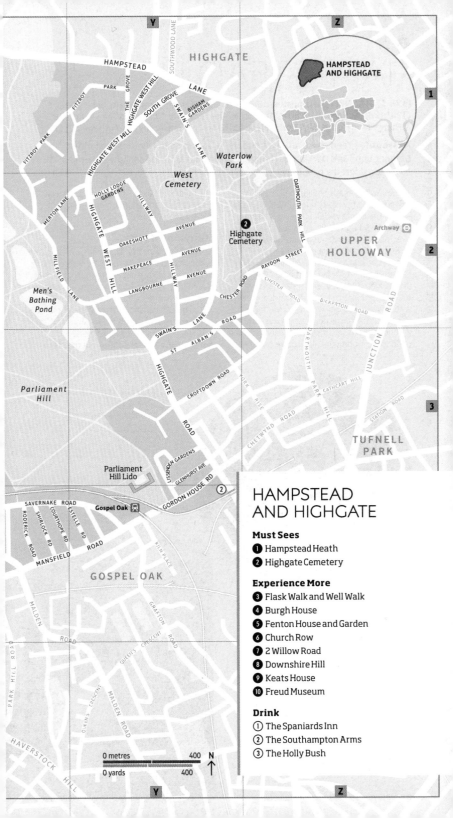

HAMPSTEAD AND HIGHGATE

Must Sees

1 Hampstead Heath
2 Highgate Cemetery

Experience More

3 Flask Walk and Well Walk
4 Burgh House
5 Fenton House and Garden
6 Church Row
7 2 Willow Road
8 Downshire Hill
9 Keats House
10 Freud Museum

Drink

① The Spaniards Inn
② The Southampton Arms
③ The Holly Bush

1

HAMPSTEAD HEATH

X3 NW3, NW5 Hampstead, Golders Green Hampstead Heath, Gospel Oak
24 hrs daily; Kenwood House: Apr-Oct: 10am-5pm daily; Nov-Mar: 10am-4pm daily
Hampstead Heath: cityoflondon.gov.uk; Kenwood House: english-heritage.org.uk

A favourite green space among Londoners, Hampstead Heath is the largest of inner London's parklands, though it is too wild and wonderfully unkempt to be considered a proper park.

The sprawling heath, separating the hilltop villages of Hampstead and Highgate, brings a slice of the countryside to the city, with large tracts of wild woodlands and meadows rolling over hills and around ponds and lakes. Covering an area of 8 sq km (3 sq miles), its natural habitats attract a wealth of wildlife, including bats and some 180 species of birds. There are also all kinds of landscaped areas, most notably the Hill Garden, a charming Edwardian garden with a raised pergola walkway, flowering plants and beautiful formal pond, which was once the grounds to Lord Leverhulme's house, but is now open to all. Among the many other features of the heath are Vale of Health, an isolated village tucked inside the southern boundary, and the picturesque Viaduct Pond.

Kenwood House

Located on Hampstead Lane is this magnificent white Neo-Classical mansion. Its walls are hung with paintings by old masters and it overlooks splendidly landscaped grounds high on the edge of the north side of the heath. This is one of the most picturesque parts of the whole area, with two large and lovely ponds, sweeping lawns and trails through the woodlands. There has been a house here since 1616, but the present

↑ Taking a dip in the men's bathing pond (there are women's and mixed ponds too)

→ View over London from the green environs of Hampstead Heath

GREAT VIEW
Hillside Heights

Parliament Hill, in the southeast corner of the heath, provides one of the most spectacular views over the capital, taking in the Shard, the skyscrapers of the City, the dome of St Paul's Cathedral and Canary Wharf.

Statue by Henry Moore in the grounds of Kenwood House ↓

↑ Grand Kenwood House, on the edge of Hampstead Heath

villa was remodelled by Robert Adam in 1764 for the Earl of Mansfield. Adam transformed the interior and most of his work has survived, including the highlight, the resplendent library, with its ceiling paintings, opposing apses and Corinthian columns. Precious paintings in Kenwood's collection include works by Vermeer, Van Dyck, Hals, Reynolds, Gainsborough and Rembrandt – his *Self-Portrait with Two Circles* is the star attraction of the collection. The house has a tearoom and café with a lovely garden seating area. In summer there are ticketed, open-air concerts in the grounds, though many people pack a picnic and sit nearby to listen.

↑ Elegant rooms filled with old master paintings

2 ⬀ M3

HIGHGATE CEMETERY

📍 Z2 🚇 Swain's Lane N6 🚇 Archway 🕐 Times vary, check website 🌐 highgatecemetery.org

Opened in 1839, this is London's best-known cemetery, most famous for epitomizing the Victorian obsession with death and the afterlife.

The two leafy sections of Highgate Cemetery, divided by a country lane, are full of flowerbeds, statues, elaborate tombs and overgrown gravestones, bathed in a light suitably subdued by the shade from the small forests of trees. For well-off Victorians, preoccupied with death and insistent on burial rather than cremation, this was the graveyard of choice, where you could lie shoulder to shoulder with poets, artists and intellectuals. Both sections contain the graves of numerous iconic figures but it is the West Cemetery (guided tour only) that is the more atmospheric, and architecturally interesting. Its showpiece is the restored Egyptian Avenue, a street of family vaults styled on ancient Egyptian tombs, leading to the Circle of Lebanon, a ring of vaults topped by a cedar tree.

↑ Statue of an angel, one of many found among the tombs and trees

Did You Know?

Original cemetery regulations required tombs to be encased in lead, which caused some to explode.

↑ Karl Marx's tomb in its tranquil surroundings in Highgate Cemetery

TOP 5 NOTABLE RESIDENTS

Karl Marx (1818-83)
German political philosopher.

George Eliot (1819-80)
The pen name of Mary Ann Evans, author of *Middlemarch*.

Douglas Adams (1952-2001)
Author of the cult-classic *The Hitchhiker's Guide to the Galaxy*.

Christina Rossetti (1830-94)
Romantic poet.

Malcolm McLaren (1946-2010)
Manager of the notorious Sex Pistols.

↑ Fenton House, whose treasures can be explored in the summer months

EXPERIENCE MORE

3

Flask Walk and Well Walk

📍W3 🏠NW3 🚇Hampstead

Flask Walk is named after the Flask pub. Here, in the 18th century, the area's therapeutic spa water was put into flasks and sold to visitors or sent to London. A disused fountain now marks the site of the well in nearby Well Walk. There have been many notable residents of Well Walk: artist John Constable, novelists D H Lawrence and J B Priestley, and the poet John Keats. At the High Street end, Flask Walk is narrow and lined with old shops. Beyond the Flask pub it broadens into a row of fine Regency houses.

4

Burgh House

📍W3 🏠New End Sq NW3 🚇Hampstead 🕐Noon-4pm Wed-Fri & Sun 🚫3 weeks at Christmas 🌐burghhouse.org.uk

Since 1979, an independent trust has run Burgh House as the Hampstead Museum, which illustrates the history of the area and some of its notable residents. The museum owns a significant art collection, which includes works by Duncan Grant and Helen Allingham, along with furniture and archive material on the area. In the 1720s, Dr William Gibbons, chief physician to the spa, lived at this address.

5

Fenton House and Garden

📍V3 🏠20 Hampstead Grove NW3 🚇Hampstead 🕐Mar-Oct: 11am-5pm Wed-Sun, public hols & some days in Dec 🌐nationaltrust.org.uk

Built in 1686, this handsome William and Mary house is the oldest mansion in Hampstead. It contains the Benton Fletcher collection of early keyboard instruments – a harpsichord dating from 1612 is said to have been played by Handel – and a collection of porcelain. The instruments are kept in full working order and concerts are sometimes given. The porcelain was largely accumulated by Lady Binning who, in 1952, left the house and its contents to the National Trust. Don't miss the splendid walled garden.

↑ The buildings of Church Row, Hampstead, a perfect slice of Georgian history

6

Church Row

◉ V4 ⌂ NW3 ⊖ Hampstead

Church Row is one of the most complete Georgian streets in London. Much of its original detail has survived, notably the ironwork. At the west end is St John's, Hampstead's parish church, built in 1745. The iron gates are earlier and come from Canons Park in Edgware, Middlesex. Inside the church is a bust of poet John Keats. Artist John Constable's grave is in the churchyard, and a long list of other Hampstead luminaries are buried in the adjoining cemetery.

7

2 Willow Road

◉ W3 ⌂ NW3 ⊖ Hampstead ⊜ Hampstead Heath ◷ Mar–Oct: 11am–5pm Wed–Sun ⊠ nationaltrust.org.uk

The striking modernist 1930s home of Hungarian architect Ernö Goldfinger – designer of a number of Brutalist London tower blocks – is preserved almost exactly as he designed and lived in it, complete with many of his beguiling possessions. The relatively plain, unremarkable façade makes the sleek, stylish yet warm interior all the more memorable. Steps from the ground floor delicately fan out in a spiral leading up to the open-plan, beautifully efficient living space. Bathed in a natural light perfect for viewing Goldfinger's precious 20th-century art

↑ The Regency façade of St John's Downshire Hill, completed in 1823

collection, the geometrically designed rooms are full of innovative touches – removable walls, for example, that allow interior spaces to be reconfigured. Admission from 11am to 2pm is limited to hourly tours.

8

Downshire Hill

◉ W4 ⌂ NW3 ⊖ Hampstead

A beautiful street of mainly Regency houses, Downshire Hill lent its name to a group of artists, including Stanley Spencer and Mark Gertler, who would gather at No 47 between the two World Wars. The same house had been the meeting place of Pre-Raphaelite artists, among them Dante Gabriel Rossetti and Edward Burne-Jones. A more recent resident, at No 5, was the late Jim Henson, the creator of The Muppets.

The church on the corner (the second Hampstead church to be called St John's) was built in 1823 to serve the Hill's residents. Inside, it still has its original box pews.

Keats House

W4 **10 Keats Grove NW3** **Hampstead, Belsize Park** **Hampstead Heath** **11am-5pm Wed-Sun** **Christmas week** **cityoflondon.gov.uk/keats**

Originally two semi-detached houses built in 1816, the smaller one became Keats's home in 1818, when a friend persuaded him to move in. Keats spent two productive years here: perhaps his most celebrated poem *Ode to a Nightingale* was said to have been written under a plum tree in the garden. The Brawne family moved into the larger house a year later and Keats became engaged to their daughter, Fanny. However, the marriage never took place: Keats died of consumption in Rome before two years had passed. He was only 25 years old. A copy of one of Keats's love letters to Fanny, the engagement ring he offered her and a lock of her hair are among the mementos exhibited at the house, whose displays were revamped for its 200th anniversary in 2018. Visitors are also able to see copies of some of Keats's manuscripts, part of a collection that serves as a tribute to his life and work. Thirty-minute tours begin at 1:30pm and 3pm.

Did You Know?

The Freud Museum has a collection of contemporary art open for public viewing.

Freud Museum

V5 **20 Maresfield Gdns NW3** **Finchley Rd** **Noon-5pm Wed-Sun** **1 Jan, 25-26 Dec** **freud.org.uk**

In 1938, Sigmund Freud, the founder of psychoanalysis, fled from Nazi persecution in Vienna to this Hampstead house. Making use of the possessions he brought with him, his family re-created the atmosphere of his Vienna consulting rooms.

After Freud died in 1939 his daughter Anna (who was a pioneer of child psycho-analysis) kept the house as it was, and in 1986 it was opened as a museum dedicated to her father. On display is the couch on which patients lay for analysis. A series of 1930s home movies shows Freud with his dog as well as more distressing footage of Nazi attacks on his apartment. There's a bookshop and free tours take place at 2pm on Wednesdays and on the first Sunday of the month. The museum also puts on regular talks.

In 2016 Anna Freud was commemorated with her own blue plaque on the house, joining that of her father; it is the only 19th-century building in the city to have been awarded the rare "double blue" accolade.

DRINK

The Spaniards Inn

Dickensian pub on Hampstead Heath with a colourful 500-year history, a beer garden for summer and an open fire in winter.

W1 **Spaniards Rd NW3** **thespaniards hampstead.co.uk**

The Southampton Arms

A relaxed traditional pub with a dinky beer garden, offering a superior range of ales from independent breweries.

Y3 **139 Highgate Rd NW5** **thesouthampton arms.co.uk**

The Holly Bush

A cosy 18th-century pub with low ceilings on a charming backstreet in Hampstead. Great pub grub too.

V3 **22 Holly Mount NW3** **hollybush hampstead.co.uk**

← A stained-glass skylight illuminating the library of Keats House

A SHORT WALK
HAMPSTEAD

Distance 1.5 km (1 mile) **Time** 30 minutes
Nearest Tube Hampstead

Perched awkwardly on a hilltop, with its broad heath to the north, Hampstead has kept its village atmosphere and sense of being outside the city. This has attracted artists and writers since Georgian times and long made it one of London's most desirable residential areas. Its mansions and town houses are perfectly maintained, and a stroll through Hampstead's narrow streets is one of London's quieter pleasures.

Did You Know?

Admiral's House was the inspiration for the home of Admiral Boom in P L Travers' *Mary Poppins*.

*A welcome retreat from the city, **Hampstead Heath's** broad open spaces include bathing ponds, meadows and lakes (p290).*

Whitestone Pond *takes its name from the old white milestone nearby.*

Admiral's House *dates from about 1700. Built for a sea captain, its name derives from its external maritime motifs. No admiral ever actually lived in it.*

LOWER TERRACE

HEATH

HAMPSTEAD GROVE

UPPER TERRACE

ADMIRAL'S WALK

Grove Lodge *was home to novelist John Galsworthy (1867–1933), author of* The Forsyte Saga, *for the last 15 years of his life.*

*Summer visitors should seek out the late 17th-century **Fenton House** and its exquisite walled garden, which are well hidden in the jumble of streets near the heath (p293).*

← Stunning views of the city from a hillside on Hampstead Heath

0 metres 100
0 yards 100

↑ Browsing the characterful
shops on Flask Walk

Locator Map
For more detail see p288

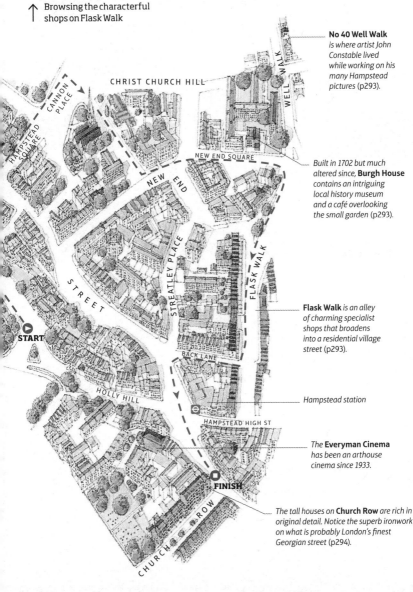

No 40 Well Walk
*is where artist John
Constable lived
while working on his
many Hampstead
pictures (p293).*

*Built in 1702 but much
altered since,* **Burgh House**
*contains an intriguing
local history museum
and a café overlooking
the small garden (p293).*

Flask Walk *is an alley
of charming specialist
shops that broadens
into a residential village
street (p293).*

Hampstead station

The **Everyman Cinema**
*has been an arthouse
cinema since 1933.*

The tall houses on **Church Row** *are rich in
original detail. Notice the superb ironwork
on what is probably London's finest
Georgian street (p294).*

GREENWICH AND CANARY WHARF

In the mid-15th century, Henry IV's son Humphrey, Duke of Gloucester and the brother of Henry V, first established the royal foothold in Greenwich when he built himself the Palace of Placentia, originally known as Bella Court. Henry VIII was born in the palace, as were his daughters, Mary and Elizabeth. The palace was demolished at the end of the 17th century and the land where it stood is now occupied by the Old Royal Naval College; the royal hunting grounds are now the gorgeous Greenwich Park. The buildings of the Naval College, the centrepiece of the UNESCO World Heritage Site referred to as Maritime Greenwich, started life as Greenwich Hospital, a home for wounded and retired sailors opened in 1692. The conversion to a Royal Navy college in 1873 cemented an already well-established maritime heritage in Greenwich, one shared by Canary Wharf over the river, the site of the historic docklands since the early 19th century.

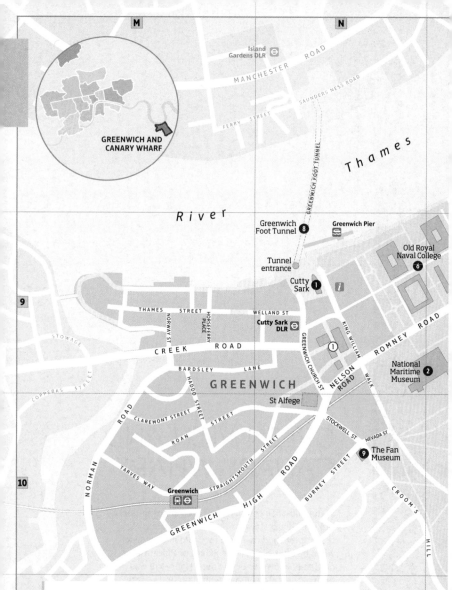

GREENWICH AND CANARY WHARF

Experience
1. Cutty Sark
2. National Maritime Museum
3. Greenwich Park
4. Royal Observatory
5. The Queen's House
6. Old Royal Naval College
7. Ranger's House – the Wernher Collection
8. Greenwich Foot Tunnel
9. The Fan Museum
10. The O2 Arena
11. Emirates Air Line
12. Museum of London Docklands
13. Canary Wharf

Eat & Shop
① Greenwich Market

Drink
② Trafalgar Tavern

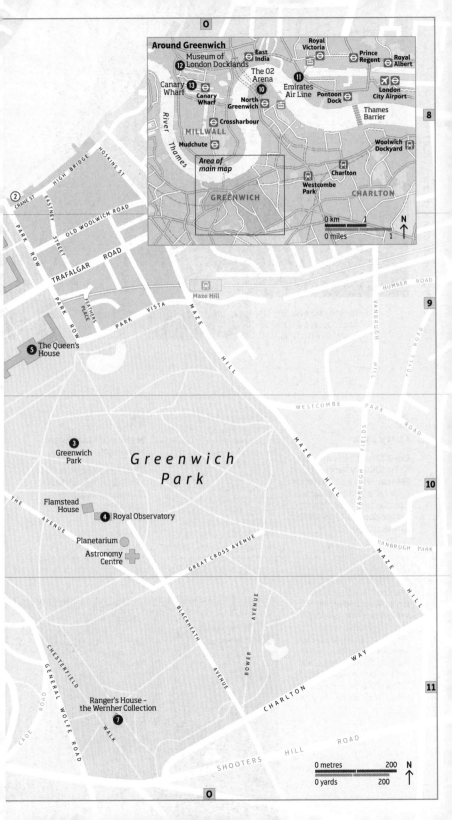

Around Greenwich

Royal Victoria

East India

Museum of London Docklands

Prince Regent

Royal Albert

The O2 Arena

Canary Wharf

Emirates Air Line

London City Airport

Canary Wharf

North Greenwich

Pontoon Dock

Crossharbour

Thames Barrier

MILLWALL

Mudchute

River Thames

Woolwich Dockyard

Area of main map

GREENWICH

Westcombe Park

Charlton

CHARLTON

0 km 1

0 miles 1

N

CRANE ST

PARK ROW

EASTNEY STREET

HIGH BRIDGE

HOSKINS ST

OLD WOOLWICH ROAD

TRAFALGAR ROAD

PARK ROW

FEATHERS PLACE

PARK VISTA

MAZE HILL

Maze Hill

HUMBER ROAD

VANBRUGH HILL

FOYLE ROAD

5 The Queen's House

WESTCOMBE PARK ROAD

3 Greenwich Park

Greenwich Park

VANBRUGH FIELDS

THE AVENUE

Flamstead House

4 Royal Observatory

Planetarium

Astronomy Centre

GREAT CROSS AVENUE

VANBRUGH PARK

MAZE HILL

BLACKHEATH AVENUE

BOWER AVENUE

CHESTERFIELD

CADE ROAD

GENERAL WOLFE ROAD

Ranger's House – the Wernher Collection

7

WALK

CHARLTON WAY

SHOOTERS HILL ROAD

0 metres 200

0 yards 200

N

The structure holding the copper hull of the impressive *Cutty Sark* ↑

EXPERIENCE

1 Cutty Sark

📍N9 🏠King William Walk SE10 🚉Cutty Sark DLR 🚢Greenwich Pier 🕐10am–5pm daily (mid-Jul-Aug: to 6pm; last adm: 45 mins before closing) 🚫24–26 Dec 🌐rmg.co.uk

This majestic vessel is a survivor of the clippers that crossed the Atlantic and Pacific oceans in the 19th century. Launched in 1869 as a tea carrier, it was something of a speed machine in its day, returning from Australia in 1884 in just 83 days – 25 days faster than any other ship. It made its final voyage in 1938 and was put on display here in 1957. In 2006 the *Cutty Sark* was closed to visitors for renovation

work, which suffered a major setback in May 2007 when the ship was severely damaged by fire. It was reopened by the Queen in 2012, fully restored and slightly raised in a glass enclosure. Visitors can explore the cargo decks and sleeping quarters below deck, take the ship's wheel, and be entertained by tales from the costumed "crew". There are interactive displays on navigation and life on board.

2 National Maritime Museum

📍N9 🏠Romney Rd SE10 🚉Cutty Sark DLR 🚢Greenwich 🕐10am–5pm daily 🚫24–26 Dec 🌐rmg.co.uk

This substantial museum, which was built in the 19th century as a school for sailors' children, celebrates Britain's

→ Portrait of a young Nelson, National Maritime Museum

3 Greenwich Park

📍010 🏛SE10 🚇Cutty Sark DLR, Greenwich DLR 🚆Greenwich, Maze Hill, Blackheath ⏰6am-6pm or dusk 🌐royalparks.org.uk

Originally the grounds of a royal palace and still a Royal Park, Greenwich Park was enclosed in 1433 and its brick wall built in the reign of James I. Later in the 17th century, the French royal landscape gardener André Le Nôtre was invited to redesign the park. The broad Avenue, rising south up the hill, was part of his plan. It's a steep climb up the hilltop but one well rewarded by sweeping views across London and more green space to explore.

4 Royal Observatory

📍010 🏛Greenwich Park SE10 🚇Cutty Sark DLR 🚆Greenwich ⏰10am-5pm daily (mid-May-Jun: to 5:30pm; Jul & Aug: to 6pm) 🚫24-26 Dec 🌐rmg.co.uk

The prime meridian (0° longitude) that divides Earth's eastern and western hemispheres passes through here, and millions of visitors come to be photographed standing with a foot on either side of it. In 1884, Greenwich Mean Time became the basis of time measurement for most of the world. Here you can journey through the history of time, explore how scientists first began to map the stars and see world-changing inventions, including the UK's largest refracting telescope. Visitors can even touch a 4.5-billion-year-old asteroid.

→

The onion dome of the Royal Observatory Greenwich, housing a colossal telescope

The stately original building, Flamsteed House, was designed by Christopher Wren for the first Astronomer Royal, John Flamsteed. It contains original instruments belonging to his successors, including Edmond Halley, as well as the celebrated sea clocks of John Harrison, including the H4 – arguably the most important timepiece ever made. There is also a state-of-the-art planetarium here, the only one in London. An entry fee is charged for Flamsteed House and the planetarium shows; access to the Astronomy Centre is free.

seafaring heritage, from early British trade through its emergence as a leading maritime nation to the expeditions of Captain Cook, and from the Napoleonic Wars through to the modern day. Unveiled in 2018, its superb East Wing galleries support an impressive array of historical objects. In the Tudor and Stuarts Seafarers gallery, theatrical trickery brings a re-creation of the Deptford royal dockyard from 1690 to life, while the Polar Worlds section draws together artifacts from the quests of Shackleton and Scott in the Arctic and Antarctic.

In the Nelson, Navy, Nation gallery, the star exhibit is the uniform that Lord Horatio Nelson was wearing when he was shot at the Battle of Trafalgar in October 1805. Rather more spectacular is the royal barge built for Prince Frederick in 1732, decorated with gilded mermaids and his Prince of Wales feathers on the stern. Throughout the museum there are numerous activities for children, such as navigating a ship around the world on a huge floor map.

5

The Queen's House

09 Romney Rd SE10
Cutty Sark DLR Greenwich 10am–5pm daily
24–26 Dec rmg.co.uk

The Queen's House was designed by Inigo Jones and completed in 1637. It was originally intended to be the home of Anne of Denmark, wife of James I, but she died while it was still being built and it was finished for Charles I's queen consort, Henrietta Maria.

Period highlights of the bare interior include the square Great Hall, enlivened by Turner Prize-winner Richard Wright's gold-leaf ceiling, added in 2016, and the spiral cantilevered "tulip staircase", which curves sinuously upwards without a central support. The main focus of interest, though, is the superb art collection of the National Maritime Museum, including works by Turner, Canaletto and Lowry. The famous Armada Portrait of Elizabeth I is on display in the Queen's Presence Chamber, beneath an opulent ceiling fresco that dates from the room's earliest incarnation as Henrietta Maria's bedchamber.

These ambitious buildings by Christopher Wren were built on the site of the old 15th-century royal palace, where Henry VIII, Mary I and Elizabeth I were born.

6

Old Royal Naval College

N9 King William Walk SE10 Cutty Sark DLR, Greenwich DLR Greenwich, Maze Hill 10am–5pm daily; grounds: 8am–11pm daily 24–26 Dec, some early closures for events ornc.org

A landmark of Greenwich, these ambitious buildings by Christopher Wren were built on the site of the old 15th-century royal palace, where Tudors Henry VIII, Mary I and Elizabeth I were born, to house naval pensioners. At its peak, the then hospital was home to some 2,700 veterans. In 1873, the hospital was acquired by the Naval College in Portsmouth and remained a training post for officers until 1997. It also trained thousands of Wrens during World War II.

The Painted Hall is the highlight of a visit. Originally intended as a dining room for the retired seamen, it was opulently decorated by Sir James Thornhill in the early 18th century with allegorical scenes. The tremendous ceiling mural, sometimes dubbed Britain's Sistine Chapel, is the largest figurative painting in the country. In 1805, the hall was the location of a lavish lying-in-state ceremony for Lord Horatio Nelson, who was killed at the Battle of Trafalgar.

The hall reopened in 2019 following an extensive conservation project, which rejuvenated the paintings' lavish colours, now illuminated with state-of-the-art lighting.

↓ One of Wren's twin buildings that form the Old Royal Naval College

EXPERIENCE Greenwich and Canary Wharf

→ Statue by Bergonzoli and Chinese-themed tapestries at the Ranger's House

The renovation also restored the vaulted King William Undercroft to something close to its original Baroque splendour. Tickets include a multimedia guide and expert talks, as well as guided walking tours of the college grounds.

Housed in the east wing, Wren's Chapel was destroyed by fire in 1779 and its interior was redesigned in Greek Revival style with decorative detailing by James Stuart.

There is a pub next to the visitor centre with a terrace overlooking the *Cutty Sark*, but visitors are also welcome to picnic in the grounds.

---

7 (bike) (EH)

Ranger's House – the Wernher Collection

📍 O11 🏠 Chesterfield Walk, Greenwich Park SE10 🚇 Cutty Sark DLR 🚆 Blackheath 🕐 Apr–Oct: 11am–5pm Sun–Thu 🌐 english-heritage.org.uk

The Wernher Collection is located in the Ranger's House (1688), an elegant building southwest of Greenwich Park (*p303*). It is an enchanting array of over 700 pieces accumulated by Sir Julius Wernher, who made a fortune from South African mines, in the late 19th century and developed a passion for collecting mostly medieval and Renaissance art. The collection is displayed across 11 rooms and includes paintings, jewellery, tapestries, furniture and porcelain. Highlights include Renaissance masterworks by Hans Memling and Filippo Lippi, over 100 Renaissance jewels, an opal-set lizard pendant jewel and a fantastic sculpture of a woman and angel by 19th-century artist Giulio Bergonzoli.

8

Greenwich Foot Tunnel

📍 N9 🏠 Between Greenwich Pier SE10 and Isle of Dogs E14 🚇 Island Gardens, Cutty Sark DLR 🚆 Greenwich Pier 🕐 24hrs daily

This 370-m- (1,200-ft-) long tunnel was opened in 1902 to allow south London labourers to walk to work in Millwall Docks. It is well worth making the crossing from Greenwich for the wonderful views, once above ground, back across the river, of Christopher Wren's Royal Naval College and of Inigo Jones's Queen's House.

Matching round red-brick terminals, with glass domes, mark the top of the lift shafts

---

DRINK

Trafalgar Tavern

A Victorian pub where visitors flock in their hundreds. Images of the area's maritime heritage, including Horatio Nelson, are scattered about.

📍 O8 🏠 Park Row SE10 🌐 trafalgartavern. co.uk

200,000

White glazed tiles were needed to line the Greenwich Foot Tunnel.

on either side of the river. Both ends of the tunnel are close to stations on the Docklands Light Railway (DLR). Although there are security cameras, the tunnel can be eerie at night.

9

The Fan Museum

📍 N10 🏠 12 Crooms Hill SE10 🚆 Greenwich 🕐 11am–5pm Tue–Sat, noon–5pm Sun 🕐 Jan, Yom Kippur, 24–26 Dec 🌐 thefan museum.org.uk

This unusual museum owes its appeal to the enthusiasm of Hélène Alexander, whose personal collection of fans has been augmented by donations; the museum's collection now numbers over 5,000 from the 12th century onwards. A small permanent exhibition looks at types of fans and fan-making, while the collection is rotated in temporary displays. On some days, afternoon tea is served in the orangery.

10 (🍴) (☕) (🛍️)
The O2 Arena

📍 08 🚇 North Greenwich SE10 🚆 North Greenwich 🚢 North Greenwich Pier 🕐 9am–1am 🌐 theo2.co.uk

The former Millennium Dome was the focal point of Britain's celebration of the year 2000. Controversial from its earliest days, it is nonetheless an amazing feat of engineering. Its canopy is made from 100,000 sq m (109,000 sq yards) of Teflon-coated spun glass-fibre, and is supported by over 70 km (43 miles) of steel cable rigged to a dozen 100-m (328-ft) masts. Now London's largest indoor concert venue, the O2 also has bars, restaurants, a cinema and Indigo at The O2, a smaller venue. You can also don climbing gear and ascend the outside along a long, bouncy walkway to the very top.

11 (🏷️)
Emirates Air Line

📍 08 🚇 Western Gateway E16/Edmund Halley Way SE10 🚆 Royal Victoria DLR, North Greenwich 🕐 7am–10pm Mon–Fri, 8am–10pm Sat, 9am–10pm Sun (Oct–Mar: to 9pm Sun–Thu) 🌐 emirates airline.co.uk

This cable car, crossing the Thames between the Royal Victoria Dock and the O2, is

Did You Know?

Sponsored by airline Emirates, the construction of the cable car cost a whopping £60 million.

a magnificent way to cross the river, providing spectacular views during the five-minute trip. Travelcards and Oyster cards provide a 25 per cent discount. In the evenings the "flights" slow down, giving you more time to enjoy the panorama of city lights.

12 (🍴) (☕) (🛍️)
Museum of London Docklands

📍 08 🚇 No 1 Warehouse, West India Quay E14 🚆 Canary Wharf, Westferry 🕐 10am–6pm daily 🌐 museumoflondon.org.uk/ museum-london-docklands

Occupying a late Georgian warehouse, this museum tells the story of London's docks and their links from Roman times to the present. A highlight is the re-creation

of the dark and dangerous "Sailortown" of Wapping in the 1850s.

↑ The Emirates cable car and the O2 Arena - the roof of which can be climbed *(inset)*

Canary Wharf

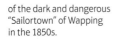 08 E14 Canary Wharf, West India Quay DLR

Home to many of London's tallest skyscrapers, this ambitious commercial development opened in 1991, when the first tenants moved into One Canada Square. At 235 m (770 ft), it is still a dominant feature of the city's eastern skyline with its pyramid-shaped top. The tower stands on what was the West India Dock, closed, like all the London docks, between the 1960s and the 1980s, when trade moved to Tilbury. Today, Canary Wharf is thriving, with a major shopping complex, cafés and restaurants.

THE THAMES BARRIER

In 1236, the Thames rose so high that people rowed across Westminster Hall; London flooded again in 1663, 1928 and in 1953. Something had to be done, and in 1984 the Thames Barrier, 520 m (1,700 ft) across, was unveiled. Its 10 gates swing up to 1.6 m (6 ft) above the level reached by the tide in 1953, and have been used over 190 times. Some boat tours go to the barrier, and there's also a small visitor centre.

A SHORT WALK
GREENWICH

Distance 1.5 km (1 mile) **Time** 25 minutes
Nearest Tube Cutty Sark DLR

Maritime Greenwich, with its illustrious royal and naval connections, is a UNESCO World Heritage Site. In Tudor times it was the site of a palace enjoyed by Henry VIII, near a fine hunting ground. The old palace is gone, but your walk will take you past Inigo Jones's exquisite Queen's House, completed for Charles I's queen consort. The route also takes in the superb National Maritime Museum and Wren's glorious Royal Naval College, making this an enjoyable short stroll.

START

Greenwich Pier is a boarding point for boats to Westminster, the O2 and the Thames Barrier.

Greenwich Foot Tunnel (p305) *is one of two remaining tunnels under the Thames that were built solely for pedestrians.*

Clipper ships such as the **Cutty Sark** (p302) *once traded across the oceans.*

Greenwich Market, *in the heart of Greenwich, sells crafts, antiques and books (p303).*

COLLEGE APPROACH

KING WILLIAN WALK

GREENWICH CHURCH STREET

NELSON ROAD

STOCKWELL STREET

NEVADA STREET

Did You Know?

The Old Royal Naval College had a starring role in Marvel's *Thor: The Dark World.*

There has been a church on the spot on which **St Alfege Church** *stands since 1012.*

← *Cutty Sark*, impressively restored and raised to allow visitors to explore above and below deck

Locator Map
For more detail see p300

George II Statue

The **Old Royal Naval College** *(p304), a stately structure by Wren, was built in four parts so that the Queen's House could keep its river view.*

The **Painted Hall** *contains 18th-century murals by Sir James Thornhill, who painted the interior of the dome of St Paul's Cathedral.*

FINISH

ROMNEY ROAD

↑ The stunning ceiling of the Painted Hall at the Old Royal Naval College in Greenwich

On his return from Italy, the **Queen's House** *(p304) was the first building Inigo Jones designed in the Palladian style.*

Real and model boats, digital displays and instruments like an 18th-century compass illustrate naval history at the **National Maritime Museum** *(p302).*

| 0 metres | 100 |
| 0 yards | 100 |

N ↑

A deer in Richmond Park

Must Sees

1 Queen Elizabeth Olympic Park

2 Hampton Court

3 Kew Gardens

4 Warner Bros. Studio Tour: The Making of Harry Potter

Experience More

5 BAPS Shri Swaminarayan Mandir

6 Victoria Park

7 Alexandra Palace

8 William Morris Gallery

9 Charlton House

10 Sutton House

11 Eltham Palace

12 Horniman Museum

13 Wimbledon Lawn Tennis Museum

14 Wimbledon Windmill Museum

15 Dulwich Picture Gallery

16 Dulwich Park

17 Brixton

18 Ham House

19 Orleans House Gallery

20 Marble Hill House

21 Richmond

22 Richmond Park

23 Syon House

24 Musical Museum

25 Osterley Park and House

26 Pitzhanger Manor House and Gallery

27 London Museum of Water & Steam

28 Fulham Palace

29 Chiswick House

30 Hogarth's House

BEYOND
THE CENTRE

London's high and mighty once sought refuge
from the city in their country manor houses,
located a short distance away from the centre.
Consumed by the rapid expansion of the Victorian
era, these stately homes and royal estates became
intertwined with sprawling suburbs, leading
to the boroughs of today. Postwar immigration
contributed to the identity of each of London's
neighbourhoods – from the West Indian
population in Brixton to the Hindu community
in Neasden – and their local characters continue
to evolve as the regeneration of the city and
gentrification push ever further outwards.

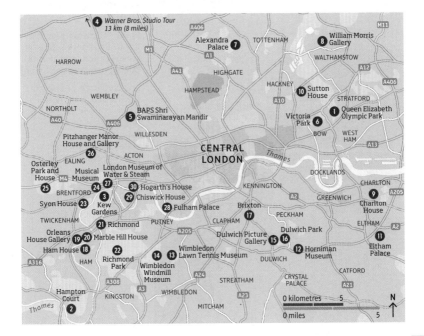

① Ⓜ Ⓨ ▢

QUEEN ELIZABETH OLYMPIC PARK

🔲 E20 ⊖ Hackney Wick, Stratford, Pudding Mill Lane 🚆 Stratford International 🚌 308, 339, 388, 108 🕐 24 hrs daily; information point 10am–3pm daily 🌐 queenelizabetholympicpark.co.uk

Home of the 2012 London Olympic Games, this east London site has been transformed from an area of industrial wasteland into a verdant park with top-quality sporting venues.

As the only city to have hosted the Olympic Games three times – in 1908, 1948 and 2012 – London is justifiably proud of its place in Olympic history. The main site for the 2012 Olympics and Paralympics was a 225-hectare (560-acre) area of former industrial land stretching along the River Lea in east London. The main attractions today are immediately familiar to anyone who watched the events: a series of large, functional but striking venues dotted amid meandering waterways and surrounded by quintessentially English wildflower gardens cut through by various trails. Renamed the Queen Elizabeth Olympic Park to commemorate the Queen's Diamond Jubilee in 2012, the site has been transformed into a permanent leisure attraction. There is plenty to see and do, particularly if you catch one of the numerous events hosted here or want to try out some sports. East Village, originally the Athlete's Village, and the former media hub, Here East, are home to restaurants and cafés.

① ⊛ ▢

Lee Valley VeloPark

🕐 9am–10pm Mon–Fri, 8am–10pm Sat, 8am–9pm Sun; book taster sessions online in advance
🌐 visitleevalley.org.uk

The Velodrome is the hub of a large cycling activity centre, with BMX and road tracks, and mountain-bike trails. Visitors can book taster sessions.

② ⊛ ▢

London Aquatics Centre

🕐 6am–10pm daily (to 5pm Sat & Sun); check online for swim sessions and events
🌐 londonaquaticscentre.org

The late architect Zaha Hadid was inspired by the flow of water for her sweeping design for the Aquatics Centre. Everyone can swim in the competition and training pools here.

③ ⊛ ▢ 🏛

ArcelorMittal Orbit

🕐 11am–5pm Mon–Fri, 10am–7pm Sat & Sun
🌐 arcelormittalorbit.com

Designed by artist Anish Kapoor, the twisting steel tower is part sculpture, part viewing platform, with a thrilling 178-m (580-ft) slide.

① The 6,000-seat velodrome is an iconic building in the Olympic Park and contains the fastest cycling track in the world.

② The pools at the London Aquatics Centre lie beneath the curving roof of this attractive building.

③ Visible from all over the Olympic Park, the ArcelorMittal Orbit tower gives visitors great views.

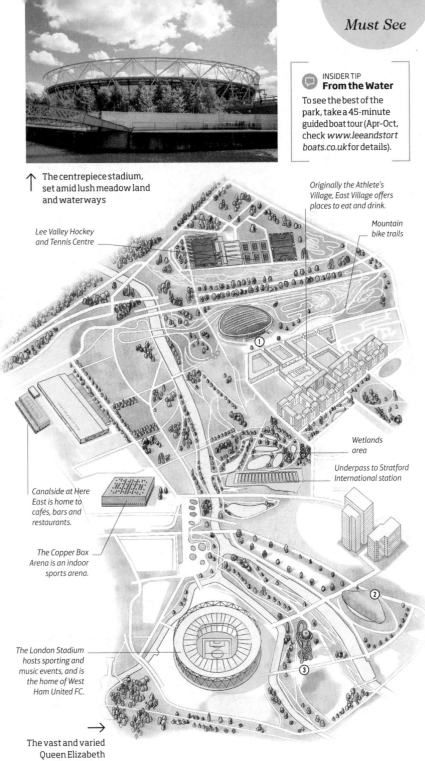

💬 INSIDER TIP
From the Water
To see the best of the park, take a 45-minute guided boat tour (Apr-Oct, check *www.leeandstort boats.co.uk* for details).

↑ The centrepiece stadium, set amid lush meadow land and waterways

Originally the Athlete's Village, East Village offers places to eat and drink.

Mountain bike trails

Lee Valley Hockey and Tennis Centre

Wetlands area

Underpass to Stratford International station

Canalside at Here East is home to cafés, bars and restaurants.

The Copper Box Arena is an indoor sports arena.

The London Stadium hosts sporting and music events, and is the home of West Ham United FC.

→ The vast and varied Queen Elizabeth Olympic Park

2 🏃 🅜 🍴 🖥 🎒

HAMPTON COURT

📍East Molesey, Surrey 🚆Hampton Court ⛴Hampton Court pier (summer only) 🕐Times vary, check website 📅24–26 Dec 🌐hrp.org.uk

With its impressively preserved palace, beautifully manicured gardens and location on the River Thames, the former stomping ground of Tudor king Henry VIII makes for an irresistible attraction.

Glorious Hampton Court began life in 1514 as the riverside country house of Cardinal Wolsey, Henry VIII's Archbishop of York. Later, in 1528, in the hope of retaining royal favour, Wolsey offered it to the king. Hampton Court was twice rebuilt and extended, first by Henry himself and then, in the 1690s, by King William and Queen Mary, who employed Christopher Wren as architect. There is a striking contrast between Wren's Classical royal apartments and the Tudor turrets, gables and chimneys elsewhere. The inspiration for the gardens comes largely from the time of William and Mary, who created a vast, formal Baroque landscape, with avenues and exotic plants.

↑ The sunken Pond Gardens, once ponds that stored fish for Henry VIII's table

> **FLOWER SHOW**
>
> The world's biggest flower show takes place each year at Hampton Court in July. Displays are on either side of Long Water and focus on environmental issues and growing your own food. Book tickets at rhs.org.uk.

↑ Spectacular Hampton Court, seen from the Privy Garden

← An example of the formal and ordered style of the palace gardens

→ Fresh produce from the Kitchen Garden, sold to visitors once a week

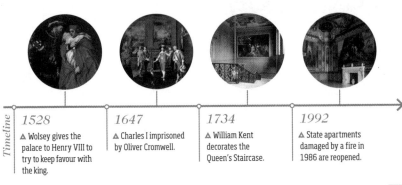

Timeline

1528
△ Wolsey gives the palace to Henry VIII to try to keep favour with the king.

1647
△ Charles I imprisoned by Oliver Cromwell.

1734
△ William Kent decorates the Queen's Staircase.

1992
△ State apartments damaged by a fire in 1986 are reopened.

Exploring the Palace

As a historic royal palace, Hampton Court bears traces of many of the kings and queens of England from Henry VIII to the present day. The building itself is a harmonious blend of Tudor and English Baroque architecture. Inside, visitors can see the Great Hall, built by Henry VIII, as well as the state apartments of the Tudor court. Many of the Baroque state apartments, including those above Fountain Court, are decorated with furniture, tapestries and old masters from the Royal Collection.

1

2

3

① The Tudor kitchen prepared up to 1,000 meals a day for the court, which often included dishes of fresh game, lamb, venison and swan - at a time when most people only ever ate preserved meat.

② The King's Staircase has wall paintings by William Kent, re-creating the court of George I with real people of the time.

③ The Great Hall was used as a banqueting room and a theatre – William Shakespeare's King's Men performed here for James I over Christmas and New Year in 1603–4.

The Tudor Chapel Royal, refitted by Wren, except for the gilded vaulted ceiling.

Queen's Guard Chamber

The ghost of Catherine Howard is said to run through the Haunted Gallery

Hung with tapestries beneath a hammer-beam roof, the Tudor Great Hall is sumptuously decorated.

→

The vast Hampton Court with its mix of Tudor and English Baroque architecture

CARDINAL WOLSEY

Thomas Wolsey (c 1475–1530), who was simultaneously a cardinal, Archbishop of York and Lord Chancellor, was, after the king, the most powerful man in England. However, when he was unable to persuade the pope to allow Henry VIII to divorce his first wife, Catherine of Aragon, Wolsey fell from royal favour. He died while making his way to face trial for treason.

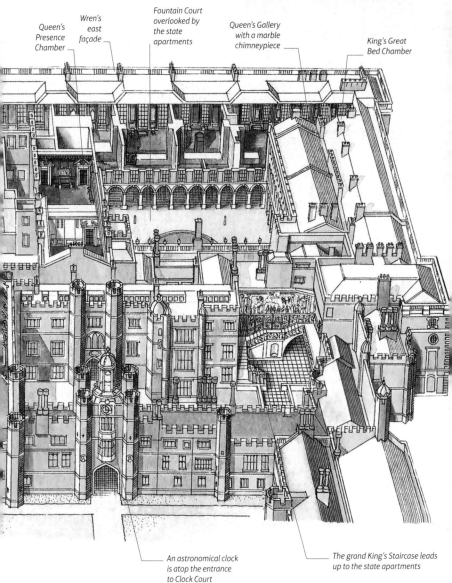

Queen's Presence Chamber

Wren's east façade

Fountain Court overlooked by the state apartments

Queen's Gallery with a marble chimneypiece

King's Great Bed Chamber

An astronomical clock is atop the entrance to Clock Court

The grand King's Staircase leads up to the state apartments

Immaculately manicured flowerbeds in front of the iconic Palm House ↑

3 🥾 🚫 🍴 🖥 🛍

KEW GARDENS

📍 Royal Botanic Gardens, Richmond 🚇 Kew Gardens 🚋 Kew Bridge ⏰ Gardens: from 10am daily (closing times vary, check website); Kew Palace & Great Pagoda: Apr-Sep 10:30am-5:30pm daily; Queen Charlotte's Cottage: Apr-Sep: 11am-4pm Sat, Sun & public hols 🚫 24-25 Dec 🌐 kew.org; hrp.org.uk

The Royal Botanic Gardens, Kew, are a World Heritage Site. Given to the nation in 1841, they display about 30,000 plants.

Kew's reputation was first established by the British naturalist and plant hunter, Sir Joseph Banks, who worked here in the late 18th century. The former royal gardens were created by Princess Augusta, the mother of George III, on the 3.6 ha (9-acre) site in 1759. The world's largest Victorian-era glasshouse, the magnificent Temperate House showcases over 1,500 rare or endangered plant species from across the globe. The Palm House, designed by Decimus Burton in the 1840s, houses exotic plants in tropical conditions.

↑ Fine views from up in the canopy on the Treetop Walkway

🔍 HIDDEN GEM
Hive of Activity

An unusual construction set in a wildflower meadow, The Hive gives visitors a multi-sensory experience of life inside a beehive.

↑ The 1762 Great Pagoda, standing almost 50 m (164 ft) high

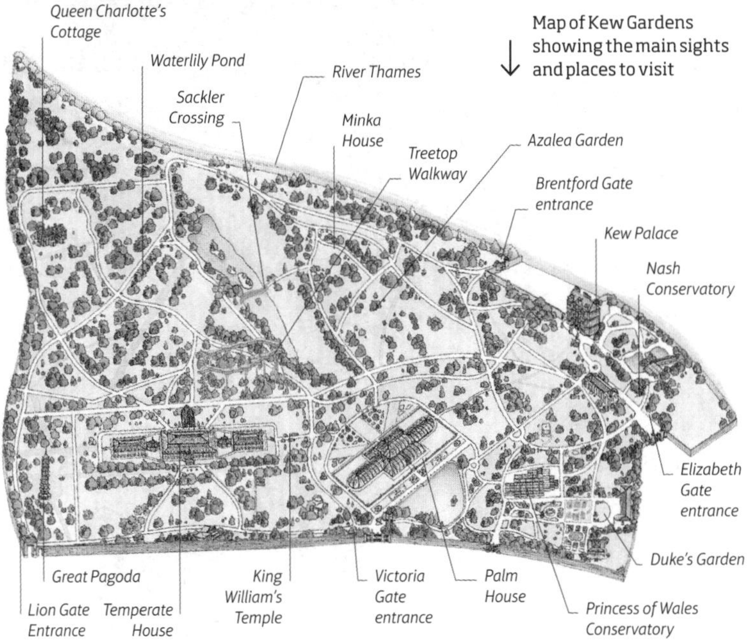

Map of Kew Gardens ↓ showing the main sights and places to visit

Queen Charlotte's Cottage

Waterlily Pond

Sackler Crossing

River Thames

Minka House

Treetop Walkway

Azalea Garden

Brentford Gate entrance

Kew Palace

Nash Conservatory

Elizabeth Gate entrance

Duke's Garden

Princess of Wales Conservatory

Palm House

Victoria Gate entrance

King William's Temple

Temperate House

Great Pagoda

Lion Gate Entrance

WARNER BROS. STUDIO TOUR: THE MAKING OF HARRY POTTER

🏠 Studio Tour Drive, Leavesden ⬛ Watford Junction (shuttle buses run from the station every 20 mins) 🕐 9:30am–8pm Mon–Fri (final tour begins 4pm), 8:30am–10pm Sat, Sun & school holidays (final tour begins 6:30pm) 🚫 25 & 26 Dec 🌐 wbstudiotour.co.uk

Walk the streets of Diagon Alley, enjoy a frothing glass of Butterbeer and admire the animatronics behind your favourite characters – this behind-the-scenes and in-the-scenes tour is an absolute must for budding wizards and witches.

Housed in a building adjacent to the studios where all eight of the Harry Potter films were created, the Making of Harry Potter tour brings you up close to the original sets, props, models and costumes used in the world-famous films. Visitors can wander into the imposing Great Hall at Hogwarts, walk up Diagon Alley, sneak into Dumbledore's office, explore the

← The front entrance of the Warner Bros. Studio Tour: The Making of Harry Potter

The set of Platform 9¾, departure point for the Hogwarts Express ↓

Did You Know?

The Harry Potter novels have sold more than 500 million copies, in 80 languages.

← Diagon Alley, home to the wand shop Ollivanders and Weasley's Wizard Wheezes

Forbidden Forest and admire the Hogwarts Express locomotive at Platform 9¾. Just as impressive as the real-life sets is the huge, jaw-droppingly detailed scale model of Hogwarts School, used for the exterior shots in the films.

There's much more to marvel at throughout the tour, from costumes for the students at Beauxbatons Academy and the Yule Ball to Harry's broomstick and Hagrid's motorcycle, as well as animatronic creatures, including Buckbeak, a 6-m- (20-ft-) wide Aragog and a full-size Basilisk head. Secrets of the special and visual effects departments reveal how the Invisibility Cloak works and what role the green screen played. As you might expect, the three shops on site offer a huge range of take-home souvenirs.

↑ The office of Albus Dumbledore, first created for *Harry Potter and the Chamber of Secrets*

EAT

The Food Hall
Enjoy classic British fare at this quite basic canteen. Breakfast is well catered for, with the Full English setting you up for the day. At lunch, tuck into hot or cold meals – soups, salads, burgers and the like.

£££

Backlot Café
This is the place to stop for Butterbeer, whether as a drink or an ice cream. There is hot food available here too.

£££

EXPERIENCE MORE

⑤ 🏛️ Ⓜ️ 🛍️

BAPS Shri Swaminarayan Mandir

📍 105-119 Brentfield Rd NW10 ⊖ Harlesden then bus 206 or 224 (or Stonebridge Park and bus 112) 🕐 Daily; Mandir and Haveli: 9am-6pm; Deities: 9-11am, 11:45am-12:15pm & 4-6pm (to 5pm Sat) 🌐 londonmandir.baps.org

Right out in northwest London, not far from Wembley Stadium, stands one of the most incongruous – and beautiful – religious buildings in the city, often known simply as the Neasden Temple. The intricately carved Hindu temple was completed in 1995, after a small army of volunteers from the local community banded together to raise funds and build it. Thousands of tonnes of Bulgarian limestone and Italian Carrara marble were shipped to India to be carved, then assembled on site like a giant jigsaw. The result is a staggeringly detailed, intricately carved temple. When the Mandir's inner sanctum is not closed for prayer, you can inspect some

of the shrines to the deities close-up. The Haveli, the cultural education centre, features yet more beautiful carving, this time in Burmese teak and English oak.

Leave any large bags at the baggage cabin in the car park, dress modestly (with your shoulders, upper arms and knees covered) and leave your shoes in the cloakroom before you enter the main building.

---

⑥

Victoria Park

📍 Grove Rd E3 ⊖ Mile End 🚆 Hackney Wick, Cambridge Heath 🚌 277, 425 🕐 7am-dusk 🌐 towerhamlets.gov.uk

Victoria Park opened in 1845 as London's first public park, and is now part of the largest belt of green space in the East End. The venue for many political rallies in the 19th century and beyond, it became known as the "People's Park" and remains hugely popular. There are boats for hire on one of its two lakes, and gardens, cafés, playgrounds, splash pools, tennis courts and a skate park. Footpaths along the Hertford Union and Regent's canals hug two of its sides, linking up with the River Lea on its journey around the Olympic Park.

⑦ 🏛️ 🍴 🍽️

Alexandra Palace

📍 Alexandra Palace Way N22 🚆 Alexandra Palace ⊖ Wood Green then bus W3 🕐 Daily 🌐 alexandrapalace.com

Built as the People's Palace in 1873, Alexandra Palace has a slightly chequered history – it has burned down twice, once just 16 days after it opened, and again in 1980. From 1936 until 1956 the BBC's television studios were housed at Alexandra Palace, and in 1936 the first television transmission took place from here. Affectionately known as Ally Pally, the large, ornate Victorian halls now host a wide variety of events, from

---

DRINK

Crate Brewery

This canalside brewery is the place to go to sample the east London hipster scene: post-industrial styling and great craft beer.

📍 Queens Yard, Hackney Wick E9 🌐 cratebrewery.com

trade and antiques fairs to large-scale concerts. Set in parkland, the building sits majestically exposed on a hill, so the views are spectacular, and it's a good spot for fireworks and funfairs (the website has details of events). There's a permanent ice rink and the grounds have a pitch-and-putt golf course, a boating lake and playgrounds.

8 William Morris Gallery

⌂ Lloyd Park, Forest Rd E17
⊖ Walthamstow Central
🕐 10am–5pm Tue–Sun
🚫 25 & 26 Dec, 1 Jan
🌐 wmgallery.org.uk

The most influential designer of the Victorian era, born in 1834, lived in this 18th-century house as a young man. It is now a beguiling and well-presented museum giving a full account of William Morris the artist, designer, writer, craftsman and socialist. It has examples of his work and that of other members of the Arts and Crafts movement – tiles

←

Victoria Park, part of a 3 km (1.5-mile) band of green space that opens up east London

by William De Morgan and paintings by members of the Pre-Raphaelite Brotherhood.

Interactive exhibits introduce visitors to techniques such as hand-printing and dyeing. There are regular special exhibitions, workshops and lectures.

9 Charlton House

⌂ Charlton Rd SE7
🚆 Charlton 🕐 9am–10pm Mon–Fri, 9am–5pm Sat
🚫 Public hols 🌐 greenwich-heritage.org/visit/charlton-house

Completed in 1612 for Adam Newton, tutor to Prince Henry, Charlton House is the best-preserved Jacobean mansion in London. It is now used as a community centre, but many of the original ceilings and fireplaces survive, as does the carved main staircase and parts of the wood panelling. Other ceilings have been restored using the original moulds. The house has walled gardens and the grounds contain a summer house reputedly designed by architect Inigo Jones, and a mulberry tree said to have been planted by James I in 1608.

↑ The exquisite, and intricately detailed *(inset),* BAPS Shri Swaminarayan Mandir

10 Sutton House

⌂ 2–4 Homerton High St E9 ⊖ Bethnal Green then bus 253 🕐 Selected dates noon–4:30pm Wed–Sun; check website 🌐 nationaltrust.org.uk

One of the very few Tudor merchants' houses in London to have survived in something like its original form, Sutton House was built in 1535 for Ralph Sadleir, a courtier to Henry VIII. Though the front was altered in the 18th century, the Tudor fabric remains surprisingly intact, including brickwork, fireplaces and wood panelling. The house has spent time as a school and an anarcho-punk squat, a history that is explored on regular tours (book ahead).

The clock tower of the Horniman Museum, designed in Arts and Crafts style ↑

11

Eltham Palace

⌂ Court Yard SE9 🚆 Eltham then a 15-minute walk ⏰ Apr–Sep: 10am–6pm Sun–Fri (Oct: to 5pm; Mar: to 4pm); Nov–Feb: 10am–4pm Sun only; daily during Christmas week & half-term 🌐 english-heritage.org.uk

This unique property lets visitors relive the grand life of two very different eras. In the 14th century English kings spent Christmas in a splendid palace here. The Tudors used it as a base for deer-hunting, but it fell into ruin after the English Civil War (1642–51). In 1935 Stephen Courtauld, of the wealthy textile family, restored the Great Hall and, next to it, he built a house described as "a wonderful combination of Hollywood glamour and Art Deco design". The palace has been superbly restored – especially the circular glass-domed entrance hall. The lush grounds are particularly lovely, especially the carp-filled moat and the 1930s garden.

12

Horniman Museum

⌂ 100 London Rd SE23 🚆 Forest Hill ⏰ 10am–5:30pm daily; animal walk: 12:30–4pm daily; gardens: 7:15am–sunset Mon–Sat, 8am–sunset Sun & public hols 🚫 24–26 Dec 🌐 horniman.ac.uk

Frederick Horniman, a tea merchant, had this museum built in 1901 to house the curios he had collected on his travels in the 1860s. It features a music gallery, an aquarium (for a fee) and world culture displays, but the highlight is a natural history gallery that contains a remarkable collection of taxidermy and skeletons, including the famous Horniman Walrus. The gardens have a Victorian conservatory, a bandstand, nature trails and a sunken garden as well as a Butterfly House (for a fee) and Animal Walk, a small petting zoo.

13

Wimbledon Lawn Tennis Museum

⌂ Church Rd SW19 🚆 Southfields ⏰ 10am–5:30pm daily (winter: to 5pm) 🚫 1 Jan, 24–26 Dec 🌐 wimbledon.com

Even those with only a passing interest in tennis will find plenty to enjoy here. The museum explores tennis's development from its early incarnation in the 1860s as a diversion for country house parties to the sport it is today. Equipment and tennis fashion from the Victorian era are on display and visitors can watch clips and recent matches in the video theatre. It's advisable to book ahead to take one of the tours, which include a visit to Centre Court.

14

Wimbledon Windmill Museum

⌂ Windmill Rd SW19 🚆 Wimbledon then bus 93 ⏰ Apr–Oct: 2–5pm Sat, 11am–5pm Sun & public hols 🌐 wimbledon windmill.org.uk

Built in 1817, the mill on Wimbledon Common now houses a museum exploring windmills, rural life and local history. Boy Scout founder Robert Baden-Powell wrote part of *Scouting for Boys* here

Did You Know?

In 2018 the *New York Times* named the Horniman one of the "10 coolest museums in the world".

in 1908, and there are display cases of early memorabilia from the scouting and Girl Guide movements.

The mill came out of service in 1864, but you can see some of the original workings on the upper floors, as well as try your hand at grinding grain on old mortars and querns, an activity popular with young children. There are also some beautifully crafted cutaway models of this and other mills.

Dulwich Picture Gallery

🏛 Gallery Rd SE21 🚆 West Dulwich, North Dulwich 🕐 10am-5pm Tue-Sun & bank hols 🚫 1 Jan, 24-26 Dec 🌐 dulwichpicture gallery.org.uk

England's oldest public art gallery, which opened in 1817, was designed by Sir John Soane *(p143)*, and was built to house the royal collection of the King of Poland, who had been forced to abdicate in 1795. Its imaginative use of skylights made it the prototype of most galleries created since. The grand collection has works by Rembrandt (his *Jacob III de Gheyn* has been stolen from here four times), Canaletto, Poussin, Watteau, Raphael and Gainsborough. The building houses Soane's mausoleum to Desenfans and Bourgeois, the art dealers who built the collection.

Dulwich Park

🏛 College Road SE21 🚆 West Dulwich, North Dulwich 🚌 P4, P13 🕐 7.30am-dusk

Just across the road from Dulwich Picture Gallery, this park was opened in 1890 on land previously owned by Dulwich College, the public school whose buildings lie to the south of the park. This is one of the prettiest of the borough parks, with paths weaving around colourful flowerbeds, sports courts and pitches, a bowling green, a central boating lake and a duck pond. Dog walkers are confined to the perimeter, making the central lawns pleasant for play and picnicking in the warmer months. At weekends the outer loop fills with kids and adults messing around on the novelty bikes rented out by the park's resident cycle hire firm, London Recumbents.

🔍 HIDDEN GEM
Sydenham Hill Wood

A short walk south of Dulwich Park, this swathe of woodland is the largest remaining tract of the ancient Great North Wood. Wander along the paths and perhaps you'll find the hidden Victorian folly.

Visitors exploring the superb Dulwich Picture Gallery ↑

A cold and frosty morning in Richmond Park

Multinational flags in Brixton Village, one of a pair of colourful covered market arcades ↑

⑰ 🍴 🖥 🛍 Brixton

📍 SW2, SW9 🚇🚆 Brixton

The unofficial capital of south London, Brixton has been characterized since the 1950s by one of the city's largest West Indian communities. Brixton Market loops around the centre along Electric Avenue, Pope's Road and Station Road, and is packed full of stalls selling Caribbean produce alongside arts, crafts, clothing and the usual market bric-a-brac. Brixton Village and Market Row, neighbouring market arcades, are filled with independent traders and an eclectic mix of food hotspots. Despite the march of gentrification, Brixton fiercely protects its roots and remains a brilliantly energetic part of the city.

⑱ 🏛 🏠 🖥 🛍 NT Ham House

📍 Ham St, Richmond 🚇 🚆 Richmond then bus 65 or 371 🕐 House: noon–4pm daily; gardens: 10am–5pm daily (Nov–Jan: to 4pm) 🚫 24 & 25 Dec 🌐 nationaltrust.org.uk

This magnificent house beside the Thames was built in 1610, but its heyday came when the Countess of Dysart inherited it from her father, who had been Charles I's "whipping boy" (in his boyhood he took the punishment for the future king's misdemeanours). From 1672, she and her husband, a confidant of Charles II, set about modernizing the house, and it was regarded as one of Britain's finest. The garden has been lovingly restored to its 17th-century form. In summer and also on winter weekends (except November), a foot-passenger ferry runs from here to Marble Hill House and Orleans House at Twickenham.

EAT

Franco Manca

Arguably London's love affair with sourdough pizza started here, at the original Franco Manca. Simple menu, perfect pizzas.

📍 4 Market Row SW9 🌐 francomanca.co.uk

£ £ £

---

⑲ 🏛 🖥 🛍 Orleans House Gallery

📍 Orleans Rd, Twickenham 🚇 🚆 St Margaret's or Richmond then bus 33, 490, H22, R68 or R70 🕐 10am–5pm Tue–Sun 🚫 1 Jan, Good Fri, 24–26 Dec 🌐 orleanshousegallery.org

This gallery occupies what remains of Orleans House, named after Louis Philippe, Duke of Orleans, who lived there from 1815 to 1817. The restored Octagon Room was designed by James Gibbs for James Johnston in 1720. It displays the Richmond Borough art collection.

---

⑳ 🏛 🖥 🛍 EH Marble Hill House

📍 Richmond Rd, Twickenham 🚆 St Margaret's 🕐 Apr–Oct: for guided tours only, check website; park and café: daily year-round 🚫 Public hols & events 🌐 english-heritage.org.uk

Built in 1729 for George II's mistress, Henrietta Howard, the house and its grounds

→

Syon House, built as a square around a central courtyard

have been fully restored to its Georgian appearance. The house has a collection of paintings by William Hogarth and a depiction of the river and house in 1762 by artist Richard Wilson, who is widely regarded as the father of English landscape painting. The house remains closed pending extensive refurbishment, but the park is currently open.

Pleasure boats plying the Thames at Richmond ↑

Richdmond

🏠 TW10 🚇🚆 Richmond

This attractive London suburb gained its name from the palace that Henry VII built here in 1500. Many early 18th-century houses survive near the Thames and off Richmond Hill; particularly noteworthy is Maids of Honour Row, built in 1724. The beautiful view of the river from the top of the hill has been captured by many artists over the years, and has remained largely unspoiled.

Richmond Park

🏠 Richmond TW10
🚇🚆 Richmond then bus 65 or 371 🕐 24 hours daily (7:30am–8pm Nov & Feb) 🌐 royalparks.org.uk

In 1637, Charles I built a 13-km (8-mile) wall round the royal park to enclose it as a hunting ground. Today the vast park is a beautiful national nature reserve and deer still graze warily among the chestnuts, birches and oaks. They have learned to coexist with the human visitors who stroll here on fine weekends.

In late spring, the highlight is the Isabella Plantation when its spectacular azaleas burst into colour, while the Pen Ponds are popular with optimistic anglers. (Adam's Pond is for model boats.) The rest of the park is covered with heath, bracken and trees (some are hundreds of years old). Richmond Gate, located in the northwest corner, was designed by John Soane (p143) in 1798.

Nearby is Henry VIII Mound, which offers superb views across the Thames Valley, with a tree-framed sightline towards the City and St Paul's (p176). The Palladian White Lodge, built in 1729, is now home to the famed Royal Ballet School.

Syon House

🏠 London Rd, Brentford
🚇 Gunnersbury then bus 237 or 267 🕐 Mid-Mar–Oct: 11am–5pm Wed–Thu, Sun & public hols; gardens: mid-Mar–Oct: 10:30am–5pm daily 🌐 syonpark.co.uk

The Earls and Dukes of Northumberland have lived here for 400 years – it is the only large mansion in the London area still in hereditary ownership. The interior was remodelled in 1761 by Robert Adam and is considered one of his masterpieces. The five Adam rooms house original furnishings and a collection of old master paintings.

The 80-ha (200-acre) park includes a lovely 16-ha (40-acre) garden, landscaped by Capability Brown, with more than 200 species of rare trees. The park's Great Conservatory inspired Joseph Paxton's designs for the Crystal Palace.

24

Musical Museum

📍399 High St, Brentford
🚆Kew Bridge 🚇Gunnersbury then bus 237 or 267, or South Ealing then bus 65
🕐10:30am–5pm Tue, Fri–Sun & bank hols 🌐musicalmuseum.co.uk

The collection, arranged over three floors, chiefly comprises large automatic instruments, including player pianos and organs, miniature and cinema pianos, and what is apparently the only surviving self-playing Wurlitzer organ in Europe.

25 (NT)

Osterley Park and House

📍Jersey Rd, Isleworth
🚇Osterley 🕐House: times vary, check website; garden: 10am–5pm daily (Nov–mid-Feb: to 4pm); park: 7am–7:30pm daily (later in summer)
🌐nationaltrust.org.uk

Osterley is ranked among Robert Adam's finest works and its colonnaded portico and ornate stuccowork

demonstrate why. Much of the furniture is by Adam; the garden and temple are by William Chambers, architect of Somerset House.

26

Pitzhanger Manor House and Gallery

📍Mattock Lane W5 🚇Ealing Broadway 🕐House: 10am–4:30pm Tue–Fri, Sun & public hols; 10am–3pm Sat; park: 7:30am–dusk daily
🌐pitzhanger.org.uk

Sir John Soane, architect of the Bank of England, rebuilt this manor house in 1804 as his own country residence. There are clear echoes of his elaborately constructed town house in Lincoln's Inn Fields (p142). Soane retained two of the principal formal rooms: the drawing room and the dining room, designed in 1768 by George Dance the Younger, with whom Soane had worked.

Set in landscaped Walpole Park, Pitzhanger reopened in 2019 following a £12-million conservation project, which returned the house to Soane's vision, with a skylit gallery for exhibitions.

27

London Museum of Water & Steam

📍Green Dragon Lane, Brentford 🚆Kew Bridge, Gunnersbury then bus 237 or 267 🕐10am–4pm Wed–Sun, daily in school hols
🚫24–28 Dec 🌐waterandsteam.org.uk

This 19th-century water pumping station near the north end of Kew Bridge is now a museum of steam power and water. Its main exhibits are five giant Cornish beam engines that pumped water here from the river, to be distributed across London. The earliest engines, dating from 1820, are similar to those built to pump water out of Cornish mines. Visitors can see them working some weekends and on public holidays (times are posted on the website). The Waterworks gallery tells the story of London's water

←

Gobelins tapestry from the "Loves of the Gods" series at Osterley

↑ Part of the Knot Garden at Fulham Palace *(inset)*, originally created by Bishop Blomfield in 1831

supply in lots of interactive detail, and there's an outdoor area where children can play with the water features.

 28

Fulham Palace

🏠 Bishops Ave SW6
🚇 Putney Bridge 🕐 Daily; times vary, check website; botanic garden: dawn–dusk daily 🚫 25, 26 & 31 Dec
🌐 fulhampalace.org

The home of the Bishops of London from the 8th century until 1973, Fulham Palace has parts that date from the 15th century. The palace stands in its own landscaped gardens, which comprise a botanical garden and a delightful walled garden, from which produce grown in the palace garden is sold from a barrow. Restored using original materials in 2019, the original Tudor courtyard lies at the heart of the palace. Renovations also reopened long-inaccessible historic rooms to the public gaze. Now home to a museum, it imaginatively retells the stories of the Bishops of London, including a "mood room" that explores the palace's history using light and sound.

 29

Chiswick House

🏠 Burlington Lane W4
🚇 Chiswick 🕐 Apr–Oct: 10am–3pm Mon & Wed, 10am–4pm Sat & Sun; gardens: 7am–dusk daily
🌐 chiswickhouseand gardens.org.uk

Completed in 1729 to the design of its owner, the third Earl of Burlington, this is a fine example of a Palladian villa. Burlington revered Palladio and his disciple Inigo Jones, and statues of both stand outside. Built around a central octagonal room, the house is packed with references to ancient Rome and Renaissance Italy.

Chiswick was Burlington's country residence and this house was built as an annexe to a larger, older house (since demolished). It was designed for recreation and entertaining – Lord Hervey, Burlington's enemy, dismissed it as "too little to live in and too big to hang on a watch chain". Some of the ceiling paintings are by architect William Kent, who also contributed to the garden design.

The house was an asylum from 1892 until 1928, when restoration began. The layout of the gardens, now a public park, is much as Burlington designed it. Tours of the house are included with admission and take place at noon, plus 2:30pm on weekends.

DRINK

The Bell and Crown
Lots of riverside outdoor seating and a rustic interior are found here.
🏠 11–13 Thames Rd, Chiswick W4

The City Barge
Great food and beer is available here daily, and the Saturday brunch is legendary.
🏠 27 Strand-on-the-Green, Chiswick W4

Bull's Head
Cosy pub with good Sunday roasts as well as riverside picnic benches.
🏠 15 Strand-on-the-Green, Chiswick W4

 30

Hogarth's House

🏠 Hogarth Lane W4
🚇 Turnham Green 🕐 Noon–5pm Tue–Sun & bank hol Mon 🚫 1 Jan, Good Fri, Easter Sun, 25 Dec 🌐 hogarths house.org

When the painter William Hogarth lived here from 1749 until his death in 1764, he called it "a little country box by the Thames" and painted rural views from its windows – he had moved here from Leicester Square *(p115)*. It has now been turned into a small museum and gallery, filled with engraved copies of the moralistic cartoon-style pictures with which Hogarth made his name. Salutary tales such as *Marriage à la Mode*, *An Election Entertainment*, *A Harlot's Progress* and many others can all be seen here.

NEED TO KNOW

Transport in London city centre

BEFORE
YOU GO

Things change, so plan ahead to make the most of your trip. Be prepared for all eventualities by considering the following points before you travel.

AT A GLANCE

CURRENCY
Pound Sterling (GBP)

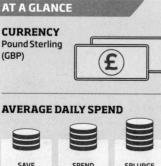

AVERAGE DAILY SPEND

SAVE	SPEND	SPLURGE
£75	£125	£200

BOTTLED WATER	COFFEE	BEER	DINNER FOR TWO
£1	£2.80	£5	£70

CLIMATE

The longest days occur May–Aug, while Oct–Feb sees the shortest daylight hours.

The heaviest rainfall is in October and November, but showers occur all year round.

Daytime highs average 22°C (75°F) in summer. Winter can be cold and icy.

ELECTRICITY SUPPLY
Power sockets are type G, fitting three-pronged plugs. Standard voltage is 230 volts.

Passports and Visas

For entry requirements, including visas, consult your nearest British embassy or check the **UK Government** website. Post-Brexit arrangements for citizens from EEA countries will vary depending on the terms agreed; rights of Irish citizens will not change.
UK Government
🅦 gov.uk/check-uk-visa
🅦 gov.uk/guidance/visiting-the-uk-after-brexit

Government Advice

Now more than ever, it is important to consult both your and the UK government's advice before travelling. The **UK Foreign and Commonwealth Office**, the **US State Department**, and the **Australian Department of Foreign Affairs and Trade** offer the latest information on security, health and regulations.
Australia
🅦 smartraveller.gov.au
UK
🅦 gov.uk/foreign-travel-advice
US
🅦 travel.state.gov

Customs Information

You can find information on the laws relating to goods and currency taken in or out of the UK on the **UK Government** website.
UK Government
🅦 gov.uk/duty-free-goods

Insurance

We recommend that you take out a comprehensive insurance policy covering theft, loss of belongings, medical care, cancellations and delays, and read the small print carefully.

Emergency treatment is usually free from the National Health Service, and there are reciprocal arrangements with Australia, New Zealand and some others (check the **NHS** website for details). Healthcare arrangements for EEA citizens – currently covered by the

EHIC (European Health Insurance Card)– are likely to change in 2021. Check the NHS website for the most up-to-date information.
EHIC
🔟 gov.uk/european-health-insurance-card
NHS
🔟 nhs.uk

Vaccinations

No inoculations are needed for the UK.

Money

Major credit and debit cards are accepted in most shops and restaurants, while prepaid currency cards are accepted in some. Contactless payments are widely accepted in London, including on public transport. However, it is always worth carrying some cash, as some smaller businesses and markets still operate a cash-only policy. Cash machines are conveniently located at banks, train stations, shopping areas and main streets.

Tipping in London is discretionary. In restaurants it's customary to tip 10–12.5 per cent for good service. It is usual to tip taxi drivers 10 per cent and hotel porters, concierge and housekeeping £1–2 per bag or day.

Booking Accommodation

London offers a huge variety of accommodation to suit any budget, including luxury five-star hotels, family-run B&Bs and budget hostels.

Lodgings can fill up and prices become inflated during the summer, so it's worth booking well in advance.

A comprehensive list of accommodation to suit all needs can be found via **Visit London**, London's official tourist information website.
Visit London
🔟 visitlondon.com

Travellers with Specific Requirements

Accessibility information for public transport is available from the TFL website (*p337*). In the City, Westminster, Camden and Kensington and Chelsea, a disabled-driver badge allows you to park in Blue Badge bays only. The Visit London website offers handy tips on the city's accessibility

provisions. **AccessAble** has a useful searchable online directory. Museums and galleries offer audio tours, which are useful to those with impaired vision. **Action on Hearing Loss** and the **RNIB** (Royal National Institute of Blind People) can also offer useful information and advice.
AccessAble
🔟 accessable.co.uk
Action on Hearing Loss
🔟 actionhearingloss.org.uk
RNIB
🔟 rnib.org.uk

Language

English is the official language spoken in London. However, it is a multicultural city, in which you will hear many languages spoken. Many attractions and tour companies offer foreign language tours.

Opening Hours

COVID-19 The pandemic continues to affect London. Some museums, tourist attractions and hospitality venues are operating on reduced or temporary opening hours, and require visitors to make advance bookings for a specific date and time. Always check ahead before visiting.

Mondays Some museums and attractions close.
Sundays Most shops operate limited opening.
Public holidays Public services are closed for the day; some shops, museums and attractions either close or operate shorter hours.

PUBLIC HOLIDAYS 2021	
1 Jan	New Year's Day
2 Apr	Good Friday
5 Apr	Easter Monday
3 May	Early May Bank Holiday
31 May	Spring Bank Holiday
30 Aug	Summer Bank Holiday
25 Dec	Christmas Day
26 Dec	Boxing Day
27 Dec	In lieu of Christmas Day
28 Dec	In lieu of Boxing Day

GETTING AROUND

London has one of the busiest public transport systems in Europe; understanding how it works will help you make the most of your trip.

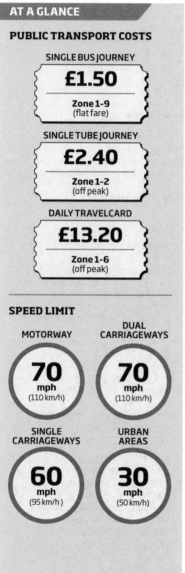

AT A GLANCE

PUBLIC TRANSPORT COSTS

SINGLE BUS JOURNEY
£1.50

Zone 1-9
(flat fare)

SINGLE TUBE JOURNEY
£2.40

Zone 1-2
(off peak)

DAILY TRAVELCARD
£13.20

Zone 1-6
(off peak)

SPEED LIMIT

MOTORWAY
70 mph
(110 km/h)

DUAL CARRIAGEWAYS
70 mph
(110 km/h)

SINGLE CARRIAGEWAYS
60 mph
(95 km/h)

URBAN AREAS
30 mph
(50 km/h)

Arriving by Air

Five major airports serve London: Heathrow, Gatwick, Stansted, Luton and City. With the exception of City Airport, all are situated a significant distance from central London, with good transport connections to the city centre. For the best rates, book train or bus tickets in advance. For a list of transport options, approximate journey times and travel costs for transport to and from London's airports, see the table opposite.

Train Travel

International Train Travel
St Pancras International is the London terminus for Eurostar, the high-speed train linking the UK with the Continent.

You can buy tickets and passes for multiple international journeys via **Eurail** or **Interrail**; advance reservations are usually not required but always check that your pass is valid on the service on which you wish to travel before attempting to board.

Eurostar runs regular services from Paris, Brussels and Amsterdam (via Brussels) to London via the Channel Tunnel.

Eurotunnel operates a drive-on-drive-off train service between Calais and Folkestone, in southeast England.

Eurail
W eurail.com
Eurostar
W eurostar.com
Eurotunnel
W eurotunnel.com
Interrail
W interrail.eu

Domestic Train Travel
The UK's railway system is complicated and can be confusing. Lines are run by several different companies, but they are coordinated by **National Rail**, which operates a joint information service.

London has eight main railway termini serving different parts of Britain (Charing

GETTING TO AND FROM THE AIRPORT

Airport	Transport to London	Journey Time	Price
London City	DLR	30 mins	from £2.80
	Taxi	20 mins	from £25
London Heathrow	Heathrow Express	15 mins	from £22
	London Underground	50 mins	from £3.10
	National Express Coach	1 hr	from £5
	Taxi	1 hr	from £40
London Stansted	Stansted Express	50 mins	from £9.45
	National Express Coach	1 hr 50 mins	from £5
	Taxi	1 hr 10 mins	from £75
London Gatwick	Gatwick Express	30 mins	from £17.80
	London Thameslink	40 mins	from £11
	National Express Coach	1 hr 50 mins	from £6
	Taxi	1 hr 30 mins	from £60
London Luton	Bus & London Thameslink	45 mins	from £17.40
	National Express Coach	1hr 20 mins	from £7
	Taxi	1hr 10 mins	from £75

Cross, Euston, King's Cross, London Bridge, St Pancras, Paddington, Waterloo and Victoria. There are also over 300 smaller London stations. Each main terminus is the starting point for local and suburban lines that cover the whole of southeast England.

London's local and suburban train lines are used by commuters every day. For visitors, rail services are most useful for trips to the outskirts of London and areas of the city without nearby Underground connections (especially in south London). If you are planning to travel outside of the capital, always try to book rail tickets in advance.
National Rail
w nationalrail.co.uk

Long-Distance Bus Travel

Coaches from European and UK destinations arrive at Victoria Coach Station. The biggest operator in the UK is **National Express**. **Eurolines** is its European arm, offering a variety of coach routes to London from other European cities. Fares start from around £17 and vary depending on distance. Book in advance.
Eurolines
w eurolines.de
National Express
w nationalexpress.com

Public Transport

Transport for London (**TFL**) is London's main public transport authority. Safety and hygiene measures, timetables, ticket information, transport maps and more can be found on their website.
TFL
w tfl.gov.uk

Fare Zones
TFL divides the city into six charging zones for Underground, Overground and National Rail services, radiating out from Zone 1 in the centre. On buses, there is a flat fare for each trip, no matter how far you travel.

Tickets

Tube and rail fares are expensive, especially individual tickets. If you expect to make multiple trips around the city in a short space of time, you can buy a one-day off-peak Travelcard, which gives unlimited travel on all systems after 9:30am on weekdays (or any time on Saturday, Sunday and public holidays) until 4:30am the next morning within Zones 1–4 or 1–6 for a flat fee.

If you wish to travel more freely, purchase a pay-as-you-go Oyster card or Visitor Oyster card (valid for all London zones, as well as Heathrow and Gatwick Express), which you can preload and top up with credit (note that a £5 deposit is required when buying an Oyster card and you will need one card per person). You can also use contactless credit or debit cards in the same way as the Oyster card. It is cheaper to pay as you go using contactless or Oyster as fares are subject to daily and weekly caps.

When using public transport, you "touch in" with your card on a yellow card reader, and the corresponding amount is deducted. On Underground, DLR and Overground trains, you must also remember to "touch out" where you finish your journey, or you will be charged a maximum fare, though the excess can usually be reclaimed via the website if you forget. Prices rise during peak times: 6:30–9:30am and 4–7pm Mon–Fri.

Buy Travelcards and Oyster cards at Underground and local rail stations, or any shop that has the TFL "Ticket Stop" sticker in the window. Many smaller stations just have self-service machines. You can also buy them from overseas agents in around 30 countries.

The Underground and DLR

The London Underground (commonly referred to as "the Tube") has 11 lines, all named and colour-coded, which intersect at various stations. The construction of an additional line, the Elizabeth line, is currently underway. Following setbacks, this will open in late 2021 at the earliest.

Some lines, like the Jubilee, have a single branch; others, like the Northern, have more than one, so it is important to check the digital boards on the platform and the destination on the front of the train.

Trains run every few minutes 7:30–9:30am and 4–7pm, and every 5–10 minutes at all other times. The Central, Jubilee, Northern, Victoria and Piccadilly lines offer a 24-hour service on selected routes on Fridays and Saturdays. All other lines operate roughly 5am–12:40am Mon–Sat, with reduced hours on Sun.

The DLR (Docklands Light Railway) is a mostly overground network of trains that run from the City to stops in east and southeast London, including City Airport and Greenwich. It operates roughly 5:30–12:30am Mon–Sat, 7am–11:30pm Sun, with trains departing every 3 minutes.

Stations with step-free access are marked on Tube maps, which are located on all trains and at every station.

The Overground

Marked on Tube maps by an orange line, the Overground connects with the Underground and main railway stations at various points across the city. It operates in much the same way as the Underground, and covers most areas of the city without nearby Underground connections. The line between Highbury & Islington and New Cross Gate runs 24 hours Friday and Saturday.

Bus

Slower but cheaper than the Tube, buses are also a good way of seeing the city as you travel.

Bus routes are displayed on the TFL website and on maps at bus stops. The destination and route number is indicated on the front of the bus and the stops are announced on board.

Buses do not accept cash so a ticket, Oyster card or contactless payment is required.

A single fare costs £1.50, while unlimited bus travel caps out at £4.50 – just use the same card each time you use the bus to reach the daily cap.

The hopper fare allows you to make unlimited bus journeys for free within an hour of travel. Travel is free on buses for under-16s as long as they carry a Zip Oyster photocard. Apply for one on the TFL website at least four weeks before you are due to arrive.

The Night buses (indicated by the letter "N" added before the route number) run on many popular routes from 11pm until 6am, generally 3–4 times per hour up to 2 or 3am.

Taxis

London's iconic black cabs can be hailed on the street, booked online or over the phone, or picked up at taxi ranks throughout the city. The yellow "Taxi" sign is lit up when the taxi is free. The driver's cab licence number should be displayed in the back of the taxi.

All taxis are metered, and fares start from £3. Taxi apps such as Uber also operate in London.

The following services can be booked by phone or online:

Dial-a-Cab
w dialacab.co.uk
Licensed London Taxi
w licensedlondontaxi.co.uk

Driving

Holders of non-UK licences, including EU citizens, may need to apply for an International Driving Permit. Check with your local automobile

association before you travel, or consult the UK Driver and Vehicle Licensing Agency (**DVLA**).
DVLA
w gov.uk/driving-nongb-licence

Driving in London

Driving in London is not recommended. Traffic is slow-moving, parking is scarce and expensive, and in central London there is the added cost of the **Congestion Charge** – a £15 daily charge for driving in central London 7am–10pm daily.

In the event of an accident, contact the **AA** for roadside assistance.
AA
w theaa.com
Congestion Charge
w tfl.gov.uk/modes/driving/congestion-charge

Parking

Parking is prohibited at all times wherever the street is marked with double yellow or red lines by the kerb.

If there is a single yellow line, parking is normally allowed from 6:30pm–8am Mon–Sat and all day Sun, but exact hours vary, so always check the signs along each street before leaving your vehicle. Where there is no line at all, parking is free at all times, but this is rare in central London. Rental car drivers are still liable for parking fines.

Car Rental

To rent a car in the UK you must be 21 or over (or in some cases, 25) and have held a valid driver's licence for at least a year.

Driving out of central London will take about an hour in any direction, more during rush hours; if you want to tour the countryside, it can be easier to take a train to a town or city outside London and rent a car from there. Airports tend to offer cheaper car rental.

Rules of the Road

Drive on the left. Seat belts must be worn at all times by the driver and all passengers. Children up to 135 cm tall or the age of 12 or under must travel with the correct child seat for their weight and size.

Mobile telephones may not be used while driving except with a "hands-free" system, and third-party insurance is required by law.

Overtake on the outside or right-hand lane, and when approaching a roundabout, give priority to traffic approaching from the right, unless indicated otherwise. All vehicles must give way to emergency services vehicles.

It is illegal to drive in bus lanes during certain hours. See roadside signs for restrictions.

The drink-driving legal limit (*p341*) is strictly enforced and penalities upon conviction can be severe.

Cycling

You need a strong nerve to cycle in London's traffic, but it can be a great way to see the city. **Santander Cycles**, London's self-service cycle hire, has docking stations in central London. Bikes can also be rented from the **London Bicycle Tour Company** and other rental companies throughout the city.

Be aware that drink-drive limits (*p341*) also apply to cyclists.
Santander Cycles
w tfl.gov.uk/modes/cycling/santander-cycles
London Bicycle Tour Company
w londonbicycle.com

Walking

Walking is a rewarding way to get around in London. The centre is not large, and you will be surprised at how short the distance is between places that seem far apart on the Tube.

Boats and Ferries

Car ferries departing from Calais and Dunkirk arrive in Dover or Folkestone, around 2 hours' drive from London.

Passenger and car-ferry services also sail from other ports in northern France to the south of England, as well as from Bilbao and Santander in Spain to Portsmouth or Plymouth.

Ferry services also run to other ports around the country from the Netherlands and the Republic of Ireland.

London by Boat

Some of London's most spectacular views can be seen from the River Thames.

MBNA Thames Clippers runs river services every 20 minutes on catamarans between Westminster and North Greenwich in both directions, via the London Eye, Bankside and Tower Bridge. Running between Battersea Power Station and London Bridge, the Tate Boat, or RB2, is also operated by MBNA Thames Clippers and connects the Tate Britain and Tate Modern museums.

Standard tickets cost £9 in the central zone, but discounted fares apply if bought online, via the Thames Clippers app or when using a Travelcard, contactless or Oyster card (pay as you go).

A number of providers offer **river tours** and experiences available on the Thames, with numerous options available, from dining experiences to hop-on-hop-off services.
MBNA Thames Clippers
w thamesclippers.com
River Tours
w tfl.gov.uk/modes/river/about-river-tours

PRACTICAL
INFORMATION

A little local know-how goes a long way in London. Here you will find all the essential advice and information you will need during your stay.

AT A GLANCE

EMERGENCY NUMBERS

GENERAL
EMERGENCY

999

TIME ZONE
GMT/BST
British Summer
Time (BST) runs
28 Mar–31 Oct 2021
EST -5; AEDT +11

TAP WATER
Unless otherwise
stated, tap water
in the UK is safe
to drink.

APPS

Citymapper
Covers all urban modes of transport,
including cycling and walking routes, to
help you navigate the city.

TFL Oyster and contactless
Top up and manage your Oyster card on
the go with this app from TFL.

Trainline
Use this app to find the cheapest train
tickets and check journey times.

Visit London
Includes offline maps, area guides plus
exclusive deals and offers.

Personal Security

London is a relatively safe city to visit. Pick-
pocketing is less of a problem than in many other
European capitals. Keep your belongings in a safe
place and with you at all times, use your common
sense and be alert to your surroundings.

If you have anything stolen, report the crime
as soon as possible to the nearest police station.
Get a copy of the crime report in order to claim
on your insurance.

Contact your embassy if you have your
passport stolen, or in the event of a serious
crime or accident.

As a rule, Londoners are very accepting of
all people, regardless of their race, gender or
sexuality. Homosexuality was legalized in
England in 1967 and in 2004, the UK recognized
the right to legally change your gender. If you
do feel unsafe, the **Safe Space Alliance**
pinpoints your nearest place of refuge.
Safe Space Alliance
🅦 safespacealliance.com

Health

The UK has a world-class healthcare system.
Emergency medical care in the UK is generally
free. It is important to arrange comprehensive
medical insurance before travelling. If you have an
EHIC card (p334), be sure to present this as soon
as possible. You may have to pay after treatment
and reclaim the money later. Those without
an EHIC may have to pay upfront for medical
treatment and reclaim on insurance at a later
date; check the NHS website (p335) for details
of reciprocal agreements in place for treatment
between your home country and the UK.

For minor ailments go to a pharmacy or
chemist. These are plentiful throughout the
city; chains such as Boots and Superdrug have
branches in almost every shopping district.

If you have an accident or medical problem
requiring non-urgent medical attention, you
can find details of your nearest non-emergency
medical service on the NHS website (p335).
Alternatively, you can contact **NHS 111** (the
NHS emergency care service) at any hour online

or by calling 111, or go to your nearest Accident and Emergency (A&E) department.

You may need a doctor's prescription to obtain certain pharmaceuticals; the pharmacist can inform you of the closest doctor's surgery or medical centre where you can be seen by a GP (general practitioner).

NHS 111
w 111.nhs.uk

Smoking, Alcohol and Drugs

The UK has a smoking ban in all public places, including bars, cafés, restaurants, public transport, train stations and hotels.

The UK legal limit for drivers is 80 mg of alcohol per 100 ml of blood, or 0.08 per cent BAC (blood alcohol content). This is roughly equivalent to one small glass of wine or a pint of regular-strength lager; however, it is best to avoid drinking altogether if you plan to drive. The possession of illegal drugs is prohibited and could result in a prison sentence.

ID

There is no requirement for visitors to carry ID, but in the case of a routine check you may be asked to show your passport and visa documentation. Anyone who looks under 18 may be asked for photo ID to prove their age when buying alcohol.

Local Customs

Always stand to the right on escalators or stairwells. Allow passengers to exit before you board public transport. On the Tube, it is customary to offer your seat to passengers who are less able-bodied, pregnant or elderly.

Visiting Places of Worship

Dress respectfully when entering places of worship: cover your torso and upper arms. Ensure shorts and skirts cover your knees.

Mobile Phones and Wi-Fi

Free Wi-Fi hotspots are widely available in the city centre. Cafés and restaurants will give you their Wi-Fi password, though you should make a purchase beforehand.

Visitors travelling to the UK with EU tariffs after the UK leaves the European Union should check whether they are affected by data roaming charges.

Post

Standard post in the UK is handled by Royal Mail. There are Royal Mail post office branches located throughout London, which are generally open 9am–5:30pm Mon–Fri and until 12:30pm Sat.

You can buy 1st-class, 2nd-class and international stamps in post offices, shops and supermarkets. Distinctive red post boxes are located on main streets throughout the city.

Taxes and Refunds

VAT (Value Added Tax) is charged at 20% and almost always included in the marked price. Stores offering tax-free shopping display a distinctive sign and will provide you with a VAT 407 form to validate when you leave the country. EU residents should check www.gov.uk for the latest advice.

Discount Cards

London can be an expensive city, but there are a number of ways in which costs can be reduced, and many museums are free. Students and under-18s pay lower admission to many exhibitions, and holders of an ISIC (International Student Identity Card) or IYTC (International Youth Travel Card) are eligible for a range of other discounts.

A number of visitor passes and discount cards are available online and from participating tourist offices. These cards are not free, so consider carefully how many of the offers you are likely to take advantage of before buying one. For a full list of the options available, consult the **Visit London** website.

One such card is the **London Pass**, which offers free entry to more than 80 of the city's top attractions, fast-track entry to some busier sights, money off selected tours and discounts in participating shops and restaurants, with the option of adding unlimited travel.

London Pass
w londonpass.com
Visit London
w visitlondon.com

INDEX

Page numbers in **bold** refer to main entries

Index

ACKNOWLEDGMENTS

DK would like to thank the following for their contribution to the previous edition: Edward Aves, Alice Fewery, Michael Leapman, Matt Norman, Alice Park, Helen Peters

The publisher would like to thank the following for their kind permission to reproduce their photographs:

Key: a-above; b-below/bottom; c-centre; f-far; l-left; r-right; t-top

123RF.com: bloodua 280tl; Alexey Fedorenko 271br; flik47 157clb; Christian Mueller 23tc, 260–61.

4Corners: Olimpio Fantuz 20tl, 172–3; Maurizio Rellini 8–9b; Alessandro Saffo 21bl, 218–19.

Alamy Stock Photo: age fotostock / Lluìs Real 44–5t; Alan King engraving 181bl; Andrew Orchard sports photography 38tr; Arcaid Images / Diane Auckland 131bl,/ Richard Bryant 200tr, 267tl; ART Collection 317tr; A. Astes 121tl, 284cl; Colin Bain 140–41b; Rob Ball 46–7t; John Baran 176cr; Richard Barnes 38b; Peter Barritt 257cr; Guy Bell 302–3t, 321tl; Nigel Blacker 128–9t; John Bracegirdle 309cr; Eden Breitz 212tr; Michael Brooks 96–7b; Matthew Bruce 330cra, 330–31t; Jason Bryan 307cr; Colin Burdett 252cr; Paul Carstairs 225tr; Matthew Chattle 99tc; Chronicle 61tr, 65tr, 74bc, 75bl; Classic Image 179tl; Vera Collingwood 293t; Danielle Connor 25, 310; Lindsay Constable 56–7b; csimagebase 37b; Ian Dagnall 36bl, 183bl, 246cra; DavidCC 187tl; Kathy deWitt 146bl; Chris Dorney 253tl; V. Dorosz 291tl; dpa picture alliance archive 75br; Adam Eastland 59bl; Greg Balfour Evans 120bl; Everett Collection Inc 73br; Exflow 266–7b; eye35.pix 318–19t; Malcolm Fairman 156–7b; Andrew Fare 60t; John Farnham 290clb; Tony Farrugia 49cla; Nicola Ferrari 20cb, 194–5; Fotomaton 268br; Garden Photo World / David C Phillips 21tl, 204–5; Roger Garfield 103tr; Marc Gascoigne 32–3t; Goss Images 28bl; Granger Historical Picture Archive 61br, 74ca, 77ca; Grant Rooney Premium 42–3t; Alex Hare 303br; Cath Harries 43br, 146t; Heritage Image Partnership Ltd 75bc, 77tc, 180br; Jeremy Hoare 294bc; Angelo Hornak 179cl, 179cr, 179bl; Ianni Dimitrov Pictures 90–91b; Yanice Idir 119tc; imageBROKER / Helmut Meyer zur Capellen 246br, / Werner Lang 320cl; Imagedoc 52bl; incamerastock 49crb; INTERFOTO 64br, 77tl; Jansos 12bl, 22tl, 232–3; Benjamin John 93br, 162cl, 278t; Johnny Jones 53cr; Bjanka Kadic 246clb; John Kellerman 176–7; Sung Kuk Kim 47b; Norman Krimholtz 170bc; Elitsa Lambova 155tl; Peter Lane 280–81b; LatitudeStock 225cla; Lebrecht Music & Arts 110br, 179tr, 183c; Geraint Lewis 211cla; London Picture Library 19tl, 150–51; Londonstills.com 291tr; De Luan 74br; M.Sobreira 230br; mauritius images GmbH / Steve Vidler 108clb, 183cra, 203cr, 214t, 302br; Neil McAllister 74cla; Trevor Mogg 10bl; Frank Molter 39br; Luciano Mortula 34bl; adam parker 39tl; Pawel Libera Images 35bl; Mark Phillips 158–9t; Photopat / Tate Modern, London / SUPERFLEX © DACS, 2018 One Two Three Swing! 208–9b; picture 230tl; The Picture Art Collection 110tl; Enrico Della Pietra 18tl, 122–3; PjrTravel 179ftl, 231t; PjrWindows 18bl, 136, 147tl; Portrait Essentials 143tl; Laurence Prax 113tl; Prisma by Dukas Presseagentur GmbH 55tr, 155tr; RealyEasyStar / Rodolfo Felici 133t; Richard Wareham Fotografie 40–41t; robertharding / Chris Mouyiaris 201tr,/ Adina Tovy 11cr,/ Adam Woolfitt 77br; Roger Cracknell 01 / classic 238t, 240bl; Marcin Rogozinski 56–7t; Grant Rooney 41crb, 127clb, 225tl; Amanda Rose 34ca; Peter Scholey 186b, 236cl; Scott Hortop Travel 101br, 160tl; Adrian Seal 198–9t; Marco Secchi 90bl; Alex Segre 30tl, 43cl, 54–5b, 103br, 291cra, 322br, 325b; Ian Shaw 213t; Mick Sinclair 271bc; Trevor Smithers ARPS 140–41t; Kumar Sriskandan 96t, 157tr; Robert Stainforth 98–9b; Stockimo / Neil Juggins 228–9b; Stockinasia 297tl; Adam Stoltman 65br; Sunshine 320–21b; Homer Sykes 159br, 294t; Erik Tham 8clb, 108–9; Roger Tillberg 210clb; Tim Gartside London 35cr; travelibUK 74cl; travelpix 246–7; Simon Turner 50br; Pat Tuson 37cr, 241tr, 269bl; V&A Images 330bl; Steve Vidler 44tl, 59br, 183br, 295bl; Monica Wells 169tl; Tim E White 57cl; Mark Wiener 183crb; World History Archive 60–61cla, 181br; Gregory Wrona 17tl, 33br, 86–7, 329tr; Chris Yates 48tl; Marc Zakian 171crb; Zoonar / Michal Bednarek 132b; Zoonar GmbH 237tr; Justin Kase zsixz 48b.

AWL Images: David Bank 66–7, Alan Copson 82br; PhotoFVG 239cra; Alex Robinson 23cb, 272–3, 281t; Mark Sykes 254tl; Travel Pix Collection 16, 68–9.

Barbican Centre: Max Colson 184br.

Bridgeman Images: Christie's Images 315bl; Mirrorpix 77cra; Royal Academy of Arts, London / Joshua Reynolds Self portrait (c 1779–80) oil on panel (1723–92) 93tl, / Michelangelo Buonarroti Tondo Taddei (16th century) 93tr; Universal History Archive / UIG 63br.

Coca Cola London Eye: Dave Bennet 229cl.

Courtesy of BFI: 45cl.

© DACS 2018: SUPERFLEX © DACS 2018 One Two Three Swing! at Tate Modern, London 208–9b, 216bl.

Depositphotos Inc: georgios 64bl; jovannig 26cr; masterlu 51b; VictorHuang 32br.

TM & © Warner Bros. Entertainment Inc.
Harry Potter Publishing Rights © JKR.:
Harry Potter characters, names and related
indicia are trademarks of and © Warner Bros.
Entertainment Inc. All Rights Reserved. 321cra.

Truman Markets: Haydon Perrior 199tr

ZSL London Zoo: 277tr.

Photographic Reference The London Aerial
Photo Library, and P and P F James.

Front flap images:
Alamy Stock Photo: Garden Photo World /
David C Phillips br; Enrico Della Pietra t; Jansos
bl; AWL Images: Alex Robinson c; Getty Images:
oversnap cra; iStockphoto.com: oversnap cla.

Sheet map cover images:
Alamy Stock Photo: John Kellerman.

Cover images:
Front and Spine: Alamy Stock Photo: John
Kellerman.
Back: 4Corners: Alessandro Saffo cl; Alamy
Stock Photo: John Kellerman b; AWL Images:
Nadia Isakova c, Alex Robinson tr.

For further information see: www.dkimages.com

Cartographic Data ERA-Maptec Ltd (Dublin)
adapted with permission from original survey
and mapping by Shobunsha (Japan).

Illustrators:
Brian Delf, Trevor Hill, Robbie Polley, Ann Child,
Gary Cross, Tim Hayward, Arghya Jyoti Hore,
Fiona M Macpherson, Janos Marffy, David More,
Chris Orr, Richard Phipps, Rockit Design, Michelle
Ross, John Woodcock.

Penguin
Random
House

This edition updated by
Contributor Darren Longley
Senior Editor Alison McGill
Senior Designers Stuti Tiwari Bhatia,
Tania Da Silva Gomes, Laura O'Brien
Project Editors Dipika Dasgupta, Lucy
Sara-Kelly
Editors Nayan Keshan, Manjari Thakur, Avanika
Assistant Designer Bandana Paul
Senior Picture Researcher
Sumita Khatwani
Picture Researcher Vagisha Pushp
Jacket Coordinator Bella Talbot
Jacket Designer Laura O'Brien
Senior Cartographic Editor
Mohammad Hassan
Cartography Manager Suresh Kumar
DTP Designer Rohit Rojal
Senior Production Editor Jason Little
Production Controller Rebecca Parton
Managing Editors Shikha Kulkarni,
Hollie Teague
Deputy Editorial Manager Beverly Smart
Managing Art Editors Bess Daly,
Priyanka Thakur
Art Director Maxine Pedliham
Publishing Director Georgina Dee

First edition 1993

Published in Great Britain by Dorling Kindersley Limited,
One Embassy Gardens, 8 Viaduct Gardens, London SW11 7BW

Published in the United States by DK Publishing,
1450 Broadway, Suite 801, New York, NY 10018

Copyright © 1993, 2021 Dorling Kindersley Limited
A Penguin Random House Company

21 22 23 10 9 8 7 6 5 4 3 2

A CIP catalog record for this book
is available from the British Library.

A catalog record for this book is available
from the Library of Congress.

ISSN: 1542 1554
ISBN: 978 0 2415 0967 8

Printed and bound in Latvia.

www.dk.com

A NOTE FROM DK EYEWITNESS

The rapid rate at which the world is changing is
constantly keeping the DK Eyewitness team on our
toes. While we've worked hard to ensure that this
edition of London is accurate and up-to-date, we
know that opening hours alter, standards shift, prices
fluctuate, places close and new ones pop up in their
stead. So, if you notice we've got something wrong or
left something out, we want to hear about it.
Please get in touch at travelguides@dk.com